Shakespearian Players and Performances

KEAN AS SHYLOCK
"A sentence! Come prepare."

Shakespearian Players and Performances

ARTHUR COLBY SPRAGUE

With a new preface to the
Greenwood reprint by the author

GREENWOOD PRESS, PUBLISHERS
NEW YORK

To W. Bridges-Adams

PREFACE TO THE
REPRINT EDITION

During the fifteen years since the appearance of this book, important work has been completed on Garrick, Macready, and Poel. The Harvard University Press has brought out Garrick's *Letters*, in three volumes, edited by David Little and Dr. George M. Kahrl. Garrick's productions have been ably defended by Professor Kalman Burnim (*David Garrick, Director,* Pittsburgh, 1961). Macready has been the subject of a biography by Mr. J. C. Trewin, who has also edited a happily chosen volume of selections from the actor's diaries. Two of Macready's Shakespearian promptbooks have been published, with valuable commentaries by Professor Charles Shattuck; and Professor Alan Downer has brought out his long-awaited book on Macready, *The Eminent Tragedian* (1966). Finally, in Mr. Robert Speaight's *William Poel and the Elizabethan Revival,* a Society for Theatre Research volume, published by Heinemann in 1954, we have what might be called the official biography of Poel, and a very fine one indeed.

Arthur Colby Sprague
New York, 1968

PREFACE

The present chapter on Booth's Iago appeared originally in *Theatre Annual* and that on William Poel in *The University of Toronto Quarterly*, and I am grateful to the editors for permission to include them here. Both chapters have been considerably added to and revised. Some paragraphs, also, which now come at the end of Chapter I were first printed in the form of a brief essay, or query, "Did Betterton Chant?" in *Theatre Notebook*.

For most of the illustrations, I am indebted to the Harvard Theatre Collection. That of a scene from *Hamlet* on Poel's Elizabethan stage (from the Enthoven Collection) was very kindly sent me by Miss M. St. Clare Byrne. The photograph of Gielgud as Leontes was furnished by Angus McBean, and the photograph of John Neagle's sketch of Kean as Shylock, once in the possession of Charles Durang, is reproduced by permission of the Pennsylvania Academy of Fine Arts. In a letter of Neagle's this last is described as a sketch "executed rapidly in the earliest part of my professional career" (in 1821, according to Durang). "It represents the great Tragedian in the very attitude and costume of the moment, as I saw him. It was sketched in oil colors, early in the morning after I had seen him play the part & while my recollection was clear & my mind was filled with the subject. The scene is in the 4th act — The passage, '*A sentence! Come prepare.*' "

I have been privileged to talk at length with a number of Shakespearian actors and with such wise and experienced directors as Mr. Nugent Monck, Mr. Robert Atkins, and Mr. W. Bridges-Adams. It is a happiness, as well, to remember the kindness of old friends: of Professor Samuel C. Chew, who listened patiently to each chapter, upon its completion, and gave me many valuable suggestions; of Mr. F. W. C. Hersey, who read and shrewdly criticized my account of Edwin Booth; and of Dr. William Van Lennep, who came to my assistance more than once with the generosity he has shown to so many historians of the stage. I must add that a grant from the Madge Miller Fund was of much help in procuring needed photostats, and that a Fulbright grant gave me, what might have been very difficult for me to have otherwise, a long spring of Shakespearian playgoing in England.

ARTHUR COLBY SPRAGUE

Bryn Mawr College

CONTENTS

ILLUSTRATIONS

Frontispiece

John Neagle's sketch in oils of Kean as Shylock. *Pennsylvania Academy of Fine Arts.*

Following page 176

Betterton. *From a mezzotint by R. Williams after a painting by Kneller. Harvard Theatre Collection.*

Garrick as Lear. *From the mezzotint by James MacArdell after the painting by Benjamin Wilson. 1754. Harvard Theatre Collection.*

Kemble as Hamlet. *From a line engraving by T. Cook after a drawing by J. H. Ramberg. 1785. Harvard Theatre Collection.*

Mrs. Siddons as Lady Macbeth. *From a line engraving by C. Rolls after a painting by G. H. Harlow. Harvard Theatre Collection.*

Drury Lane Playbill, February 20, 1817. *Harvard Theatre Collection.*

Macready as Macbeth. *From a line engraving published by John Tallis. Harvard Theatre Collection.*

Booth as Iago. *From a photograph in the Harvard Theatre Collection.*

Irving as Shylock. *From a photograph, published in* The Theatre, *January 1, 1880. Harvard Theatre Collection.*

A scene from the First Quarto *Hamlet* on Poel's Elizabethan stage. *Photograph in the Enthoven Collection, Victoria and Albert Museum.*

John Gielgud as Leontes. *Photograph by Angus McBean.*

Troilus and Cressida at the Brattle Theatre, Cambridge, Massachusetts. *Photograph by Peter Rossiter.*

"When we say that So-and-so's performance was a good one, we mean that it was good on such-and-such a night. Each night our performances die; each night they must be born again" (Robert Speaight, *Acting: Its Idea and Tradition*).

"Actors never can abrogate their right to claim Shakespeare as their fellow, nor forget that they are personally responsible to the public for the justice and honour, or the lack of either, that is meted out to him, and more especially for the invaluable legacy Shakespeare left in their custody" (William Poel, *Monthly Letters*).

INTRODUCTION

During the summer of 1943 I was writing on the stage business in Shakespeare's plays, and my thoughts were much upon the old actors. I promised myself a single holiday. For word had come early in July that Margaret Webster was producing *Othello*, with Paul Robeson as the Moor, first at Cambridge, then for a week at Princeton — and Princeton was not too far away. Presently, there came reports of the first night. It had been, I heard, an exciting one, and I waited more and more eagerly for the performance I was to see. When the day arrived it brought difficulties — a train-connection almost missed, the worst heat of a very hot summer — and it was with some sense of achievement that I found myself in the theatre, at last, and hearing the first words of the play. It may well be that the pleasure I experienced in Mr. Robeson's acting owed something to all these circumstances I have been describing. Certainly, I was left at the close wondering whether his performance had not approached the greatness attributed to actors in other times.

My thoughts turned, once more, to them — to Betterton and Garrick and the rest. Was it possible to imagine them as they really were? It seemed to me that each attempt implied its own limits. Garrick on the stage was only to be imagined in a particular rôle, as Richard, say, or King Lear, and on a particular night. Garrick on the night of June 8, 1776, when he played Lear for the last time, was what one would conjure up! And it was with the idea of recreating a series

1

of great Shakespearian performances that I set to work, two or three years later, on the present book.

The choice among parts had first to be made. Hamlet for Betterton was obvious, and Lear for Garrick, and Lady Macbeth for Mrs. Siddons. Macbeth is peculiarly associated with the grim-visaged, saturnine Macready; and though for a time I was tempted to write on Kean as Shylock — Shylock, on that January night in 1814 when the new romantic acting triumphed in London — I decided upon Othello as the rôle in which his genius found its most complete expression. Shylock, a "character part," as they used to call it, Irving had made his very own, adapting it to the tastes of a late-Victorian public — reconceiving it, in fact — and playing it more successfully even than Hamlet. Irving as Shylock! It was concerning John Kemble and Edwin Booth that I had most doubt. Was not Hamlet the perfect part for Booth? and Coriolanus, for that "last of all the Romans," Kemble? Yet I chose otherwise.

Kemble bade farewell to the stage in Coriolanus, was famous in the part and, I am sure, deserved his fame. His Roman presence served to identify him with Shakespeare's hero, as also that suggestion of the aristocrat which set him apart from "common players." Kemble, defying for weeks the mob that besieged his theatre, is easy to think of as Coriolanus! Against the choice was the mutilated state of the play as it was given in his time — not only cut, as they then cut Shakespeare, but with its closing scenes quite shamelessly rewritten. It was not as if there were no alternative. Kemble's Hamlet could be described in 1808 as "now the most finished piece of acting on the English stage." [1] Lamb, indeed, expostulated against the identification of part and player: "It is diffi-

2

cult for a frequent play-goer to disembarrass the idea of Hamlet from the person and voice of Mr. K." [2] For Mary Mitford, Kemble's Hamlet remained the only satisfactory one she had ever seen—"owing much to personal grace and beauty — something to a natural melancholy, or rather pensiveness of manner — much, of course, to consummate art." [3]

It was with Hamlet that Edwin Booth was associated in the popular imagination, and Booth's own gentleness and melancholy made the association natural enough.[4] He looked like Hamlet. Yet several American critics in whom I have confidence, Towse and Henry Austin Clapp, Otis Skinner and the late Professor Copeland, were left unsatisfied. Copeland maintains that Booth's impersonation "probably kept to the last more of his early artificiality than was allowed to linger in other rôles": in Hamlet, "more often than in any of his performances within my recollection, he smote his brow, tragedian fashion, to signify deep thought"; or "took the stage" in the manner of "the old school." [5] First among Booth's Shakespearian performances, he put Iago; [6] and English criticism in 1880–81 bears out his preference.

The selecting of performances was a pleasant task. I took for Betterton's Hamlet that evening in 1709 when Dick Steele saw it and praised the old master's simulation of youth. Garrick's Lear and Macready's Macbeth are their final appearance in those parts, and Macready's performance his last on the stage. Othello and Iago are described as they were played competitively: Othello by Kean in bitter contention with Booth the elder; Iago by Edwin Booth in friendly rivalry with Irving, the old school of acting against the new. Three other chapters are on first London appearances: those of Irving as Shylock; Mrs. Siddons as Lady Macbeth; and her

3

brother, a young actor from the provinces making his début at Drury Lane, as Hamlet, September 30, 1783. It was, Kemble's latest biographer tells us, "probably the most important night" in his life.[7]

The material I have felt I could use has varied greatly in amount, and indeed in quality, from performance to performance. Thus in the case of Betterton's Hamlet, it was a matter of making the most of a little — that little, however, coming from the actor's last years. Far more was written, of course, about Garrick's Lear. A few very early descriptions seemed to me too early to be admissible, but I have not hesitated to draw on several which antedate Garrick's last season. To have done otherwise would, I thought, have savored of pedantry.[8]

There is next to nothing about the appearances of Mrs. Siddons as Lady Macbeth before she undertook the part in London, and in her case it was only necessary to decide how far to use valuable but very late accounts, like that of Sheridan Knowles. She herself is variously quoted as having said that "she never read over the part without discovering in it something new," [9] and that she believed she had "gradually improved in all her characters"; [10] but also, "that over-exertion in large theatres had injured her power of expression, which was much greater in her earlier days." [11] This last remark has special interest. To what degree was Mrs. Siddons forced to modify a style formed and perfected before the enlargement of the theatres, to meet the new demands of great distances? [12] Drury Lane in 1794 was a very different playhouse from that in which she had first represented Lady Macbeth. To Lord Torrington, her Katherine in *Henry VIII* now seemed

lost and sent to waste in this wild wide theatre, where close observation cannot be maintain'd, — nor quick applause received!

4

. . . The nice discriminations, of the actors face, and of the actors feeling, are now all lost in the vast void of the new theatre of Drury Lane.

Garrick — thou didst retire at the proper time — for wer't thou restor'd to the stage, — in vain, would now thy finesse, — thy bye play, thy whisper, — thy aside, — and even thine eye, assist thee.[13]

Minor variations there were, unquestionably, but we have Boaden's word for it that in all essentials her Lady Macbeth remained the same through the years.[14]

There were changes in Irving's Shylock from the very beginning, and with the passing of time — for Irving returned to the Jew again and again — the interpretation darkened.[15] The outlines were retained, it is true. To the last there was pathos, and much dignity. William Winter's extraordinarily full description in *Shakespeare on the Stage* is, nevertheless, of a different Shylock, from that of the first performance — a Shylock, for instance, who spoke the word "ducats" as a money-lender might, caressingly.[16] Both Ellen Terry and Bram Stoker mention this idea as having been suggested to Irving by a blind man, and Stoker says it was adopted only after he had been acting the part for "a good many years." [17] It was characteristic of Irving, and a measure of his fine integrity as an artist, that he was never quite satisfied with what he had done.

In Kean's characters, on the other hand, it is hard to detect any development. One performance differed from another only, it was said, in quality. The design, however much it might be marred in execution, remained fixed. Yet even with him there might be a surprise in store for the unwary, the overconfident. Neagle, the painter, seeing Kean's Othello in Philadelphia, was impressed by a passage in the third act:

"I had rather be a toad,
And live upon the vapor of a dungeon,
Than keep a corner in the thing I love
For others' uses. *Desdemona* comes."

Kean read this with

a mixture of heartfelt sorrow and frantic rage. At the exclamation at its end, "*Desdemona* comes!" he struck one of the most splendid attitudes that perhaps was ever witnessed on the stage of any country. The delivery of the latter part of the passage was given with a peculiar, snarling, sardonic laugh, but yet extremely quiet in manner. The sudden ejaculation, "*Desdemona* comes!" was a climax that ever struck the audience like the lightning, instantaneously.[18]

Determining to make a rapid sketch of the actor at this moment in the play, Neagle returned on the second night, secured a place in the pit, about the fourth bench from the orchestra, and waited. But when Kean reached the lines, he so completely altered his manner of speaking them that Neagle let fall his paper in despair.

Enough has been said to suggest the difficulties of one who would recreate for himself performances of long ago. It should be added that in each case I have gone on to say something about the actor's style and particular achievement. Such judgments as are passed will be unlikely to satisfy readers who have already made up their minds. Irving's limitations may seem to have been insisted upon; Kemble to have been defended too ardently. Where, it may be asked, is Ellen Terry's Beatrice, Macklin's savage Jew; or why is Macready included but not Phelps? If purely historical considerations had come first, it would have been impossible to leave out Charles Kean. The book might well have become a very long one.

As it is, the last two chapters stand a little apart from the rest; but I was anxious to carry the story farther, beyond the actors of the past and their ways with Shakespeare to performances I had been privileged to see with my own eyes. The chapter on William Poel's revolutionary *Hamlet* of 1881 makes a little less abrupt this transition from Irving and Booth to Bridges-Adams and John Gielgud. For Poel, whose name is known to few playgoers in America and who is not much more than a name to many in England, stood for ideals which are still alive in our theatre, if only as an incentive and a challenge.[19]

My own playgoing began earlier than the earliest modern performance I have attempted to describe. But such recollections as I have of Julia Marlowe in *Twelfth Night*, for instance, or of John Barrymore in *Hamlet*, were, I decided, too dim and untrustworthy to record; nor had I in those days formed the habit of taking notes on what I saw. Barrymore I recall vividly in certain passages, some of which he executed brilliantly, though I was convinced that another, immediately contemporary Hamlet, Mr. Walter Hampden's, was the more *right* of the two. I have begun, accordingly, with productions of the later nineteen-twenties, giving to each the exact date when I saw it. The book, indeed, becomes increasingly personal, and much of the last chapter is concerned with what a lover of Shakespeare feels he has learned about the plays from seeing them where they belong, on the stage.

7

Betterton as Hamlet

IT is the evening of September 20, 1709. At Will's Coffee House Isaac Bickerstaff is reading a letter for *The Tatler* about the "irregular practices" of a country clergyman when he is interrupted by Mr. Greenhat, who has just seen *Hamlet*.

"Mr. Bickerstaff," said he, "had you been to-night at the playhouse, you had seen the force of action in perfection: your admired Mr. Betterton behaved himself so well, that, though now about seventy, he acted youth; and by the prevalent power of proper manner, gesture, and voice, appeared through the whole drama a young man of great expectation, vivacity, and enterprise."

"Expectation, vivacity, and enterprise": the terms chosen are a little surprising, and it is a temptation to read meanings into them. But Mr. Greenhat is insisting that an old actor had succeeded splendidly in a young part, not explaining to us how he had interpreted it.[1]

Thomas Betterton had been on the stage since 1660. He first played Hamlet in 1663. Instructed in the traditions of the rôle by Davenant, who remembered Joseph Taylor's Hamlet before the wars, he had won in it "Esteem and Reputation, Superlative to all other Plays." So writes old Downes the prompter;[2] and Pepys, who saw Betterton's Hamlet often

9

in the sixties, calls it "the best part . . . that ever man acted." [3] But that was a long while ago, and to some of those who had seen the actor recently, if not to Mr. Greenhat, the effects of age were visible enough. Even Colley Cibber is at pains to point out that when he writes of Betterton he is thinking of him at fifty — "tho' to the last he was without his Equal." [4] Other actors, young Robert Wilks for instance, had been appearing as the Dane of late. Did playgoers assemble long beforehand, on this September evening, to see their old favorite once more in the part? A few months later, when Betterton was to tread the boards for the last time — as Melantius in *The Maid's Tragedy* for his own benefit — it is reported that "the curiosity of the public was so much excited, that many spectators got into the playhouse by nine o'clock in the morning, and carried with them provisions for the day." [5] The great actor died a fortnight later.

To a person acquainted with subsequent acting versions of *Hamlet,* Betterton's text might not at first glance seem strange. Many of the cuts are those, once warranted by tradition, which have been introduced in countless performances of the tragedy. Voltemand and Cornelius are gone, and Reynaldo, and Polonius's advice to Laertes. Hamlet has no meeting with the Norwegian Captain and is deprived of the thoughts which it inspires,

How all occasions do inform against me. . . .

On the other hand, Shakespeare's martial closing, with Fortinbras and the bearing away of the hero, is retained. English audiences were hardly to see it again until Forbes-Robertson's time.

It is only when one settles down to reading this version attentively that there comes a sense of disquietude. Surely,

Hamlet, telling derisively of the King's manner of drinking, should not say:

The Kettle Drum and Trumpet thus proclaim. . . .

Nor does his soliloquy when he comes upon Claudius praying begin:

Where is this murderer, he kneels and prays.

Nor is it in just these words that Claudius defies the rebels:

There's such divinity doth hedge a King,
That treason dares not reach at what it would.

This is a Restoration version, after all; and so convinced was the Restoration of its own superior refinement that it did not hesitate to "improve" the masterpieces of the past. *Hamlet*, indeed, was comparatively fortunate. Yet the raciness of its idiom must give place every so often to what is starched and stuffed, or deadly literal — to the approved diction of neo-classical tragedy. *"Bray out"* is what Shakespeare wrote, in the lines I have quoted, and *"Now might I do it pat,"* and *"can but peep to what it would."* [6] Hamlet's "inky cloak" is now "this mourning cloke"; and "Popp'd in" —

Popp'd in between th'election and my hopes —

has become "Stept in." [7]

Mr. Greenhat names passages which Betterton had brought home to the audience: the soliloquy, "To be, or not to be"; the expostulation with Gertrude in the Closet Scene; "the noble ardour, after seeing his father's ghost; and his generous distress for the death of Ophelia." It is of the Ghost scenes alone that we have detailed accounts. Colley Cibber, in the admirable fourth chapter of his *Apology*, is painfully aware of the difficulty which confronts anyone who would set down in words the "particular Excellence" of an actor. "How shall I shew you *Betterton?*" Of what avail were it to "tell you that all the *Othellos, Hamlets, Hotspurs, Mackbeths,* and *Brutus's* whom you may have seen since his Time, have fallen far short of him?" Then he tries what a comparison will do.

You have seen a *Hamlet* perhaps, who, on the first Appearance of his Father's Spirit, has thrown himself into all the straining Vociferation requisite to express Rage and Fury, and the House has thunder'd with Applause.

But this was to sacrifice meaning (as "the late Mr. *Addison,*" sitting next Colley in the theatre, once remarked) and "in this beautiful Speech the Passion never rises beyond an almost breathless Astonishment, or an Impatience, limited by filial Reverence," to learn why the Ghost is here.

This was the Light into which *Betterton* threw this scene; which he open'd with a Pause of mute Amazement! then rising slowly to a solemn, trembling Voice, he made the Ghost equally terrible to the Spectator as to himself! and in the descriptive Part of the natural Emotions which the ghastly Vision gave him, the boldness of his Expostulation was still govern'd by Decency, manly, but not braving; his Voice never rising into that seeming Outrage or wild Defiance of what he naturally rever'd.[8]

Barton Booth once grumbled at rehearsal that Wilks had bullied him, in *Hamlet,* the night before. "When I acted the Ghost with Betterton," Booth went on, "instead of my awing him, he terrified me. But divinity hung round that man!" [9]

Some further details come from *The Laureat* (1740) and from Tony Aston. A gentleman who had "frequently seen" Betterton play Hamlet assured the author of *The Laureat* that in the Closet Scene he had

observ'd his Countenance (which was naturally ruddy and san-
guin) . . . turn instantly on the Sight of his Father's Spirit, as
pale as his Neckcloath, when every Article of his Body seem'd to
be affected with a Tremor inexpressible. . . . And when *Hamlet*
utters this Line, upon the Ghost's leaving the Stage. . . *See*
———— *where he goes* ———— *ev'n now — out at the Portal*: The
whole Audience hath remain'd in a dead Silence for near a
Minute, and then, ———— as if recovering all at once from their
Astonishment, have joined as one Man, in a Thunder of universal
Applause.[10]

Aston, on the other hand, had "often wish'd" that Betterton
in his later days would resign the part. "When he threw
himself at *Ophelia's* Feet, he appear'd a little too grave for
a young Student . . . and his *Repartees* seem'd rather as
Apopthegms [*sic*] from a *sage Philosopher*, than the *sporting
Flashes* of a Young HAMLET." [11] Here, at last, is adverse criticism, and how little it amounts to! No more, indeed, than that
Aston remained conscious of what Steele could forget — the
actor's years.

Any consideration of the characteristics of Betterton's art
must begin with his range, a range unmatched by that of any
comparable English actor, save only Garrick and possibly
Phelps. Among the rôles Betterton created were Dorimant
(in *The Man of Mode*), Philip II (in *Don Carlos*), Sir John
Brute (in *The Provoked Wife*), and Jaffier (in *Venice Preserved*). He played Bosola (in *The Duchess of Malfy*), and
Othello, and Brutus (in *Julius Caesar*). Downes calls his
Henry VIII unapproachable, and he was famous in *Henry IV*
first as Hotspur, then as the fat knight.

That Betterton's powers of impersonation were highly de-
veloped seems beyond question. *Henry IV,* revived in 1700,
is immensely successful, and "the criticks allow that Mr. Bet-

terton has hitt the humour of Falstaff better than any that have aimed at it before." [12] ("Humour" does not, of course, have its modern meaning. Today, we might assure the actor of a difficult part that he had "got the man.") Or there is the striking statement of Aston's that *"Betterton*, from the Time he was dress'd, to the End of the Play, kept his Mind in the same Temperament and Adaptness, as the present Character required." [13] Or there is Dick Steele in *The Tatler* telling of his burial. "The perfection of an actor," Steele remembers, "is only to become what he is doing." And waiting in the Abbey cloisters he had felt a deep concern for the characters Betterton had once personated, grieving that Brutus had quarrelled with Cassius; "that Hotspur's gallantry was so unfortunate; and that the mirth and good humour of Falstaff could not exempt him from the grave." [14]

Restraint in acting is, of course, relative. What was considered "the modesty of nature" by one age might seem a good deal like "o'erdoing Termagant" to another. Yet some of the descriptions in Cibber's *Apology* give us pause. One of these has already been quoted, the description of Betterton's Hamlet in the first scene with the Ghost. Another is of his Brutus. "It was a farther Excellence of *Betterton*," writes Cibber, "that he could vary his Spirit to the different Characters he acted. Those wild impatient Starts, that fierce and flashing Fire, which he threw into *Hotspur*, never came from the unruffled Temper of his *Brutus*." In the Quarrel Scene in *Julius Caesar*,

his steady Look alone supply'd that Terror which he disdain'd an Intemperance in his Voice should rise to. Thus, with a settled Dignity of Contempt, like an unheeding Rock he repelled upon himself the Foam of Cassius. [15]

From another source come the suggestive details that "his Actions were few, but just," and that he seldom raised his arms "higher than his Stomach." Even as Alexander, in Lee's tempestuous play *The Rival Queens*, he "kept his Passion under." [16]

A curious anecdote picked up by Tom Davies concerns Betterton's assumption of this last rôle. Before the union of the companies in 1682, Alexander had been the property of an elder actor, Charles Hart. At rehearsal Betterton, dissatisfied, apparently, with his own speaking of one of the lines, asked whether anyone present could recall what Hart's emphasis had been.

At last, one of the lowest of the company repeated the line exactly in Hart's key. Betterton thanked him heartily, and put a piece of money in his hand as a reward for so acceptable a service.[17]

If the anecdote had any significance for Davies, it was merely as an instance of the actor's modesty. But are not other qualities implied as well — a desire for rightness in details; the idealism of an artist? It is in keeping with Betterton's practice of consulting even "the most indifferent Poet" about a character he had accepted; whereas many actors took it "amiss to have the Author give them any Instruction." [18] By the same token, he was a student of Shakespeare, though he played him in the versions, often monstrous, of his own day. Nicholas Rowe, in the famous Introduction to his edition of 1709, writes that he

cannot leave *Hamlet*, without taking notice of the Advantage with which we have seen this Master-piece of *Shakespear* distinguish it self upon the Stage, by Mr. *Betterton's* fine Performance of that Part. . . . No Man is better acquainted with *Shakespear's*

15

manner of Expression, and indeed he has study'd him so well, and is so much a Master of him, that whatever Part of his he performs, he does it as if it had been written on purpose for him, and that the Author had exactly conceiv'd it as he plays it.[19]

It is the same Betterton, the true artist, whom we find talking with Cibber about the different kinds of applause. "I have heard him say," Colley reports, "he never thought any kind of it equal to an attentive Silence; that there were many ways of deceiving an Audience into a loud one; but to keep them husht and quiet was an Applause which only Truth and Merit could arrive at." Such applause was the due of his acting and it was bountifully bestowed. "Upon his Entrance into every Scene," we read, "he seem'd to seize upon the Eyes and Ears of the Giddy and Inadvertent! To have talk'd or look'd another way would then have been thought Insensibility or Ignorance." [20] Even those who were accustomed to dispute, not about "the turn of the expression, the elegance of the style, and the like," but only about cards — "the very gaming part" of the house — experienced pity for "those illustrious personages" whom Betterton enacted.[21] Tony Aston describes him, unflatteringly, in his later years. He had a large head, a short neck. Though "his Aspect was serious, venerable, and majestic," he was corpulent and "clumsily made"; his voice, "low and grumbling." But "he could Tune it by an artful *Climax*, which enforc'd universal Attention, even from the *Fops* and *Orange-Girls*." [22] And Cibber goes even farther, declaring that

in all his Soliloquies of moment, the strong Intelligence of his Attitude and Aspect drew you into such an impatient Gaze and eager Expectation, that you almost imbib'd the Sentiment with your Eye before the Ear could reach it.[23]

Thus we may say with confidence that Betterton's range was extraordinary and that the varied characters in which he appeared were impersonated rather than merely represented. We may grant him restraint: certainly, many of his effects were gained through underplaying. He sought conscientiously to ascertain his author's meaning. And, without recourse to claptrap, he was able to hold the hushed attention of a frivolous audience.

There were persons in Betterton's time who found, indeed, that acting was on the decline, that the "new Scenes, and Decorations of the Stage," which were introduced soon after the Restoration, had been "the Destruction of good Playing." [24] To attempt at this distance to compare Betterton with Burbage is to venture from the security of a little knowledge into the hazardous ways of conjecture. The eighteen years during which the theatres remained closed would have facilitated innovation. The regular employment of scenery, often of a spectacular sort, and the approximation to something like the picture-frame stage of later times must, one feels, have affected the style of acting. Yet the persistence of a sizable apron is also to be reckoned with; for upon this apron where visibility was greatest, the players are certain to have stationed themselves whenever possible.[25]

That acting reflected the growing artificiality of tragedy is equally certain. Not, of course, that Betterton played his Shakespearian parts precisely as he played Alvaro in *Love and Honour*, or Alexander. We may grant that he differentiated between styles; indeed, it was remarked as a peculiar merit in his acting that he excelled in both Shakespeare and Nat Lee. Yet the desire to modernize, to bring Shakespeare into accord with the current fashions in plays, was a tendency in performance then as now. In *The Spectator*, Addison describes with amusement the pompous regalia, and in particular, the towering plumes, which distinguished the hero of tragedy from lesser men.[26] An uncompleted comedy of Steele's, *The School of Action*, contains a passage which is even more to the point. Buskin, one of those who "pretend to the stage," recites a blustering speech, and for his pains is told to strip.

Buskin. How, strip me!

Humber. Ay, strip you — for if it be not sense in your doublet, it is not in your long robe. High heels on your shoes, or the feathers on your beaver, cannot exalt you a tittle. . . . Such stuff as this is only a tragedy of feathers — it is only lace and ribbon in distress; undress the actor, and the speech is spoiled. . . .

Buskin. Give me my truncheon at least; I got it by heart with a stick in my hand.[27]

Betterton himself would often have worn such plumes and have wielded a truncheon. Is it safe to assume that no trace of the heightened manner of delivery which was in keeping with them remained when he played Hamlet?

Cibber praises Betterton's reading; and the fact that he does so is a little ominous, Cibber himself and those he taught being notorious for affecting a sort of chant or recitative. The *"good old Manner of singing and quavering out their tragic Notes"* is a description of the style as it was practiced by them in the forties,[28] when "the unnatural swelling" of Colley's "words displeased all who preferred natural elocution to artificial cadence." [29] Or there is what Davies tells us of Mrs. Porter. The career of this actress, the legitimate successor, as she came to be regarded, of the great Mrs. Barry, began under Betterton; and when she was a child Betterton saw to it that she spoke and acted "as he would have her" and not otherwise. "Her recitation of fact or sentiment was so modulated," when Davies saw her, "as to resemble musical cadence rather than speaking," though "where the passion predominated, she exerted her powers to a supreme degree" and "seemed then to be another person." [30] Were there no more to it than this, the inference would be clear. But Victor, too, saw Mrs. Porter. She was handicapped, he writes, by "a *plain Person* and a *bad Voice*."

She had naturally a tender Voice, which was enlarged by Labour and Practice into sufficient Force to fill the Theatre; but, by that Means, that *Tremor* was contracted, which was a Singularity that nothing but Custom could reconcile.[31]

Betterton, in the opinion of Cibber, preserved a "medium, between mouthing and meaning too little." Mouthing is bad enough; yet is not "this Extreme . . more pardonable than its opposite Error? I mean that dangerous Affectation of the Monotone, or solemn Sameness of Pronounciation, which, to my Ear, is insupportable." An actor must himself feel "the passion he would raise"; and it had often amazed Cibber that "those who soon came after" Betterton should in many passages "have heavily dragg'd the Sentiment along like a dead Weight, with a long-ton'd Voice and absent Eye, as if they had fairly forgot what they were about." Even Barton Booth he finds lacking in that "requisite Variation of Voice" which made everything Betterton spoke appear "his own natural self-deliver'd Sentiment." Booth "seem'd too much to heave up his Words," paid "too solemn a Regard to Harmony." [32] Charles Gildon in 1710 and Aaron Hill six years later agree that what was chiefly wanting in stage speech was variety of inflection. Neither writer mentions a musical cadence; it is a deadening monotony which they condemn.

"As this Variation of the Voice is founded in Nature," Gildon observes, "so the nearer you approach to Nature, the nearer you come to Perfection. . . . A natural Variation is much the best; the easiest way of arriving at which, is a just Observation of common Discourse, and to mind how you speak your self in Conversation." [33] And Hill blames the obstinacy of the players, who *"are so accustom'd to a horrible,* Theatric,. *way of speaking"* that you almost never *"hear so much as an Endeavour, at those thrilling* Breaks, *and* Changes *of the* Voice; *the only possible Expression of our Passions, in their Variations and Degrees."* [34] Finally, there is the testimony of the usually reliable Tony Aston. Writing of Mrs. Barry, who so often played opposite Betterton, he assures us that "neither she, nor any of the Actors of those Times, had any Tone in their speaking, (too much, lately, in Use.)" [35]

Betterton may have chanted. But the evidence that he did so stops far short of proof. Cibber, excellent critic of acting as he was, never satisfied his contemporaries that he could, himself, perform tragic parts; and it may well be that his speaking of verse was little more than a travesty of Betterton's. The predominant style of Betterton's successors — a solemn and monotonous declamation — is expressly distinguished from his. Tragic acting was, indeed, falling into decadence — to be revived, after the passing of a full generation, by the genius of David Garrick.

Garrick as King Lear

D AVID GARRICK was fond of the Burneys and they delighted in his unceremonious calls. One early morning in the spring of 1775 he had been taking off Dr. Johnson for them and was full of pranks. "He would not be prevailed with to lengthen his visit," Fanny Burney writes:

We all followed him instinctively down stairs; though he *assured* us he would not pilfer anything! "Here is a certain maid here," said he, "whom I love to speak to, because she is *cross.* Egad! Sir, she does not know the *Great Roscius*; but I frightened her this morning a little. Child, said I, you don't know who you have the happiness to speak to! Do you know I am one of the first Geniuses of the Age? Why, child, you would *faint away*, if you knew who I am!" [1]

The old actor spoke lightly of what was infinitely dear to him. His fame reached far beyond the little circle of playwrights and playgoers who had esteemed Betterton or Betterton's predecessors. Like Shakespeare — and their names were now most commonly linked — Garrick had become a national institution.[2]

It is possible to forget that his reputation was founded upon achievement in the art which he professed. Garrick both talked and wrote well — or well enough — and he was not in the least above self-advertisement, which he practised skillfully. His tact, vivacity, and amiability made him generally welcome. Consorting little with his fellow players, he found a place for himself in polite society, just as he was at last elected to membership in The Club. Today, it is safe to say that he is known to many persons merely as a rather prominent character in Boswell's *Johnson*, or as the sitter for portraits by Gainsborough and Sir Joshua Reynolds.

Coming forward, as he did, at the close of a decadent period in tragic acting, Garrick had triumphed splendidly and at once. Something has already been said of the style which his superseded.[3] Cibber and others had approached chanting, or *recitative*, in their delivery. The great Quin, that "Dr. Johnson of the stage," was cold and declamatory.[4] "Sir" John Hill, in *The Actor* (1750), defending Quin against the already familiar charge of monotony, made the point that many of the rôles with which his name was associated — Cato, for instance — admitted of little variety. Yet Garrick, even in passages where "the author carefully delivers a sentence in every line," as if to compel the reader to repeat "the same tone and cadence," avoided singsong:

he lengthens or shortens the pause at every period, according to the circumstances, so that the rests are too much varied from one another to affect the ear as the same thing: he delivers an equal number of syllables in two succeeding lines in very unequal time; and while he gives a more than common force to such passages as will bear it, he delivers others of more familiar import with a naked simplicity, which, tho' the very reverse of that pomp we generally expect in tragedy, is not less just or affecting.[5]

Garrick himself is said to have remarked that Quin was able to "find many words on which to lay an emphasis" where he could find none.[6]

An illuminating comparison between the old school of acting and the new appeared in Colman and Thornton's periodical *The Connoisseur* in 1754. Something like a balance is struck, since neither school is held free from fault. "The generation of players that immediately preceded the present, prided themselves on what they called fine speaking; the emotions of the soul were disregarded for a distinct delivery." Glancing at Quin, the writer remembers "when every line of Othello, a character remarkable for variety of passions, was drawn out in the same pompous manner." It might be urged that "the dignity of the buskin would be degraded by talking in a strain too low and familiar." But "the manner of elocution in a tragedy should not, on the other hand, be more remote from our natural way of expressing ourselves than blank verse . . . is from prose"; and rightly "our present set of actors have, in general, discarded the dead insipid pomp applauded in their predecessors." If, however, there had been improvement in the art of speaking, this was attended by lapses of another sort. "The tragedians of the last age" used little action beyond "strutting with one leg before the other" and waving their arms. Those of the present "have perhaps run into a contrary extreme," employing violent and unnatural gestures and throwing their bodies into attitudes unwarranted by "any of the paintings or sculptures of the best masters." [7]

As for Betterton, he was too distant in time — a full generation — to be of much use for purposes of comparison. Horace Walpole admits grudgingly that the Duke of Argyll considered young Garrick "superior to Betterton." [8] Dibdin and Percival Stockdale were able to find old men with long memories who said the same thing. [9]

Colley Cibber's famous description of Betterton's Hamlet

has already been quoted.[10] It is of the moment when Hamlet first sees the Ghost. We are not told whether Betterton started, whether he introduced action of any sort. Cibber confines himself to the manner in which this great actor spoke Shakespeare's lines. They were an expression of Hamlet's awe and solicitude, not of terror; were deeply impressive without recourse to rant. An equally famous passage, in Lichtenberg's *Letters*, describes Garrick's treatment of the same episode. This time, the details are almost wholly visual. Hamlet, his arms folded beneath his black cloak, his hat pulled down over his eyes, had turned his back to the audience and was moving up stage, "slightly to the left," when Horatio's cry, "Look, my lord, it comes!" reached him. At sight of the Ghost, who had appeared unnoticed on the right and now stood motionless, he staggered back two or three steps "with his knees giving way under him; his hat falls to the ground and both his arms, especially the left, are stretched out nearly to their full length, with the hands as high as his head, the right arm more bent and the hand lower, and the fingers apart." In this strained position, supported by Horatio and Marcellus, he spoke at last, "not at the beginning, but at the end of a breath, with a trembling voice: 'Angels and ministers of grace defend us!' " But this ejaculation merely completed such an effect of terror as made the observer's flesh creep.[11]

The implications of the two passages insofar as styles of acting are concerned, seem clear. They must not, however, be pressed too far. Cibber is making comparisons. Lichtenberg has the eye of an ever-observant traveller. And if Garrick, as I am sure he did, spoke admirably when he came to speak, Betterton is not likely to have trusted to elocution alone. But though the latter "made the Ghost equally terrible to the Spectator as to himself," it was by means less obviously contrived. What Lichtenberg describes is a very elaborate piece of byplay, brilliantly effective but purely histrionic, the invention, there is every reason to suppose, of the actor himself.[12] And he closed the scene with business that was almost as exciting: following the Ghost slowly, and pausing as he went, with his sword drawn and the point advanced as if for protection. "You can well imagine," writes Lichtenberg, "what loud applause accompanies this exit. It begins as soon as the ghost goes off the stage and lasts until Hamlet also disappears." [13]

At its simplest, then, the revolution which Garrick effected was the substitution of a pantomimic style for a declamatory one.[14] Hostile critics, in the actor's own time, attack his starts and attitudes even more fiercely than the "false stops" in his reading. Cibber (not Colley, this time, but his son, the quite impossible Theophilus) cites the start at sight of the very monument "he went to look for," in the last act of *Romeo and Juliet*, and, a moment later, his *"Cyclopedian* Attitude," with iron crow heaved aloft, on the appearance of Paris. (Would not a gentleman, Cibber asks maliciously, have had instinctive recourse to the gentleman's weapon, his sword?) [15] Yet the same starts and attitudes won vast applause in the theatre and were promptly imitated by other actors, with whom they long remained as part of their stock-in-trade.

As for the "false stops," they too imply innovation. Writing to Peter Whalley in 1748, Garrick explains that upon his "first setting out in the Business of an Actor" he had "endeavour'd to shake off the Fetters of Numbers," and had in consequence "been often accus'd of neglecting the Harmony of the Versification, from a too close Regard to the Passion, and the Meaning of the Author." Whalley had found fault with his reading of a number of lines. Garrick admits the justness of the objections in some cases, believes his correspondent mistaken in one, and excuses himself for slips in *Venice Preserved* as owing to his illness on the night when Whalley saw him: "I am often troubled with Pains in my Breast, arising from Colds; and at such Times I have it not in my Power to speak as I would; my Breath often fails me, and I am oblig'd to stop in wrong Places, to enable me to finish the Sentence." [16]

Garrick's pauses were sometimes involuntary; more often they were determined by an alert intelligence. In another letter, he sets forth a few principles of acting, for the benefit of an aristocratic amateur. "In the speaking of soliloquies," he writes, "the great art is to give variety." This "can only be obtained by a strict regard to the pauses. The mixing of the different parts of a monologue together will necessarily give a monotony." [17] He had far more nearly mastered Shakespeare's verse, with its subtle interrelations of rhythm and meaning, than had those drowsy tragedians of the generation before. Moreover, with his unfailing histrionic sense, he made the rhetorical pause an important means of commanding attention.[18] Thus, in the second scene of *Hamlet* where Horatio explains why he has returned to Elsinore,

> My lord, I came to see your father's funeral,

Hamlet says:

> I prithee do not mock me, fellow student.
> *I think it was to see — my mother's wedding.*

In speaking this last line, Garrick protests,

I certainly never *stop* . . . (that is close the *sense*,) but I as certainly *suspend* my voice, by which your ear must know that the sense is suspended too; for Hamlet's grief causes the break, and with a sigh, he finishes the sentence — "my mother's wedding." I really could not from my feelings act it otherwise.[19]

If we are tempted to use the word "natural" of his style, it must be with immediate reservations. Tragedy, though lately she had given up some of her regalia, was still Tragedy and heedful of decorum. Garrick's Macbeth might appear with his wig slightly disarranged after the murder of Duncan, but Macbeth's guests and retainers must not, upon the discovery of the murder, suggest through "half, or even disordered, dress" that they had been startled from their beds.[20]

Garrick, as we have seen, "endeavour'd to shake off the Fetters of Numbers" — he hated singsong. He also hated rant. William Powell, a young actor in whose progress he was interested, had been appearing in Nat Lee's violent old play *The Rival Queens*.

I am very angry with *Powell*, [Garrick writes,] for playing that detestable part of Alexander — Every Genius must despise it, because that, & such fustian-like Stuff, is the bane of true merit — If a man can act it well, I mean to please y[e] People, he has something in him that a good actor sh[d] not have. . . . I hate your Roarers — Delane was once a fine *Alexander* — damn y[e] Part — I fear 'twill hurt him.[21]

But as if to demonstrate that naturalness in acting is always relative, he tried a curious experiment. He had been talking to Joseph Cradock and others about Shakespeare. "The scene of Iago's working Othello up to jealousy" was, he thought, the finest single scene; the first three acts of *Hamlet*, the finest acts; and *Macbeth*, "altogether the finest tragedy." Then, turning to Cradock, "let us now," he said, "try those scenes, as easy and natural as possible, I mean divested of all stage strut and trick, beginning, 'Excellent wench,' &c." At the close of the recital he asked for opinions and was not, I should judge, in the least surprised to hear that though it might be "strictly natural" it would never do on the boards.[22]

Closely related to the welcome variety of his speaking was his power of passing with the utmost rapidity from one emotion to another. "He falls from fury into tears with a breath; and is pure and entire in both sensations" — the words carry added weight coming as they do from William Shirley, a writer who was very ready indeed to find fault.[23] And old Mrs. Abington, an actress who had caused Garrick plenty of annoyance in her time, said that "his excellence lay in the bursts and quick transitions of passion. . . ."[24] *Hamlet* affords two striking instances:

> I say, away! — Go on, I'll follow thee,

where "his variation from extreme passion to reverential awe" was "forceably expressed in eyes, features, attitude, and voice"; and, in the Closet Scene, "his turning short from looking after the apparition with wildness of terror, and viewing his mother with pathetic concern."[25]

At such moments, the unmatched expressiveness of his face came into full play. It was, indeed, his face which was likely to impress most deeply those who saw him.[26] Churchill, the satirist, in that once famous poem *The Rosciad* (1761) alludes to the frequent criticism of Garrick's unnatural starts and affected pauses. But, he answers:

> When in the features all the soul's portray'd,
> And passions, such as Garrick's, are display'd,
> To me they seem from quickest feelings caught:
> Each start is Nature; and each pause is Thought.[27]

It was only to be expected that Garrick would make the most of this extraordinary gift, yet the fact that he did so was remarked, and not always charitably. William Mason, who wrote classical tragedies, maintains that the actor-manager was uninterested in plays which gave him no opportunity to express "strong, but sudden effects of passion." Indeed, if *Hamlet* itself had been a new play, submitted to Garrick for revision, not many of the great soliloquies

would have been admitted by him without the most licentious pruning. For though no man did more to correct the vicious taste of the preceding age in theatrical declamation than he did . . . yet this was not his principal excellence, and he knew it, and therefore disliked to perform any part whatever, where expression of countenance was not more necessary than recitation of sentiment.[28]

David Williams addresses him sarcastically in 1772, when Roscius was growing old: "You almost always present your whole face, and the broad glare of your eye, to the audience," who must not be denied a *full view of the wonderful Garrick.*" [29]

The face they were privileged to study was dark, with something of a Gallic cast bespeaking the actor's French blood. The eyes were black, or very nearly so, brilliant, piercing; and "they looked," it was said, "the very soul." [30] Nor could any fault be found with the voice, which was both commanding and musical. Joshua Steele, in his curious treatise, *Prosodia Rationalis*, writes that Garrick was distinctly audible even when he spoke most softly. Steele confesses that he had once set down Hamlet's "To be, or not to be," with his own system of musical notation, "in the stile of a ranting actor, swelled with *forte* and softened with *piano*." Then he heard Garrick speak the same soliloquy, and he delivered it "with little or no distinction of piano and forte, but nearly uniform; something below the ordinary force, or, as a musician would say, *sotto voce*, or *sempre poco piano*." [31]

In every respect, save one, Garrick was superbly equipped. The deficiency, as his critics never tired of reminding him, was in height. He was a little man. His appearance as Othello — a very black Othello — was occasion for a *bon mot* of Quin's which became justly famous: *"There is the boy,"* said Quin severely, upon Garrick's entrance, *"but where is the tea-kettle?"* [32] For compensation, Garrick could count upon the grace of his every movement — denied only by those who did not want to see it, grace being the least demonstrable of gifts — and upon shoes with very high heels!

Now, as he began the season of 1775–1776, he was tired and unwell. The vexations of theatrical management had become irksome to him. It was time to give over. *Exit Roscius!* Drury Lane heard the news, in a prologue spoken by Tom King, early in March. Then came a long series of fare-well performances. London saw Garrick in a round of his famous parts: as Benedick and Archer, as Hamlet and Richard III and Abel Drugger. King Lear he performed for the last time on June 8, two nights before the final night of all when, turning once more to comedy, he appeared as Don Felix in *The Wonder*.

Places for these performances became harder and harder to get. Garrick himself was harassed with requests, demands. [33]

The eagerness of people to see him, [writes Hannah More in one of her letters,] is beyond any thing you can have an idea of. You will see half a dozen duchesses and countesses of a night, in the upper boxes: for the fear of not seeing him at all, has humbled those who used to go, not for the purpose of seeing, but of

30

being seen; and they now courtsey to the ground for the worst places in the house.[34]

The unfortunate Samuel Curwen, once of Salem, Massachusetts, "attempted to get into Drury Lane theatre, to see Mr. Garrick in the character of Archer, but the crowd," he found, was "so great, that after suffering thumps, squeezes, and almost suffocation for two hours," he gave up in despair.[35]

Tears were being shed and tender emotions experienced on the stage as well as among the spectators. *King Lear* is reviewed in *The London Chronicle*, May 21–23, 1776. Garrick had "never appeared so great in the character before. The curse at the close of the first act, and his phrenetic appeal to heaven at the end of the second . . . caused a kind of momentary petrifaction thro' the house, which he soon dissolved universally into tears." And the writer adds, what I have never quite been able to imagine: "Even the unfeeling Regan and Goneril, forgetful of their characteristic cruelty, played through the whole of their parts with aching bosoms and streaming eyes." To Hannah More it seemed as if, seeing Garrick for the last time in character after character, she had been "assisting at the funeral obsequies" of each in turn.[36]

Signs of a reaction against emotionalism are not, however, wholly wanting. Witness the astringent letter of a person who calls himself "Anti-Sycophant," in *The Morning Chronicle*, June 8. The Town, he agreed, was suffering from "Garricko-Mania," a malady which was gaining ground daily "among the *bon ton*. I admire the little great man as much as any one well can within the bounds of reason." But how is it possible to reconcile

the contradictory compliments that are so lavishly bestowed upon him. In a Morning Paper (not famous for puffing) we are told, that (as he is there termed) the *extraordinary phaenomenon*, Richard the Third, departed *his theatrical life* last night. Another evening paper of yesterday, with equal propriety, terms the King Richard, of Drury Lane, an *immortal performer*.

Who shall decide when Critics disagree?

Garrick's Lear was as fine that last spring as it had ever been. Even "Theatricus" in *St. James's Chronicle*, May 23–25, says as much; and he was capable of referring to a young actress who had appeared with Garrick in *The Suspicious Husband* as "that Abstract of Insipidity, the inanimate *Siddons*." In *The Public Advertiser* of June 6 was the notice: "Mr. Garrick will appear in King Lear for the last Time on Saturday next, being the last Time but one of his appearing on the Stage." Horace Walpole attended, and told Garrick afterwards that he was "more shocked at the rest of the company than pleased with him — which I believe was not just what he desired." [37] On that same Saturday, "his Majesty reviewed, on Wimbleton Common, Gen. Burgoyne's Regiment of Light Dragoons, who are on their March to Portsmouth, to embark for America." [38]

King Lear as it was produced by Garrick was not Shakespeare's tragedy. Nor was it, strictly speaking, the notorious version of the play composed by Nahum Tate, though it is very close to this. In a series of able studies, Dr. George Winchester Stone has argued convincingly that Garrick was not a mere exploiter of Shakespeare, an antic garnished in his colors. On the contrary, Shakespeare owes a great deal to this actor — even, we are told, in the matter of restoring his words to the stage.[39] In a moment of aberration, Garrick did alter *Hamlet*. But his alteration has proved to be less impious, now that we can judge of it for ourselves, than it used to appear from garbled descriptions.

32

In *King Lear*, the structural changes effected by Tate were chiefly three. He introduced "heart interest," a mawkish love affair between Edgar and Cordelia; he omitted the Fool, presumably out of deference to neo-classical ideas of tragic decorum; and he contrived a happy ending, in accordance with the then fashionable doctrine of poetic justice. Cordelia does not die, nor Lear, nor even Gloucester. Virtue is rewarded, as well as vice punished. In addition to these changes in the plot of the play, there is an almost incessant 'improving' of its language — cuts, additions, and appalling substitutions. And it was here that Garrick came to the poet's rescue. Too timid to brave the censure of those who still upheld Tate and the criticism of the play implied in Tate's reshaping of it, he busied himself with making verbal restorations, and not only in the lines which he himself spoke but in others as well. There were murmurers still. Tom Davies refers to "admirers of *unsophisticated Shakspeare*" who "wished to have seen *Mr. Garrick* in *Lear*, as originally written; though I believe the distress would have been more than any audience could bear." [40] (Tate's version, too, was easier on the actor cast as Lear, "who stands in need of all the relief which the conduct of the fable can afford him.") [41] Garrick at one time thought of putting back the part of the Fool, but decided not to "hazard so bold an attempt." [42] According to Cradock, he was under some pressure at the time of his last performances:

Steevens urged him to give the genuine text of Lear, which he rejected . . . as he feared, from agitation and unlearning, he might make some mistake; indeed, the morning I was with him, and heard him recite some part, he seemed quite miserable; and I told Steevens I was sorry he had been so pressed. Johnson had never interfered about the matter. He played Lear twice; after the second act I left my place, and went in tears to the Bedford

Coffee House; when Garrick heard of this he was quite affected, and shook me by the hands. I went to the Theatre during the last act, merely to inquire after him; and *here the curtain fell*; for I did not see him take his final leave in Felix.[43]

Garrick's Lear is pictured for us unkindly as a "little, old, white-haired man . . . with spindle-shanks, a tottering gait, and great shoes upon the little feet." [44] His face he made up with remarkable skill to suggest great age; [45] and, what was something of a novelty, he and the other actors in this production were "judiciously habited," not in contemporary, but "in old English dresses." [46]

How an actor represents Lear will depend to a great extent on his own physique. The hale old man who comes back from hunting with eager demands for his dinner might be more Shakespearian than a Lear already weak with age when we first see him, but Garrick could not be burly. It was found praiseworthy in his impersonation that he colored "all the Passions, with a certain Feebleness suitable to the Age of the King"; [47] that his was "an old man's passion, and an old man's voice and action"; [48] that his "strength and activity of spirit" were "judiciously united to nerveless limbs" — though "in the sudden starts of passion, you perceive the quick flow of blood giving momentary firmness to his sinews." [49] Garrick himself, in a manuscript letter quoted by Dr. Stone, dwells upon the importance of Lear's age, if only because it ensured the sympathy of an audience. "Lear is certainly a weak man, it is part of his character — violent old and weakly fond of his daughters." But "his weakness proceeds from his age . . . and such an old man full of affection, generosity, passion," enduring what he has to endure, will inevitably become an object of pity.[50] And Garrick's king was thoroughly amiable,

"an honest, well-meaning, ill-used old man," discovered
"seated upon his throne in fullness of a content, which he
shares out with infinite complacency among his *pelican
daughters.*" [51]

I have been able to learn very little about his playing of
the first scene. (It is not of much consequence to read that he
was "angry with superior Sovereignty," though it is something.) [52] Near the close of the act, when Lear clashes with
Goneril, details begin to stand out with some clearness.
Joseph Pittard was impressed by,

> "Oh *Lear*!
> Beat at that Gate which let thy Folly in,
> And thy dear Judgment out."

Garrick lent the words a power "which cannot be conceived
but with much Difficulty" by those who had not seen him
themselves. "The whole bitter Tide of Resentment pours
back on himself, and is as fully exprest, from the Fingers to
the Toes, through the flashing Eye, and keen Features, as
Raphel [*sic*] has exprest . . . in his Picture of the Transfiguration." [53] Thomas Wilkes was struck by other passages.[54]
It is noteworthy, indeed, how many different passages are
cited by different onlookers, though a few impressed all alike.
The imprecation against Goneril, which in the present version closes the act, was one of these last. Even before Garrick's
time, there is evidence of the terrible words' having been
recited kneeling, almost in the manner of a prayer.[55] Garrick
himself, despite criticism — there was a lasting controversy
as to how the lines should be spoken — interpreted them thus.
Flinging away the crutch or stick which he carried, he
dropped on one knee and with clenched hands and raised
eyes began, "Hear, Nature, hear!" As he continued to speak,

"with a broken, inward, struggling Utterance," [56] ending with a burst of tears, his face exhibited "such a combination of painful, enraged feelings, as scarce any countenance but his own could describe." [57] It was this amazing display of facial expression, no doubt, which made the actor choose "yᵉ curse in Lear," along with the Dagger Scene and the "falling asleep in Sʳ John Brute," to give in Paris, after "the *Clairon*" had been reciting from Racine.[58]

Joseph Warton acknowledges he had been more moved by Garrick's speaking of a single line in the second act —

O me, my heart, my rising heart! But down! —

than by "the most pompous declaimer of the most pompous speeches in Cato or Tamerlane." [59] And this was at a time (1753) when neo-classical tragedy was still taken seriously! Davies was grateful for the restoring of Shakespeare's lines,

Do you but mark how this becomes the house:
"Dear daughter, I confess that I am old.
Age is unnecessary. On my knees I beg
That you'll vouchsafe me raiment, bed, and food."

Garrick "threw himself on both knees, with his hands clasped, and, in a supplicating tone, repeated this touching, though ironical, petition." [60] In the parleying with Goneril and Regan, another contemporary writes, "rage and tenderness, suppressed fury and affectionate condescension" were "mingled happily till the conclusive speech, where his breaks of voice, and variation of features, surpass the finest conception that has not been impressed by him." [61] And phrases from the same speech — "I will do such things — What they are yet, I know not"; and, in its altered form, "O gods! I shall go mad" — awakened emotion long afterwards in old men who had once heard Garrick speak them.[62]

A sterner test — the hardest, it may be, that Shakespeare ever exacted of a player — comes with Lear's next scene. There, as Granville-Barker has shown, Lear himself must act the storm; and it is a striking tribute to Garrick that "the elementary conflict" was "re-imaged in his distracted looks." [63] His appearance, as described by Wilkes, was one to evoke both pity and terror:

I never see him coming down from one corner of the Stage, with his old grey hair standing, as it were, erect upon his head, his face filled with horror and attention, his hands expanded, and his whole frame actuated by a dreadful solemnity, but I am astounded, and share in all his distresses; . . . *one might interpret from the dumbness of his gesture.*[64]

Scenes of madness follow, those before the hovel and in the farmhouse, which had been combined by Tate, and the meeting with Gloucester. Garrick, according to an early description, was so skillful in suggesting the approaches of distraction that one scarcely perceived where he first began to be mad, yet found that he was mad "before *Kent* says,

'I fear'd 'twould come to this; his Wits are gone.'" [65]

The "first absolute Act of Madness" was a strange mirthless laugh, a laugh that seemed "without any Connection with the Soul; an involuntary Emotion of the Muscles," which moved the audience to tears.[66] Yet he played these scenes with an extraordinary self-denial.

He had no sudden starts, [Murphy writes,] no violent gesticulation; his movements were slow and feeble; misery was depicted in his countenance; he moved his head in the most deliberate

37

manner; his eyes were fixed, or, if they turned to any one near him, he made a pause, and fixed his look on the person after much delay; his features at the same time telling what he was going to say, before he uttered a word.[67]

A quaint and spontaneous tribute was paid his art by the poet William Julius Mickle. Offended by Garrick's rejection of a tragedy of his, Mickle had taken a scholar's vengeance and inserted in his translation of *The Lusiad* a footnote concerning the "many neglected unsufferable loads of unanimated dulness" which Garrick had honored by his approbation.[68] Sometime later, the poet, who had never seen Garrick on the stage, was taken to *King Lear*. Through the first three acts, he remained silent. Then, "in a fine passage of the fourth, he fetched a deep sigh, and, turning to his friend, 'I wish,' said he, 'the *note* was out of my book!'" [69]

Lear in Tate's version of the play, still has his exquisite scene of reconciliation with Cordelia. Garrick rose to it. Davies, after summarizing his achievement thus far, his transitions "from one passion to another," his pursuit of "the progress of agonizing feelings to madness in its several stages," adds that he was able to make this scene "more interesting," through his "superior taste," than anything that had come before.[70] And the old actor Bannister said that "the scene with Cordelia and the physician, as Garrick played it, was the most pathetic he ever saw on the stage." [71] An admired detail was Lear's "putting his finger to the cheek of Cordelia, and then looking at his finger" — [72] "Be your tears wet? Yes faith."

There remains the unhappy happy ending, as Tate had devised it, with Lear rescued while he was still defending Cordelia. Garrick's acting was impressive even in this final episode. One moment in particular was long remembered where the old king, leaning breathless and exhausted against the side of the scene, hears one of Edgar's followers say:

> Look here, my lord, see where the generous king
> Has slain two of 'em.
> *Lear.*   Did I not, fellow? [73]

This had become a touchstone for excellence when, a few years later, Mrs. Siddons was taking London by storm. "She interested her audience in a stile of acting new to us, and of such a sort, that except Mr. Garrick's rapid exclamation of 'Did I not[,] fellow?' in King Lear, in our memory never was equalled." [74]

It is as the complete actor that I think of David Garrick. He was a master of mimicry. He loved to act — off the stage as well as on it. [75] He drew tears from those who saw him, and remained quite unmoved himself. [76] His charm was such as to draw all eyes to him. It was quaintly argued that he really should not appear on the stage at all since, when he was there, the other characters ceased to exist: in the *Hamlet* Play Scene, there was no play — one saw only Hamlet; and though the object of Hamlet's scrutiny "was to have been the *King* . . . the devil a king was there." [77]

His powers of transformation were the wonder of the age. He was now King Lear, now Abel Drugger, and magnificent in both. But it is suggestive, I think, that his critics found him best in "busy or passionate characters," [78] or said that his perfection consisted *"in the extreme."* [79] Hence his inability to perform satisfactorily the colorless rôle of a fine gentleman. He wanted parts that demanded *acting*, not mere elegance, good looks — and stature! Within his legitimate province, he delighted to create. He wrote of the French actor Préville: "his genius never appears more to advantage than

39

when the author leaves him to shift for himself." [80] Almost
the same thing was said of Garrick: "Where other performers,
and good ones too, pass unnoticed, he is frequently great;
where an author is languid, he gives him spirit." [81]

Acting, he made clear by demonstration, was no poor
relation to the other arts. In its representation of the passions,
for instance, it was found comparable to painting; and such
names as Raphael and Angelo figure repeatedly in accounts
of his performances. The English Theatre, prospering greatly
under his management, became for the first time, what it was
to remain, despite protests, for more than a century — an
actor's theatre. Once past your first innocence as a playgoer,
you no longer went to see *The Fair Penitent*, but to see
Garrick as Lothario contending with old Quin as Horatio;
no longer to see *Romeo and Juliet*, but one of the rival
Romeos — and which was better, Barry or Garrick? — no
longer to see *King Lear*, but to see, if you might, Garrick for
the last time in his greatest tragic part.

Kemble as Hamlet

JOHN PHILIP KEMBLE'S place in the great succession of English actors is secure, if enigmatic. One names them over — Betterton, Garrick, Kemble, Kean — with confidence. Yet in Kemble's own time there were many who questioned his preëminence, which was challenged by George Frederick Cooke, specialist in villainous and sardonic parts, and challenged anew by the prodigious child, Master Betty. Even the warmest admirers of Kemble put his sister, Mrs. Siddons, before him; and near the close of his career he found himself eclipsed by Edmund Kean, a player whom he could only regard as a vulgar charlatan. Kean fascinated audiences and critics alike, and he still fascinates those who know him from the inspired pages of Hazlitt. Kean was unconventional, daring, "natural." Kemble is the only English actor of distinction who by his contemporaries was not called natural. History repeats itself, and as Garrick in triumphing over poor Quin had exposed something essentially false so, one feels, must it have been with Kean and Kemble.

Not that the elder actor was without apologists. But Sir Walter Scott's essay is much less known than it should be, and William Robson's *Old Play-goer* is all but forgotten. Boaden's memoir, still read for its substance, is pompous and ill-written, and the poet Campbell's once famous "Valedictory Stanzas" are chilling.

> Fair as some classic dome,
>   Robust and richly graced,
> Your KEMBLE's spirit was the home
>   Of genius and of taste;
> Taste, like the silent dial's power,
>   That, when supernal light is given,
> Can measure inspiration's hour,
>   And tell its height in heaven.
> At once ennobled and correct,
>   His mind surveyed the tragic page,
> And what the actor could effect
>   The scholar could presage.

After that, one wants to read about actors who were rogues and vagabonds!

But in the autumn of 1783 Kemble was still unknown to London, and as a brother of the celebrated Mrs. Siddons and on the strength of flattering reports from Dublin and the provinces,[1] his début was eagerly awaited. Another brother, Stephen, remembered as a Falstaff who could do without stuffing, had come out at Covent Garden a few days before. He proved to be merely the *big*, not the *great* Mr. Kemble. Then, at Drury Lane, September 30, John Philip Kemble appeared as Hamlet. "The great expectations which were formed of this gentleman drew together a most crouded audience; and the house was completely filled in a few minutes after the doors opened." [2]

At one moment, when Hamlet after stabbing Polonius cries, "Is it the King?" there were "universal Plaudits" [3] — the Closet Scene and those with the Ghost were considered Kemble's best. He was interesting. "The impression he made on his auditors was such that his performance, and no other subject, was the leading topic through the remainder of the evening." [4] They talked of his resemblance to his sister. This was a young Hamlet — of a "lad-like" appearance.[5] His style was like hers, too, in its attention to niceties of detail.

Kemble's face seemed richly expressive to some, but there was difference of opinion here. And was not his action somewhat wanting in ease; too artificial, "bordering," it might be, "upon affectation"?[6] As for the deficiencies of his voice, which were to become so serious in course of time, they do not seem to have been conspicuous. The friendly reviewer of *The Gazetteer and New Daily Advertiser* did, indeed, notice that the young man's voice lost "its music and its energy when raised to the vehement, and it is apparently with great uneasiness to himself that he reaches the necessary heights of impassioned oratory," and another critic, though he was sitting "no farther distant than the Extremity of the Boxes," could not always hear.[7] But Kemble's variety of intonation and firm intelligence as a reader were warmly praised. The malice of an anonymous contributor to *The Public Advertiser* is, indeed, patent. Though granting the new player "Good Sense and Powers of Judgment" far beyond those of his sister, he yet calls him "a strong *Mannerist*," one whose utterance at times, "sensibly approached the dull, designing Drawl of a popular Preacher, or a Methodist." Fortunately this rascal was convincingly shown not to have attended the performance he criticized! (He praised Parsons as the Gravedigger when in point of fact an apology had been made for Parsons, and Dick Suett "went through his Part.")[8] *The Gazetteer and New Daily Advertiser* finds that

43

his recitation is evidently his great talent, and here, in our mind, he has no equal. His tones are beautifully modulated, his emphasis critical and instructive, and he so accurately possesses and conveys the meanings of the Poet, that it is a feast to hear him.[9]

Only, as was pointed out even in the case of this early performance, his pauses were sometimes too long (Kemble's pauses were to be the occasion of many a joke in the years to come).

Above all, he was original: unlike Garrick, unlike Garrick's brilliant disciple and successor, Henderson, the reigning star of the moment. Not that his conception of the part was strange or heretical. Old Tom Davies, who had seen a great many Hamlets in his time, makes this clear.[10] It was in details rather than outline, tactics rather than strategy, that the novelty lay. Kemble's *style* was different. "There was nothing of . . . any man within our memory, in his delivery or deportment; he stood alone." [11]

Comparisons with Henderson were attempted immediately after the performance, but they are not very revealing. Only gradually was it realized that the Kembles had effected a revolution, that their school was in fact superseding Garrick's. Yet to most persons who had seen the earlier actor, he remained unapproachable. Bitter thrusts were levelled at players who were all *"paw and pause"* — so that on the stage one was tempted to prompt them! "The Garrick school was all *rapidity* and *passion*." [12] Its founder "never appeared solicitous to investigate a sentence, but went at once to the sentiment it enforced; his business was not to methodize words, but to express passions; he never was pertinacious, pedantic, or critical . . . he acted." [13] So the conservatives, attacking chiefly John Kemble and only rarely glancing at his sister.

And the superannuated Charles Macklin could give his bless-
ing to Holman, whose début came the season after Kemble's:
"I like the young fellow, Sir; he introduces no NEW READINGS
in the part." [14] Delight in new readings did not begin with
Kemble — it was Henderson who set his stamp on one of the
most famous of them,

> Many a time, *and oft on the Rialto —*

but they are peculiarly associated with him; and as we shall
see he introduced new readings a plenty in this performance
of 1783. [15]

Hamlet's grief and isolation were the first notes struck.
Kemble seems not to have been "discovered" (in Scene 2),
but to have come in at the end of a long procession. So, at
any rate, he entered when an American writer saw him much
later in his career.

We *have*, however, seen him in Hamlet to the very heart! We
have yearned for the last flourish of the tippling king's trumpets,
— for the passing of Mr. Murray and Mrs. Powell, — for the entrance of Mr. Claremont and Mr. Claremont's other self in Rosencrantz and Guildenstern. We have yearned for all these; because
then, after a pause, came Hamlet! — There he was! The sweet, the
graceful the gentlemanly Hamlet. . . . His mourning dress was
in unison with the fine severe sorrow of his face. . . . You could
not take your eye from the dark intensity of his: you could not
look on any meaner form, while his matchless person stood in
princely perfection before you. . . . There he stood! and when
he spoke . . . his voice fell in its fine cadences like an echo upon
the ear — and you were taken by its tones back with Hamlet to
his early days, and over all his griefs, until you stood, like him,
isolated in the Danish revel court. The beauty of his performance
of Hamlet was its retrospective air — its intensity and abstraction. [16]

45

He wore, not yet "the Vandyke costume" — that was to be adopted a little later — but "a modern court dress of rich black velvet" with his hair "in powder"; and this powdered hair was effective since, by contrast, his eyes "seemed to possess more brilliancy." [17]

In the first soliloquy, and in Hamlet's scene with Horatio, innovation began. Going back to the Folio, this young actor read:

> so loving to my mother
> That he might not *beteene* the winds of heaven
> Visit her face too roughly,

restoring "beteene" for " 'Let e'en — or 'permitted' as Garrick's better Usage was"; and he read:

> Would I had met my dearest foe in heaven,

with "*dearest* Foe — for *direst* Foe — justified by the best Copies, but on Principles too remote for a popular Audience." [18] It was the age of Malone, and Kemble was a bit of an antiquary. Nor would it ever have occurred to him that these niceties were unworthy of his attention. Hence the enduring accusation of pedantry levelled against him.

When Horatio and Marcellus began to tell of what they had seen in the night, his "fixed mute attention — not a finger moved" — was noteworthy.[19] Hamlet questions them, swiftly, incisively: "But where was this?" "Did you not speak to it?" And this second question he threw into strange prominence by laying emphasis on "you" — "Did YOU not speak to it?" Though Marcellus might not have addressed the apparition, Horatio, the scholar, Hamlet's intimate friend, must have done so! It was the most brilliant of the "new reading," sharply contested — Steevens, the redoubtable Shakespearian

46

commentator, took cognizance of it — specious, no doubt, and over-elaborate, but not for an instant absurd. Kemble, indeed, told his biographer that he had consulted Johnson on the matter and that the Doctor agreed with him: "To be sure, sir — YOU should be strongly marked. I told Garrick so, long since, but Davy never could see it." [20]

Garrick had made the scene with the Ghost one of intense excitement. His start of terror, and near collapse, and the desperate following of the apparition step by step, were still remembered and admired in 1783. It had been acting of the most sensational sort, wildly applauded. Kemble could not hope to match it. He could and did tone down its excesses: "The Disposition new, on the Ghost coming — Hamlet not starting between Horatio and Marcellus, and being held by them — but standing alone and forward." [21] There was no "studied preparation" for the start.[22] And when Kemble's Hamlet followed the Ghost out, it was without bravado, the point of his sword now trailing behind him instead of being advanced threateningly against the apparition.[23] Each change could be defended on grounds of taste. (If only, one grumbles, he had abstained from the pompousness of

And for my Soul what *can* it do to *that?*

Garrick had darted over the words — "What can it do to *that?*") [24]

Kemble's face was found well worth watching during the Ghost's long narration, though some felt there was "too much action" on the listener's part, "too frequent movement of the arms." [25] Then, an innovation which justified itself instantly, as this Hamlet swore to remember the Ghost — he knelt.[26] Noteworthy, too, was the distinction he made between Horatio, in whom Hamlet could confide, and the stranger, Marcellus. In our time, Mr. Dover Wilson has made much of this distinction, and students of the play are likely to associate it with his exciting book, *What Happens in Hamlet*. But it was not quite new even with Kemble. Henderson had certainly used it, though not Garrick.[27]

Hamlet's scenes of madness in the second act, with their swift changes and adjustments of manner, were perhaps a little beyond Kemble's powers. The madness itself was now too transparent to deceive; there was "a certain stiffness of action." [28] One invention of his, I have seen revived, and it came off well.[29] Hamlet is teasing Polonius about the offensive treatise on old men which he pretends to be reading. "Slanders, sir . . ." and he madly tore the leaf from the book! The meticulous critic who signed himself "The Rosciad," in *The Public Advertiser*, was as much puzzled by this action as Polonius might have been. He goes on to criticize the young actor for being "not only familiar, but gay and smiling," in the scene with Rosencrantz and Guildenstern. That Kemble, at any time, could be *familiar* may come as a surprise to those who have been brought up to think of him as ever stately. Yet one reviewer, Woodfall in *The Morning Chronicle*, writes with emphasis: "Again, Mr. Kemble throws so much of familiarity into his manner, that the dignity of tragedy is occasionally lost sight of, and the dialogue becomes as it were a mere colloquy between ordinary persons on an ordinary subject." This Hamlet was, unquestionably, a great gentleman, and prince, but he was quite capable of unbending. To Charles Lamb, indeed, "the playful, court-bred spirit in which he condescended to the players" was peculiarly happy.[30] Even more interesting is a comment by the German poet Ludwig Tieck. Seeing Kemble almost at the close of the actor's career, he noticed that his reading of " 'Tis not so; it begins with Pyrrhus," was applauded

because this forgetfulness, this seeking after the beginning of the verse, was expressed in such a natural way. And, indeed, when one has been listening for a length of time to a slow, measured, wailing rhythm, regularly interrupted by considerable pauses . . . one is quite taken by surprise on hearing once more the tones of nature, and the manner of everyday conversation.[31]

Kemble's style had hardened by 1817; but sudden excursions into the familiar or, as we shall see, the passionate, were an essential part of it.[32]

Edmund Kean played the Nunnery Scene with a novel tenderness for Ophelia and won vast acclaim by doing so. His treatment of her was often contrasted with Kemble's, to the latter's disadvantage. The passionate anger of Kemble's tones and looks, his violent exits and returns, belonged it may be to a still earlier time. "The Rosciad" found the scene itself "rather repulsive," but "done very delicately"; whereas *The Gazetteer* called this flatly "the worst scene of his performance" — one marred by "tricks, in the stage phrase, which have nothing to recommend them *but* their novelty." [33]

It is from a comparison with Kean, again, that we learn most about the Play Scene. But this time it is Kemble who is praised at his brilliant rival's expense. Kemble had perceived the bearing of the scene upon Hamlet's plans and was ever watching the King's face and ever avoiding being observed to be watching, so that when the King looked his way he would be preoccupied with Ophelia, or toying with her fan, and answered the King's questions carelessly.[34] In the Recorders Scene, after Guildenstern protests that he cannot "play upon this pipe," Hamlet (in 1783) turned to Rosencrantz — "I do beseech

49

you" — thus distinguishing between them as he had distinguished between Horatio and Marcellus in the first act.[35]

An amateur playgoer, Richard Twining, found Kemble's scene with Gertrude "a most capital piece of acting, or rather of *non*-acting," [36] and it was singled out for praise by other spectators. They were not, however, quite at one. Thus, "Is it the King?" was widely commended, but in *The Public Advertiser* our friend "The Rosciad" objected to the words' being spoken "with a Smile, nay more, with a Grin." This was to sacrifice the true character of the Prince: "instead of Hamlet, we see 'the Soul of Nero!' " Yet, an instant later, the same critic is questioning whether the treatment of Gertrude was not too gentle:

> In the Closet Scene, is the first Principle of the Character well analysed? — Are "the Daggers that he speaks" drawn, and as sharp, and as strongly pushed as they ought to be? . . .
> Lay not the flattering Unction to your Soul, &c.
> is preceptive, rather than supplicatory; of course the kneeling Posture of Kemble is not right.

Old Tate Wilkinson, manager of the theatre at York where Kemble had appeared often before coming to London, saw him "kneel to his mother in the third act of Hamlet, and *kiss her hand (or neck*, if he can reach it), with all the enthusiasm of filial love and duty." [37] Still another moment which aroused discussion was that of the presenting of the pictures —

> Look here upon this picture, and on this.

"The scorn and contempt" with which this Hamlet flung aside the miniature of Claudius, "and the filial affection that shews itself upon his pressing his father's portrait to his lips," were, to some at least of those who saw him, evidence of "the nicest discrimination and propriety of feeling." [38]

As for the scene with the Gravediggers, "The Rosciad" makes a single objection, that "it was not," as Kemble played it, "sufficiently *melancholy* for Hamlet." One thinks of the beplumed, funereal Prince in Lawrence's painting, Yorick's skull in his hand, his eyes lifted in mournful contemplation — no want of melancholy there, certainly! And, as certainly, an excess of solemnity. Was it not this later Hamlet who avoided the awkward and undignified action of leaping into the grave to lay hands upon Laertes? [39] Kemble was still young, and "lad-like" in appearance, on that autumn night of 1783.

Exception was taken to his studied grace as Hamlet prepared for the fencing-bout — "There was a little too much complaisance and solemnity of bowing"; and "the Prince is certainly to conduct himself with courteousness, but he is not to play the part of a dancing-master." [40] It was pointed out, however, that at the beginning of the fencing Hamlet is quite unconscious of the deadly intent of his adversary; two gentlemen are engaging in a friendly trial of skill, that is all. "The peculiar grace with which Mr. Kemble makes his first pass at Laertes shews excellent skill in the art of fencing, though it might, with great propriety, be esteemed artificial and stiff," were the Prince fighting for his life "with Richmond in Bosworth field." [41] Hamlet's last speech of all was delivered with too much vigor,[42] some thought, but "The Rosciad" seems to have been wholly satisfied: "The Dying — is a very noble Part of the Work. — The snatching elevated Tone is particularly impressing, which gives, 'The Fell Serjeant Death,' &c." And then, according to one review, the play came to an end, the audience insisting "on the curtain being dropped as soon as Hamlet pronounced the last sentence, (a compliment rarely paid to an actor)." [43] For somewhat similar reasons —

histrionic rather than dramatic — Kemble himself, as a modest newcomer to the London stage, had omitted Hamlet's advice to the players.

The mere presence of the actor lends unity to what he does on the stage, and in Kemble's case we have to reckon with an actor, splendidly handsome, whose personality was striking and memorable. Sometimes, as Sir Walter Scott admits, he was overprecise and "by giving a peculiar emphasis to every word of the sentence . . . lost the effect which to be vehement should be instant and undivided." But it was not Macbeth whom Scott saw in imagination on "the blighted heath of Forres," but "the stately step of Kemble as he descended on the stage." [44]

Kemble's interest in the minutiae of presentation was boundless. He was something of a scholar. John Taylor tells of suggesting to him that Hamlet's "Thrift, thrift, Horatio," should be spoken, not as it usually was, "in anger," but rather as ironic praise.

He immediately took down a Polyglot Dictionary, and examined the derivation and accepted meaning of the word thrift in all the languages, and finding that it was always given in a commendatory sense, he thanked me, and always after gave the passage in the manner I had suggested.[45]

Then, too, he insisted on pronouncing the word "aches" as the Elizabethans did, with two syllables — and "Kemble's aitches" became a stupid joke of the day. His rôle as a Shakespearian producer, an important rôle, pointing as it does to the ways of the future, has been well defined by Harold Child.[46] In such matters as costuming, indeed, historical accuracy still came second, with Kemble, to grace; and this has often been deplored even by writers who were conscious that the "archaeology" of Charles Kean and the eighteen-fifties was ridiculous. But *Hamlet*, as we now know, may still be *Hamlet* in dresses that are splendid to the eye yet neither of ancient Denmark nor Elizabethan England. Kemble's concern was not limited to his own part in a play. When the elder Kean was appearing in Dublin soon after his London triumphs, John Finlay grumbled about the slovenliness of some of the minor actors. We might be told, he goes on, that this was not the star's fault. "But Mr. Kemble always spent as much time at rehearsal, in marshalling and disciplining the corps dramatique, as in any other occupation"; and it was to his interference and instruction that Finlay attributes the surprising excellence of the mob in *Julius Caesar* when Kemble visited Dublin not long afterwards.[47] Many of the hitherto anonymous characters in Shakespeare even received names from Kemble as editor, and some of these names — "Marco" in *Othello*, for instance — still turn up occasionally in the casts of quite recent productions.

For an English actor to show a lively interest in such matters was novel. Garrick, indeed, had had some of them forced upon his attention by learned persons who wrote letters to him. Macklin, despite his elderly growling against Kemble's "new readings," does appear to have had a good deal of the younger player's enthusiasm about details — and in consequence was, in his own time, much ridiculed. The wonder is that Kemble, a belated classicist, an artist for whom genius could scarcely be claimed, should have won the esteem he enjoyed. The advent of Kean, in Hazlitt's phrase, "destroyed the Kemble religion." In Kean, the age found the actor it had longed for: Kemble to him was but as Jonson to Shakespeare.

At moments, as in his essay on Kemble's retirement, Hazlitt

shows himself capable of generosity. He still finds something "pedantic" about the actor's manner; "but his monotony did not fatigue, his formality did not displease, because there was always sense and meaning in what he did."

The fineness of Mr. Kemble's figure, [Hazlitt goes on,] may be supposed to have led to that statue-like appearance which his acting was sometimes too apt to assume; as the diminutiveness of Mr. Kean's person has probably compelled him to bustle too much. . . . If Mr. Kemble were to remain in the same posture for half an hour, his figure would only excite admiration.

Splendid formal acting. Shakespeare's lines were not levelled down to colloquial prose; they were declaimed, and declaimed with the confidence of understanding.[48] To a blindman sitting next to Charles Lamb in the pit at Drury Lane when Kemble was playing Richard, it was as if the actor "had been reading something out of a book." [49] But there were his gestures, too, finely expressive, very formal still, like "the double sweep" of the right arm at the close of Hamlet's soliloquy —

The play's the thing
Wherein I'll catch the conscience of the King.[50]

Gilbert Austin, author of a really formidable treatise on gesture, *Chironomia* (1806), finds in Kemble "the perfection and the glory of art, so finished, that every look is a commentary, every tone an illustration, every gesture a model for the statuary, and a study for the painter." [51]

Splendid formal acting. We have nothing like it on our stage today, and so are reluctant to accept it as good acting, even in retrospection. Yet Shakespeare, characteristically, and not in his youthful plays alone, counts upon subtle stylistic transitions and contrasts the effect of which will be lost if we play him with the single ideal of naturalness. The late Professor Morozov, in his *Shakespeare on the Soviet Stage*, tells of an experiment made some years ago in a Russian production of *Romeo and Juliet*.[52] When, at the Capulets' ball, Romeo meets Juliet and begs a kiss, the expression is stylized, even to the use of sonnet-rhymes, and the players brought out the grave formality of the speeches through their manner of delivering them, leaving to Juliet the sudden naturalness of "you kiss by th' book." Kemble's technique, even in his stateliest days, lent itself to similar effects. "Most brilliant effects," Macready calls them, "worked out with wonderful skill on a sombre ground, which only a great master of his art could have achieved."[53] There were instances in *Hamlet*. There was the speaking of Macbeth's "If I stand here, I saw him," where those who remembered the actor's "tone and gesture" knew "how truly he could hit the merely natural."[54] Or, in the fifth act, when Macbeth hears of the Queen's death — Macready, by good luck present at one of Kemble's last performances, and bored hitherto, is reporting:

When the news was brought, "The Queen, my lord, is dead," he seemed struck to the heart; gradually collecting himself, he sighed out, "She should have died hereafter!" then, as if with the inspiration of despair, he hurried out, distinctly and pathetically, the lines:
"To-morrow, and to-morrow, and to-morrow. . ."
rising to a climax of desperation that brought down the enthusiastic cheers of the closely-packed theatre. . . . At the tidings of "the wood of Birnam moving," he staggered, as if the shock had struck the very seat of life, and in the bewilderment of fear and rage could just ejaculate the words "Liar and slave!" then lashing himself into a state of frantic rage, ended the scene in perfect triumph.[55]

Without maintaining that Kemble's acting was truly great — as was his sister's, say, or Garrick's — I have tried to show why it may well have been underestimated, both in his own time and ours. The style he founded lasted long, and its virtues, those of careful study and precise execution, are demonstrable virtues. He was unfortunate in not having been born earlier in the century, when demonstrable virtues were greatly regarded. In 1817, the year of his retirement, it was remarked that "you may mention to Kean's ardent adherents every one of his faults, and the word genius stops your mouth." [56]

Mrs. Siddons as Lady Macbeth

THE season of 1783–84, John Kemble's first in London, was one of renewed triumph for his sister, Mrs. Siddons. Tragedy was very much to the fore; and the actors assured Tom Davies that the emotion excited by Mrs. Siddons's performances was so great that audiences did not laugh at the farcical after-pieces with which the long bills of that day regularly concluded.[1] (So, in 1946, when the Old Vic Company appended Sheridan's *Critic* to a magnificent *Oedipus the King,* some of us were unable to take full pleasure in the antics of Mr. Puff.) A wistful complaint appeared in *The Gazetteer* on November 10, 1783:

THEATRICAL RONDEAU

By Jack Capstern

Tragedy makes me heart-sore;
Every night 'tis a bore:
Give me to laugh and to sing.
Where's the *Abington?* Where's Tom King?
Where are the *Loves and the Graces?*
Where are the *comical faces?*
Where is the *tit for tat?*

57

Where is the *laugh and be fat?*
Killing is all out of fashion,
Peace is the joy of the nation!
Then
Comedy sure is the thing:
Where is the Abington? Where is Tom King?

King had been the first Peter Teazle, a few years back, and the delightful Mrs. Abington his Lady.

But although Mrs. Siddons no longer restricted herself to tenderness and pathos, and that season played Shakespeare's Isabella and Constance, London had not yet seen her in what was to be the greatest of all her rôles. In a letter dated Christmas 1782, Horace Walpole reports that when she had been urged to play Lady Macbeth and Medea, her reply was that "she did not look on them as female characters." [2] She herself wrote, afterwards, of her long hesitation to assume "a personage with whom no one feeling of common general nature was congenial or assistant." Then, too, there were the challenging memories of Mrs. Pritchard's Lady Macbeth to meet; and it was with "the utmost diffidence, nay terror" that she undertook the rôle.[3]

This was on February 2, 1785. The performance was for her own benefit and, according to the advertisement printed in *The Gazetteer*, part of the pit was "laid into Boxes" (Boaden speaks of the "splendour gained by the jewels and feathers of the ladies," when this was done).[4] "To prevent confusion," ladies were "desired to send their servants by half past four o'clock. To begin at a quarter after six." It proved to be "the most crowded house of the season," and Sir Joshua Reynolds was envied his special seat in the orchestra.[5] In the gallery, there was talk, I fancy, of a "shocking spectacle" which some of those present must have witnessed, the execution, on this same day, of twenty "miserable wretches" outside "the debtors door of Newgate." [6]

Years afterwards, Mrs. Siddons in her "Remarks" on Lady Macbeth,[7] took a surprisingly charitable view of the character. It was as if, aware that she had become peculiarly associated with this "fiendlike queen," she would make her as respectable as possible; if not truly amiable, at least more nearly a worthy woman than Macbeth was a worthy man. The essay is, indeed, almost painfully literary. Only by flashes are we reminded that the author is an actress writing of a part she has played. Thus, "wrenching the daggers from the feeble grasp of her husband" describes what she herself, and Mrs. Pritchard before her, actually did. It was part of the business of the scene. But what of the imaginings concerning Lady Macbeth's beauty, which was, quite unlike her own, "fair" and, "perhaps, even fragile"? And what of the Ghost's becoming visible to Lady Macbeth as well as to her husband — an idea which one rejects if only because it would make the Banquet Scene quite unplayable? An artist's knowledge is other than that of a critic, and Mrs. Siddons, descending to criticism, is no longer interesting.

On that February night in 1785, she was "at first much agitated." [8] But this was not unusual with her. According to her friend Lawrence, the painter, "she never went upon the stage . . . without a feeling of dread [of] which she could not divest Herself on Her first appearance." [9] And even as she began to read Macbeth's letter, there was novelty, brilliance. "When I burned in desire to question them further, they made themselves air," she read, with a little pause before the last word. "They made themselves — air." Sheridan Knowles, the author of *Virginius,* recalls that "in the look and tone with which she delivered that word, you recognized ten times the wonder with which Macbeth and Banquo actually beheld the vanishing of the witches." [10] It was a stroke of exactly the sort her brother delighted in, but prompted by a finer imagination.

In the soliloquy, there was a "burst of energy" when she came to "shalt be" — "and *shalt be* / What thou art promis'd" — which "perfectly electrified the house." [11] In keeping with this reading was her emphasis upon "my," in

> That I may pour my spirits in thine ear,

and again, a few lines below, upon "fate." [12] The startling news of Duncan's approach evoked the cry, "Thou'rt mad to say it," followed immediately by a corrective lowering of the voice, as if for an instant she feared that her secret had been divulged.[13] Then came a long pause before the "murmured mysteriousness" of the summoning of the spirits. Boaden pictures her as she spoke,

> Wherever in your sightless substances
> You wait on nature's mischief!

The elevation of her *brows*, the full *orbs* of sight, the raised shoulders, and the hollowed hands, seemed all to endeavour to explore what yet were pronounced no possible objects of vision. Till then, I am quite sure, a figure so terrible had never bent over the pit of a theatre; that night crowded with intelligence and beauty, in its seven front rows.[14]

An even more observant recorder, G. J. Bell, Professor of Scottish Law at the University of Edinburgh, who saw Mrs. Siddons about 1809, writes that her voice was "quite supernatural, as in a horrible dream." [15]

She made much of the exultant greeting:

> Great Glamis! worthy Cawdor!
> Greater than both, by the all-hail hereafter!

"Loud, triumphant and wild in her air," is Bell's note on the passage.[16] And as the scene proceeded she spoke, "look like the innocent flower,/*But be the serpent under't*," very slowly, with strong emphasis and a "severe and cruel expression," her voice changing to "assurance and gratulation" at the majestic,

> Which shall to all our nights and days to come
> Give solely sovereign sway and masterdom.

Only of her exit is the Scottish Professor critical: "Leading him out, cajoling him, her hand on his shoulder clapping him. This vulgar —— gives a mean conception of Macbeth, unlike the high mental working by which he is turned to her ambitious purpose." [17] Not a coldly austere Lady Macbeth, certainly! And in 1785 the dazzling beauty of the actress was still undimmed by time.

Lady Macbeth's next two scenes are those of the reception of Duncan, and her husband's wavering. Of the first, enough that Mrs. Siddons's speaking of the lines was "dignified and simple" — a delight to the ear. Macbeth was completely dominated in the second. Throughout this scene, according to the vivid account of a later time,

she feels her way, observes the wavering of his mind; suits her earnestness and whole manner to it. With contempt, affection, reason, the conviction of her well-concerted plan, the assurance of success which her wonderful tones inspire, she turns him to her purpose with an art in which the player shares largely in the poet's praise.[18]

The hideous idea of the murdered baby was presented with peculiar terror. She had been at some distance from Macbeth, but now came close to him and looked for a considerable time in his face before speaking, at first softly and with much tenderness, then, as she went on, with an appalling energy:

> I have given suck, and know
> How tender 'tis to love the babe that milks me.
> I would, while it was smiling in my face,
> Have pluck'd my nipple from his boneless gums
> And dash'd the brains out, had I so sworn as you
> Have done to this.

At that moment, writes Boaden, there stood "before us the true and perfect image of . . . a *fiend-like woman*." [19] "If we should fail?" Macbeth cries; and the "we fail" of Mrs. Siddons was already in 1785, I think, quietly fatalistic — as if she had answered, "why, then, 'We fail,' and there an end." [20] When Bell saw her, it was spoken with a "strong downward inflection, bowing with the hands down, the palm upward"; and he noticed that when, a little later in the scene, she answered another question of Macbeth's with the defiant "Who *dares* receive it other?" this was accompanied by a "look of great confidence. . . . In 'dares' great and imperial dignity." [21]

The scene of the murder — "that deadly whispering scene," as a veteran playgoer remembered it [22] — begins with Lady Macbeth waiting to hear that the deed has been accomplished. J. H. Siddons tells of how as a boy he stood just inside the O. P. door and watched Kemble putting the blood on his hands. This was in 1816, on one of those many reappearances of Mrs. Siddons's after her official retirement.

The whispered words, "he is about it," drew my attention to the half-opened door, and recalled me to the scene. . . . Mrs. Siddons . . . was bending towards the door in the act of listening — her ear so close that I could absolutely feel her breath. The words, I have said, were whispered — but what a whisper was hers! Distinctly audible in every part of the house, it served the purpose of the loudest tones.[23]

In the performance of 1785, she threw "a degree of proud and filial tenderness" into her delivery of "Had he not resembled / My father as he slept, I had done't," which was "new, and of great effect." [24] Bell's notes conjure up the very image of this Lady Macbeth as she listened to the wild speeches of her husband after his return from Duncan's chamber. When he told of the voices —

There's one did laugh in's sleep, and one cried "Murther!" —

it was as if her spirit had been "overcome by the contagion of his remorse and terror. Her arms about her neck and bosom, shuddering." This horror "became agony and alarm at his derangement, uncertain what to do." At last, she rallied: "Who was it that thus cried?" Coming close to him, she tried to recall him "to ideas of common life. Strong emphasis on *who*. Speaks forcibly in his ear, looks at him steadfastly." [25] She noticed the daggers, and snatched them from him. (Boaden remembers that her "Give ME the daggers" caused "a general start" among those near him in the crowded theatre).[26] Then she went into the chamber of death — to return again, "as calmly . . . as if she had but newly lifted her head from the pillow of innocent sleep." [27] But her confidence soon gives place to renewed fears for Macbeth, whose reason seems threatened, and she "strikes him on the shoulder, pulls him from his fixed posture, forces him away, he talking as he goes." [28]

Obeying a stupid theatrical tradition, Mrs. Siddons did not appear in the next scene, that of the discovery of the murder. Her Lady Macbeth of the third act was no longer — the actress herself tells us — "the presumptuous, the determined creature" she had once been.

Naught's had, all's spent,
Where our desire is got without content.

"The worm that never dies already gnaws her heart. . . .
Under the impression of her present wretchedness, I, from
this moment, have always assumed the dejection of countenance and manners which I thought accordant to such a state
of mind." [29] She spoke mournfully, with a single "flash of her
former spirit and energy" as she answered Macbeth's,

O, full of scorpions is my mind, dear wife!
Thou know'st that Banquo, and his Fleance, lives.
Lady. But in them Nature's copy's not eterne.[30]

A letter in *The Gazetteer* of February 3, 1785 praises "the
dresses and decorations" in *Macbeth*, as representing "the
greatest liberality in the Managers of this Theatre. The ban-
quet-scene was particularly magnificent." [31] Mrs. Siddons's
coming down from her throne, after the appearance of the
ghost, was memorable. Edward Mangin speaks of her eyes,
which "were brilliant and piercing, and could be seen to
sparkle or glare at an incredible distance on the stage; as . . .
when she rose from her throne at the solemn supper, and
was descending to chide her terrified husband." And he adds
that "the effect of her eyes was greatly assisted by a power
she had of moving her eyebrows, and the muscles of her forehead." [32]

Those only who were on the stage with Mrs. Siddons, whilst
playing a part with her, [writes Henry Curling,] could have any
idea of the power of her eye. In Lady Macbeth, it really seemed
to possess all the awful majesty of a queen. . . . She cast such a
look upon me once, when a lad, that I have never forgotten it.[33]

It was, however, her behaviour toward the guests, the "lofty courtesy" with which she received them, and "the haughty, hurried, and apprehensive manner" with which they were dismissed,[34] that came to be reckoned as one of Mrs. Siddons's finest achievements. The "inimitable grace" of "the *congé* to her guests" was, indeed, immediately recognized,[35] and it was greeted, we are assured, with thunderous applause.[36] Finally, the desolation of the close of the scene was brought out movingly. "Feeble now, and as if preparing for her last sickness," is Bell's comment.[37] The Sleepwalking Scene was already near-at-hand.

In 1785, tradition in the theatre was still a matter of consequence. When Mrs. Siddons was preparing to go on, as Lady Macbeth, Sheridan came to her dressing-room and insisted upon being admitted. He had heard, he said, that she was planning to put down her candle, in the Sleepwalking Scene, thus leaving her hands free for the washing out of the imagined blood. Mrs. Pritchard had carried her candle throughout the scene. "It would be thought a presumptuous innovation" for Mrs. Siddons to change the business. She, in turn, told him that it was too late, that she was too much agitated at this moment, to follow his advice. She had her way, and, when the curtain fell, Sheridan generously admitted that she was right.[38] But the putting down of the candle was not to escape censure. It was called a palpable trick, "an error, which would be inexcuseable in the youngest performer." [39] Her costume in this scene was also criticized. She wore, not the shroudlike garments so impressive in her later performances, but white satin. All mad heroines, according to Mr. Puff, wore white satin; it was a rule. But, since "Lady *Macbeth* is supposed to be *asleep* and not *mad*," custom did not warrant its adoption here.[40]

She was unusual in the vigor and energy of her movements. The hideous realities of the dream were now insisted upon, rather than the fact of dreaming.

She laded the water from the imaginary ewer over her hands — bent her body to listen to the sounds presented by her fancy, and hurried to resume the taper where she had left it, that she might with all speed drag her pallid husband to their chamber.[41]

Leigh Hunt, indeed, was to discover a want of refinement in her action. Was not "the dribbling and domestic familiarity with which she poured the water on her hands and slid them over each other" perhaps "even unnatural?" [42] And after she had washed them, and failed to get the blood off, "she made 'a face' in passing them before her nose, as if she perceived *a foul smell*. We venture to think that she should have shuddered and looked in despair, as recognizing *the stain on her soul*." [43]

For further details, we must go once more to Professor Bell. His notes are precise and graphic. She entered too suddenly: "A slower and more interrupted step more natural. She advances rapidly to the table, sets down the light and rubs her hand, making the action of lifting up water in one hand at intervals." "One; two," she spoke "listening eagerly," and "why then 'tis time to do't" was given in "a strange unnatural whisper." A "very melancholy tone," for "The Thane of Fife had a wife," changed to "melancholy peevishness," as her thought reverted to the stains of blood (*"What, will these hands ne'er be clean?"*), and to an "eager whisper" — "No more o' that, my lord, *no more o' that*." Finally, the "Oh, oh, oh," was "not a sigh. A convulsive shudder — very horrible. A tone of imbecility audible in the sigh." [44]

As for the effect of the scene on a sensitive spectator,

66

Knowles twice attempted to describe it. In his lecture on
Macbeth, he wrote:

Though pit, gallery, and boxes were crowded to suffocation,
the chill of the grave seemed about you while you looked on her;
—there was the hush and the damp of the charnel-house at mid-
night; you had a feeling as if you and the medical attendant, and
lady-in-waiting, were alone with her; your flesh crept and your
breathing became uneasy. . . .[45]

He did better when talking informally with the American
tragedian, Edwin Forrest. Forrest knew that his friend had
often seen Mrs. Siddons on the stage, and one day asked him
about the Sleepwalking Scene:

"I have read all the high-flown descriptions of the critics, and
they fall short. I want you to tell me in plain blunt phrase just
what impression she produced on you." Knowles replied, with a
sort of shudder. . . "Well, sir, I smelt blood! I swear that I
smelt blood!" [46]

In her own time, and after, comparisons between Mrs.
Siddons and her brother were frequently made; comparisons
with Edmund Kean are rare. Sometimes, it is true, Kean's
deficiencies seem to be slyly glanced at in panegyrics upon
the actress. Sometimes, as notably in an essay of Hazlitt's, the
things chosen for commendation in Mrs. Siddons are those
which Kean had been teaching the critic to set store by.[47] An
exception is Julian Charles Young who maintains that in
seeking effect Kean was "rather a surprising actor than a
legitimate one." Mrs. Siddons, on the contrary, "never indulged in imagination at the expense of truth." [48] Hers was a
classical style, not a romantic one. But it was a classicism
warmed by emotion and with reaches beyond those of splendid formal acting.

67

The faults which Hazlitt and Leigh Hunt came to recognize in her playing were exactly the faults [49] — pauses that endured beyond patience, an excessive slowness and solemnity — that were regularly ascribed to Kemble. Then she had a grandeur of person, like his — and a much finer voice; shared something of his delight in detail, yet like him achieved a large and heroic style. It was in the completeness with which she impersonated the characters she assumed — in what has happily been called "her powers of transubstantiation" [50] — that she stood alone.

Even at the beginning of her famous days, Davies noticed that this actress excelled "all persons in paying attention to the business of the scene"; so expressive was her face, "her eye so full of information, that the passion is told from her look before she speaks." [51] Her listening to a narrative could be more exciting than the narrative itself.[52] Her very step became different when she played Calista, and her gestures were "more frequent and more violent." [53] Goede, a visitor from the Continent, in his very observant description of English acting at the beginning of the new century, found that her voice, too, changed with the parts she assumed: "In the characters of Isabella, of Lady Macbeth, of Belvidera, you constantly remark one characteristical tone uniformly supported throughout all her declamation." [54]

Comedy lay beyond her. One woman, indeed, seeing the great actress as Rosalind in *As You Like It*, is said to have wept throughout the performance, out of habit as it were.[55] But Leslie, the painter, remembers particularly the grace with which Kemble and his sister "could descend from the stateliness of tragedy to the easy manner of familiar life," giving as instances Kemble's "conversations with the players," in *Hamlet*, and "the scene in which Mrs. Siddons, as *Volumnia*, sat sewing with *Virgilia,* and the subsequent scene with *Valeria.*" [56] And in Queen Katherine's Sick Scene, in *Henry VIII*, she employed such realism of detail as was almost shocking.[57]

The tears she shed were real.[58] Tom Moore tells of talking with Mrs. Siddons when she was an old woman:

> Among other reasons for her regret at leaving the stage was, that she always found in it a vent for her private sorrows, which enabled her to bear them better; and often she has got credit for the truth and feeling of her acting when she was doing nothing more than relieving her own heart of its grief.[59]

Equally suggestive is her account of the emotional preparation to which she had recourse before sweeping upon the stage in the third act of *King John*. She would post herself where she could not fail to hear the music, so painful to Constance, which accompanied the entrance of the army into Angiers. "The sickening sounds of that march," she writes, "would usually cause the bitter tears of rage, disappointment, betrayed confidence, baffled ambition, and, above all, the agonizing feelings of maternal affection" to start into her eyes.[60] And, after listening to it, she was able to speak, more nearly to her own satisfaction, the difficult tirade with which the act begins —

> Gone to be married? Gone to swear a peace?
> False blood to false blood join'd!

Lady Macbeth, as we have seen, she long hesitated to play in London. But as a very young actress she had essayed the part in the provinces. On the night before the earliest of these performances, she shut herself up and began to learn her lines.

As the character is very short, I thought I should soon accomplish it. Being then only about twenty years of age, I believed, as many others do believe, that little more was necessary than to get the words into my head. . . . I went on with tolerable composure, in the silence of the night, (a night I never can forget,) till I came to the assassination scene, when the horrors of the scene rose to a degree that made it impossible for me to get farther. I snatched up my candle, and hurried out of the room, in a paroxysm of terror. . . .[61]

Something of that terror she was to communicate to thousands who saw her as Lady Macbeth in the years to come.

Edmund Kean as Othello

A ND WHAT," it is often asked quite gravely when we talk of some actor of long ago, "what should we think of him if we saw him now?" It is an uncritical question, naïve, irritating. Kean, a mouthing ghost on our stage? Kean's art absurdly called worthless because it seemed old-fashioned? No, if we are to imagine, let it be with the clocks turned back! Kean at Old Drury, playing far downstage where visibility is best, the brilliant expressiveness of his face scarcely counting, even there, save with those in the front of the pit; Kean, straining to be heard in that vast theatre where he may well dread hoarseness before ever he reaches Richard's rush from the tent or the final frenzied rant of Sir Giles; Kean, at whose acting some confess they might have laughed had they not been so deeply moved — Kean, could we see him in his habit as he lived, would not disappoint us.

His lowness of stature was in his own time much talked of — more even than Garrick's had been.[1] Garrick had made up in grace what he lacked in inches. Kean was inevitably compared with the godlike Kembles. Yet when his great moments came, he seemed no longer a little man. Fitzgerald, the poet, writing to Fanny Kemble, recalls him as "heroic in spite of undersize. How he swelled up in Othello! I remem-

7 1

ber thinking he looked almost as tall as your father when he came to silence that dreadful Bell." [2] George Henry Lewes, looking back to the last time he saw Kean as Othello, speaks of "how puny he appeared beside Macready" through the first two acts. But when, in the third, moving toward Iago "with a gouty hobble," he caught him by the throat —

Villain, be sure thou prove my love a whore! —

he "seemed to swell into a stature which made Macready appear small." [3]

To the diminutiveness of Kean's person was added the frequent harshness of his voice. The lower tones were good; it was when the voice was raised that it became dissonant.[4] John Finlay, who saw the actor in Dublin soon after his first London success, found it easier to hear him when he spoke naturally: "his voice appears older than he is." [5] Nonetheless, it was a voice capable of producing extraordinary effects. Its "range of tones" was, we are assured,

from F below the line to F above it. . . . He has three distinct sets of tones; as if he occasionally played upon a flute, clarinet, and bassoon, which he uses as the passion dictates. In the scene with Lady Ann [in *Richard III*] his notes are of the most touching and persuasive kind, often springing from the harmonics of his natural voice, which he elicits with exquisite delicacy. . . . But the same voice, when moved with a ruder stroke, gave the yell and choked utterance of a savage.[6]

Kean's use of "inarticulate sounds" was remarkable — "the throttled struggle of rage, and the choking of grief — the broken laugh of extreme suffering, when the mind is ready to deliver itself over to insane joy." [7] Yet, as we shall see, he could so render the melancholy music of Othello's "Farewell"

72

that it lingered on undimmed by Time in the memories of those who had heard it.

His face, alert, intelligent, finely sensitive, was a precious asset. Hazlitt, indeed, warned him at the outset against placing "too great a reliance . . . on the expression of the countenance, which is a language intelligible only to a part of the house. . . ." Kean, it was generally recognized, must be seen from near-at-hand, from the pit, not the galleries or the more distant boxes.[8] "His face," Hazlitt writes again,

is the running comment on his acting, which reconciles the audience to it. Without that index to his mind, you are not prepared for the vehemence and suddenness of his gestures; his pauses are long, abrupt, and unaccountable, if not filled up by the expression; it is in the working of his face that you see the writhing and coiling up of the passions before they make their serpent-spring; the lightning of his eye precedes the hoarse burst of thunder from his voice.[9]

Neagle, whose terrifying portrait of Kean as Shylock is reproduced at the beginning of the present volume, has captured such a moment. The eyes themselves were "black, large, brilliant, and penetrating, and remarkable for the shortness of their upper lid, which discovered a clearly-defined line of white above the ball." [10]

With such a face, and such eyes, it is not surprising that Kean *listened* so well. Finlay, a none-too-friendly critic, calls him "the best listener on the stage," and speaks of how as Othello, for instance, he was able to "fill up the chasm of his own silence with business, emotion, and all the varied action" of "a deeply interested and attentive auditor." [11] And, according to Richard H. Dana, he knew the value of "under playing," as well. When he has no part in what is happening, "he

73

is not busy in putting himself into attitudes to draw attention, but stands or sits in a perfectly simple posture, like one with an engaged mind." [12] Such artistic self-abnegation is all the more to Kean's credit because of its unexpectedness.

His style was violent and spasmodic, counting for its effects upon startling transitions, or the singling out, for concentrated, passionate emphasis, of particular moments. He was quite capable of passing negligently over important speeches. Keats, it is true, was captivated by "the elegance, gracefulness and music" of his reading: "The sensual life of verse springs warm from the lips of Kean." [13] But the standards established by the Kembles he could not or would not meet. Sustained passages were broken up. The abruptness of his changes of tone amounted to mannerism. Stately declamation gave place to the familiar, the conversational. Kean (wrote Finlay) appears to be attempting "an extraordinary innovation . . . he would reduce the character and language of the drama to what he calls the *level of real life.*" [14]

But the great moments, the "flashes of lightning"? They were surprising, above all — a seizing upon some neglected passage for sudden illumination, sudden emotional appeal. Sometimes this was gained by vocal means alone, sometimes by vivid action as well. They became, of course, the awaited "points," dear to audiences who were accustomed to seeing the same play again and again, who compared player with player, and knew (I suspect) far more about acting than audiences today. But even though one was aware that the great moment was near, and sensed, perhaps, the careful preparation for it, it might still be startling when it came. Thus "I am a Jew" in Shylock's scene with Tubal was ever, wrote the old actor George Vandenhoff, "a cue for the most intense applause: it was the natural simplicity with which he gave it, the sort of patient appeal his tone seemed to make to your sympathy against undeserved oppression," that made it so touching.

He hurried you on through the catalogue of Antonio's atrocities and unprovoked injuries to him, enforcing them with a strong accentuation, a rapid utterance, and a high pitch of voice; and when he had reached the *climax*, he came down by a sudden transition to a gentle, suffering tone of simple representation of his oppressor's manifest un-reason and injustice, on the words —
     "I am a Jew!" —
and the effect was instantaneous.[15]

Even more characteristic was a moment in *Macbeth*, where again the method was that of contrast, dazzling in its swiftness. Dame Madge Kendal heard her father tell of it, long afterwards.

In the last act, when Macbeth rushed on the stage and spoke, "Hang out our banners on the outward walls," he shouted the command in a voice like thunder. Suddenly he paused, dropped his double-handled sword to the ground and leaning on it, whispered, "The cry is still they come, they come," at the same time seeming to become ashy grey with fear.[16]

The authenticity of this description is beyond question. It is perfect Kean!

Upon his achievement at such moments Kean's popularity was securely founded. He might descend to the sensational and the meretricious, to rant and claptrap; he might act, as was often said, only *parts of parts*, sacrificing conception to execution, the character to the passion. It scarcely mattered so long as there were, too, the flashes of lightning. Kemble's art, its stateliness and cool precision alike, seemed no longer admirable. How tame now appeared those once exciting "new readings" of his in comparison with, say, Kean's stealthy return at the end of the Nunnery Scene to kiss Ophelia's hand! The New Acting appealed directly and unashamedly to the emotions.

At the beginning of 1817, Kean seemed securely established on the throne he had seized three years before. The aging Kemble, no longer formidable, would shortly be quitting the contest. Macready was as yet scarcely to be feared. Only from a young provincial player, with whose talents Kean had become acquainted earlier in the season, was serious rivalry to be dreaded. At Brighton, one autumn evening, Kean had failed to appear in his great rôle of Sir Giles Overreach in *A New Way to Pay Old Debts*. Junius Brutus Booth, not yet twenty-one, was brought over from Worthing to take the part, and he had succeeded so well that Mr. Trotter, the sagacious Brighton manager, decided to give his audience further chances to make comparisons. Brighton, accordingly, now saw two Richards and two Bertrams. Booth essayed Othello on November 9; Kean resumed Sir Giles on the twelfth. Excitement was running high. On Christmas Eve the rivals appeared together, Kean as Othello and Booth as Iago.[17]

As might be expected, the young man was promptly brought to London, where, at Covent Garden on February 12, he made his appearance as Richard. Kean's most popular character appropriated by someone else! What was worse, this actor's style closely resembled his own. Booth even looked like him. Hazlitt might exaggerate the degree of imitation; there was no question of the extraordinary likeness in appearance.

Success went to the young man's head. In an evil hour for him, he ventured beyond his depth into the treacherous waters of theatrical politics. He decided that the terms offered him by Covent Garden were not acceptable. According to Booth's daughter, Edmund Kean himself "immediately drove in his chariot to visit Mr. Booth, overwhelmed him with congratulations, and told him to 'jump in; he had got an engagement for him.'" [18] He had, indeed, though as the sequel showed, it was not an engagement to be accepted without thought. Had the Old Master been a little below form when they appeared together in Brighton, and did Booth underestimate him now? For the contest was to be renewed immediately. At the close of Kean's performance of Hamlet at Drury Lane on Monday, February 17, it was announced that *Othello* would be given on Thursday — Othello by Kean, Iago by Booth — and the audience shouted. On Thursday afternoon, crowds gathered outside the theatre. There were no queues in those days, and the opening of the pit doors "was followed by a dangerous rush and struggle for admission." [19] It was a house crammed "to the very ceiling." The presence of "several of the Nobility" was noticed, with that of "the most eminent among literary men and critics." When Booth as Iago mentioned that he knew his price, the pit attached significance to the words and applauded them wildly, and there was another demonstration when Kean upon his entrance "spontaneously took Booth *by the hand*." [20]

Some years later, Booth told the actor Hackett that on this night "Kean's *Othello* smothered *Desdemona* and my *Iago* too." [21] Certainly, the challenger was defeated. As certainly, it had been a magnificent contest, "a night to be remembered." [22] Kean, it was generally agreed, had quite surpassed himself. It may even have been the greatest performance he ever gave.

Yet his Othello was ever the same. Nothing about it was fortuitous, nothing left unprepared. Lewes had heard on good authority that when Kean was to appear on an unfamiliar stage he would carefully count "the number of steps he had to take before reaching a certain spot, or before uttering a certain word." Such variations as occurred from performance to performance were never of the actor's seeking.

The voice on some nights would be more irresistably touching in "But, oh! the pity of it, Iago!" — or more musically forlorn in "Othello's occupation's gone" — or more terrible in "Blood, Iago; blood, blood!" but always the accent and rhythm were unchanged.[23]

And of the greatest of the speeches, Vandenhoff writes that it "ran on the same tones and semitones, had the same rests and breaks, the same *forte* and *piano*, the same *crescendo* and *diminuendo*, night after night, as if he spoke it from a musical score."[24]

Those who describe Kean's Othello dwell on single scenes, speeches, phrases; they tell us little about the impersonation as a whole. Kemble, indeed, is said to have remarked that "if the justness of the conception had been but equal to the brilliancy of the execution it would have been perfect; but the whole thing was a mistake; the fact being *that Othello was a slow man.*"[25] The American tragedian Thomas Abthorpe Cooper was of much the same opinion.[26] Even Hazlitt thought the character misconceived: "Othello was tall; but that is nothing: he was black, but that is nothing. But he was not fierce, and that is everything." Only at the end does the Moor give way to rage and despair, whereas Kean was "all passion . . . too uniformly on the verge of extravagance, too constantly on the rack."[27] Another playgoer was appalled by what he saw. Leveson Gower writes in one of his letters:

The Play — I never saw such acting. I am not sure whether I like it; admire it I must — it is nature. Should tragedy be quite so natural? There wants a spice of Dignity; the passions would be disgusting were they represented so exact. . . . Kean gives me the idea of Buonaparte in a furor. I was frightened, alarmed; I cannot account for what I felt. I wished to be away, and saw those eyes all night, and hear "D — n her! d — n her!" still — it was too horrible.[28]

Kean made little of the first two acts, saving himself, ever, for the third. Now and again, some spectator, responding more sensitively than his fellows, might be suddenly impressed. "There is an indescribable *gusto* in [Kean's] voice," a poet wrote, "by which we feel that the utterer is thinking of the past and future while speaking of the instant." And when this Othello came to,

Keep up your bright swords, for the dew will rust them,

it was as if "his throat had commanded where swords were as thick as reeds. From eternal risk, he speaks as though his body were unassailable." [29] Thus Keats. But although Finlay, in Ireland, noticed Kean's reading of the same line, it was without pleasure. To him, the actor's "pauses in the short dialogue" were

too frequent and too long. . . .
 "Keep up your bright swords,
 For the dew will rust them."
Between these two short sentences he makes a long pause; and endeavours to throw *great effect* into the last one . . . he constructs his clap-trap on the word *swords*.

And the remark to Brabantio immediately following —

Good signior, you shall more command with years
Than with your weapons —

79

was spoken mistakenly with "anger and reproof." [30]

John Kemble made, as we have seen, occasional excursions, or swoopings, into the colloquial. But they were infrequent and attracted little attention even in his own time. Kean's readiness to discard the pomps of tragic speech, to become "easy, conversational, *unstagey*," was the delight of audiences. Othello's

> Were it my cue to fight, I should have known it
> Without a prompter,

spoken simply, yet pointedly, with "a wonderful mixture of sarcasm and courtesy . . . always brought down the house." [31] A similar though less legitimate touch came in the next scene. Othello's explanation to the Venetian senators was beyond Kean. "He had little power of elocution unless when sustained by a strong emotion; and this long simple narrative was the kind of speech he could not manage at all. He gabbled over it," eager to reach the close:

> This only is the witchcraft I have us'd,
> Here comes the lady. Let her witness it.

"His delivery of this 'point' always startled the audience into applause by its incisive tone and its abrupt transition." He made it "the climax of a withering sarcasm — attacking the word 'witchcraft' with high and sudden emphasis, and dropping into an almost disrespectful colloquialism as the lady appeared." As Lewes observed, "nothing could be more out of keeping with the Shakspearian character." [32]

Act Two is through most of it Iago's act, not Othello's. One passage alone, the exquisite greeting of Desdemona in Cyprus, stood out in Kean's performance. Even there it was objected that he spoke, "not in a tone of proud, rapturous, and affecting exultation, but in the sepulchral accent, and solemn utterance, of a penitent grateful for his salvation; or a shipwrecked mariner returning thanks for his deliverance."[33] To other ears, however, the note of rapture was clearly audible, with overtones of pathos as well. The words

> if it were now to die,
> 'Twere now to be most happy,

seeming, as this Othello pronounced them, "almost to forbode the misery that awaits him."[34]

Those who knew Kean in the part waited for the third act. The intensity, the grandeur of the performance began with Iago's direct attack upon the Moor. "The whole of the latter part of the third act," Hazlitt wrote, "was a masterpiece of profound pathos and exquisite conception";[35] and Lewes was satisfied that "the lion-like fury, the deep and haggard pathos, the forlorn sense of desolation, alternating with gusts of stormy cries for vengeance," were represented by Kean "with incomparable effect."[36] Certain lines and single phrases he made peculiarly his own. Othello's farewell to the glory of war is one of these. "Not a jot, not a jot" is another, and

> I found not Cassio's kisses on her lips,

and "O, blood, Iago, blood!"

The objection that Kean was jealous too soon, occurred to Finlay. But no one else seems to have felt this, and Finlay himself admits that "in all other respects" the "picture of *jealousy*" was superb — "one of the finest exhibitions that we have seen or could imagine."[37] The *Theatrical Inquisitor*, for February 1817, praises Kean for the "peculiar tenderness" of his "prithee no more" and "I will deny thee nothing!" in the scene with Desdemona.[38] Then, when *Iago* instilled the first precepts of jealousy, by describing the monster, . . . he started at the first whisper of this insinuation, stung by alarm, and bewildered with fury, as the whole emotion spread through his shaking frame, and tinged every look, every word, with unspeakable horror.

From other accounts, it would seem that this "sudden spasmodic contortion of the body, as if he had been abruptly stabbed," was upon hearing Iago's "O beware, my lord, of jealousy." [39]

"I see this hath a little dash'd your spirits," says Iago; and Othello, "not a jot, not a jot." Kean spoke the words with a pretence of composure, or even carelessness.[40] But anguish appeared in his action, tone, and look. He "clung to the side-scene," closing his eyes as if to keep back tears.[41] In Hazlitt's words, it was "perfectly heart-rending." [42] A few speeches more, and the first application of torture is over. At "Leave me, Iago," Kean turned away and walked toward the back of the stage, "raising his hands, and then bringing them down upon his head with clasped fingers." Dana comments on the grace and "imposing grandeur in his figure," as he stood thus with his back to the audience.[43] And Lewes seems to have had the same moment in mind when he wrote, years later:

When shall we see again that lion-like power and lion-like grace — that dreadful culmination of wrath, alternating with bursts of agony — that Oriental and yet most natural gesture, which even in its *naturalness* preserved a grand ideal propriety (for example, when his joined uplifted hands, the palms being upwards, were lowered upon his head, as if to keep his poor brain from bursting) — that exquisitely touching pathos, and that lurid flame of vengeance, flashing from his eye? [44]

It was upon Othello's return, however, that Kean reached his greatest heights. The entrance was with an "abrupt and wandering step," as if he were

swallowed up in the fearful bewilderings of a heavy heart. The sound of *Iago's* voice broke his meditation. He suddenly raised his eye, and pronounced the words "avaunt, begone," with the haughty and resentful glance of a man accustomed to authority. . . . After gazing till the first burst of passion recoiled upon himself, he dropped his arms, and relapsed insensibly into a gesture finely indicative of utter exhaustion.[45]

The next speech began calmly. But the thought of Cassio's kisses roused him to desperation. He paused before "kisses," as if he could scarcely bring himself to pronounce the word ("Cassio's — kisses — on her lips"), which he spoke with an "emphatical expression of disgust." [46] The climax of the performance was near:

O, now for ever
Farewell the tranquil mind! farewell content! . . .

Kean's rendering of the great lines called forth tribute after tribute, the writers exhausting themselves to find comparisons by which to describe it. It was "as pathetic as a lover's farewell to his mistress," Henry Crabb Robinson wrote, "I could hardly keep from crying; it was pure feeling." [47] Hazlitt found that it "struck on the heart like the swelling notes of some divine music, like the sound of years of departed happiness." [48] Leigh Hunt's description, written not long before the actor's death, is one of the best.

His repeated fare-wells, with the division of the syllables strongly marked, —
"Fare-well the tranquil mind! fare-well content!
Fare-well the plumed troop," &c.

83

were spoken in long, lingering tones, like the sound of a parting knell. The whole passage would have formed an admirable study for a young actor, in showing him the beauty of sacrificing verbal painting to a pervading sentiment. . . . Mr. Kean gave no vulgar importance to "the plumed troop" and the "big wars", as commonplace actors do; because the melancholy overcomes all: it merges the particular images into one mass of regret.[49]

One even more impressive tribute remains to be quoted. It comes, this time, not from a critic but from a fellow player — Kean's rival on that momentous night in 1817.

Once and only once, [writes Edwin Booth,] my father gave me a glimpse of his reminiscences; on that occasion he, who seldom spoke of actors or the theatre, told me that in his opinion no mortal man could equal Kean in the rendering of *Othello's* despair and rage; and that above all, his not very melodious voice in many passages, notably that ending with "Farewell, *Othello's* occupation's gone," sounded like the moan of ocean or the soughing of wind through cedars. His peculiar lingering on the letter "l" often marred his delivery; but here, in the "Farewell", the tones of cathedral chimes were not more mournful.[50]

Obeying what was already a tradition of long persistence, Othello now seized Iago by the throat —

Villain, be sure thou prove my love a whore!

Kean's rage here "was nothing less than convulsion": it was "a frantic assault"; and "the feebleness which followed" gave evidence "of the intensity of suffering that had consumed him." [51] A last great moment was "O, blood, Iago, blood!" [52] Keats wrote of the exclamation that it was "direful and slaughterous to the deepest degree; the very words appear stained and gory. His nature hangs over them, making a prophetic repast." [53] Here again was the Othello whose eyes haunted Leveson Gower for hours after!

We hear much less of Kean in the last two acts, the fourth, indeed, being shockingly cut in representations of his time. Leigh Hunt, seeing him in 1831, regretted the deterioration of his acting at one point.

> "Had it pleased heaven
> To try me with afflictions, &c."

had once, he wrote, been "the finest passage in the finest performance on the stage. We remember his standing apart, when he delivered it, alone, absorbed, as if he was left desolate, and then his voice rose with calm misery as though he had tears in his eyes, and so he continued for several lines." [54]

Kean's "quietness" in the last scenes was noticed by one critic, who found it "beautifully consistent" with his manner of speaking the "farewell" in Act III. It was as if passion had " 'raved itself to rest'; even when Othello learns too late that his wife was guiltless, it scarcely moves him." [55] And Othello's repeated "Fool! fool!" this actor spoke not rantingly but "quickly, and almost inarticulately, and with a half smile of wonder." [56] There was praise, finally, for the death scene.[57] Kean, we are told, always related the manner of death to its cause. In this instance, he realized that "death by a *heart* wound is *instantaneous*," and "literally dies standing; it is the dead body only of Othello that falls, heavily and at once; there is no *rebound,* which speaks of vitality and of living muscles. It is the dull weight of clay seeking its kindred earth." [58]

Attempts were sometimes made by those who extolled Kean to find in him the legitimate successor to Garrick — or at any rate the restorer of the Garrick tradition. Elderly persons, like Jack Bannister, who remembered Roscius were eagerly consulted as to resemblances between them — both little men with magnificent eyes! [59] Kemble certainly was unlike either. But against him, as I have tried to show, Kean had every advantage. Romanticism, long kept from the stage, was bound to find its players, even if this meant setting up Eliza O'Neill as a rival to the aging Siddons. Kean himself, the vagabond and rebel, fired the imagination. His art seemed purely inspired. "Other actors," wrote Keats, "are continually thinking of their sum-total effect throughout a play. Kean delivers himself up to the instant feeling, without a shadow of a thought about anything else." [60] It was a mistaken assumption, but a quite natural one.

Kean's great moments moved men to tears. They were adventurous, laden with poetic suggestion. Better such moments, the age decided, than the monotonous accuracy of the other school. Lewes sums up in a few words the case for Kean, the romantic actor: "The greatest artist is he who is greatest in the highest reaches of his art. . . . It is not by his faults, but by his excellences, that we measure a great man." [61]

Macready as Macbeth

IN a thoughtful essay, strangely neglected, "Shakespeare's Tragedies on the Stage," the American historian and man of letters John Foster Kirk tells of a conversation he had once had with Macready. "The days of the great actors are gone," Macready remarked; and Kirk "had not the politeness to contradict him." Many of the requisites of greatness he allows him. "He had rare intelligence and a deeply-sympathetic nature." He was the only actor Kirk had seen "who was always under the apparent influence of the emotion he was depicting, and never gave the impression that he was seeking to represent what, at the time at least, he was not actually feeling." Yet somehow he had failed to do what Garrick had certainly done, and Kean, and Mrs. Siddons (Kirk would even add "the stately John Kemble and the eccentric George Frederick Cooke"): he had never captured the imagination of his own contemporaries. "All have been conscious of some lack." [1]

His progress had been slow and interrupted. Kean was already there in possession when Macready as a young actor reached London; and though once at least, with his Richard III in 1819, he had shown that the distance between them was not immeasurable, it was only after Kean's death in 1833

that he began to be regarded as the hope of "legitimacy."
Popularity had come, unlooked for, as a consequence of his
grotesque encounter with Alfred Bunn, the Drury Lane
Manager, three years later. Thenceforward, without ever
feeling so, Macready was securely established. But to the last
there were many who granted him no more than a *faute de
mieux* eminence. For them, indeed, the days of the great
actors were over.

Against him were not memories alone. Though the flat
ugly face changed for the better with time [2] — its expressiveness was always recognized — it remained vulnerable to ridicule (Lester Wallack, despite his admiration for Macready,
cannot forbear repeating the description of his Othello as
looking "like an elderly negress, of evil repute, going to a
fancy ball!") [3] It was long before he worked out a style of his
own; longer still before he perfected it. [4] An eclecticism,
doomed it might be thought to certain failure, was frequently
ascribed to him: he had attempted, it was said, to combine
the passion of Kean (whose characteristic transitions he does
seem to have imitated) with the fastidiousness of Kemble. [5]
But Kean's technique of light and shade, with much cast into
obscurity that a little might shine out the more brilliantly,
was like Kemble's in being analytical rather than synthetic.
It was left for Macready to throw emphasis upon his characters as wholes. With a painstaking regard for execution, he
put conception first. Here, far more than in the new "domestic" flavor of his acting, lay its true originality. And the
style which he finally achieved was exacting, a little ponder-
ous, and one not readily appreciated by audiences unaccus-
tomed to it. "I think I may play Othello well," he wrote in
his diary, January 8, 1835, "but the prescriptive criticism of
this country, in looking for particular points instead of con-

templating one entire character, abates my confidence in myself"; [6] and when he was enacting the part at Drury Lane, the next autumn, "the audience seemed to wait for Kean's points, and this rather threw me off my balance." [7]

Readers of his *Diaries* know Macready better than they know any other actor. The book is depressing, yet once taken up it is hard to lay aside. It contains, too, material of enduring interest on the art which he professed.[8] To the end he was learning, never standing still. "Rehearsed with care," he wrote, in Dublin, February 1, 1847. "Acted Macbeth well — yes, well — to an indifferent house. Called. . . . I never acted Macbeth better, and learned much in this night's performance. Hear this and understand it, if you can, you 'great' young actors!" [9]

The Shakespearian soliloquies were a lasting challenge. Kean's "energy," as Richard III, impressed him; but there was a "want of abstraction in his soliloquies" (June 25, 1832).[10] He was to find the same fault in his own playing of Iago, the next year, and Hamlet — "third act the soliloquy wants a more entire abandonment to thought — more abstraction." [11] During the summer of 1834 he set to work afresh:

August 7th. — Began my professional study with the soliloquy of Hamlet, which, to give with grace, earnestness, and complete abstraction, I find one of the most difficult tasks I have to master.[12]

Once at least, nine years later, he satisfied himself:

The soliloquy ending the second act was very natural, passionate, and good. That on life and death was reality — as my French friends term it, *inspiration.* I never before approached the real self-communing which possessed me during its delivery.[13]

The last phrase suggests another of Macready's convictions. He must, he believed, experience the emotions of the characters he was portraying — must, that is, identify himself with them.[14] The *Diaries* constantly recur to this self-imposed criterion of excellence. He had played most of Hamlet, he finds on one occasion, "in a really splendid style. I felt myself the man." [15] Or, he had had callers, and one of them unfortunately had praised Charles Kean. "Acted Macbeth very unequally," parts of it badly. "I cannot act Macbeth without *being Macbeth*, which I must have time to prepare my mind for. I cannot work myself into such a tempest of ever-waking thought." [16] No wonder that within the profession he gained a bad name for unnecessary violence. Fanny Kemble quite dreaded to appear with him. Nor did her fears prove groundless. In *Macbeth* he pinched her black and blue, and "almost tore the point lace" from her head.[17]

If he was to share the emotion of his character, it must be, he decided, by pausing and taking time. A significant entry is one concerning his Coriolanus, March 22, 1834:

I was most attentive to the necessity of subduing my voice, and letting the passion rather than the lungs awaken the audience. In consequence I acted well. I fail, when I allow my tongue and action to anticipate my thought.[18]

Hence his pauses — "Macready pauses," as they came to be known — which served not only to bring out the meaning, as Kemble's even more notorious pauses had been designed to do, but also to keep him in possession of himself and of his rôle. Precipitancy, to him, meant loss of conception.[19]

When in the autumn of 1850 Macready began his round of farewell performances, he was, he felt, still at the height of his powers, and he was more popular than at any moment before. In some measure, I think, this was a direct consequence of his bad treatment in America. But with the years had come appreciation — appreciation of his personal integrity as well as of his eminence as an artist. It was easy now to look back upon his periods of management, at Covent Garden and Drury Lane, as upon a golden sunset time. Now dignity had departed from the stage, along with tradition. Only, some said, at Islington, under a former member of Macready's own company, was there still a truly legitimate theatre; and Islington was remote and very unfashionable.

His last weeks on the stage found Macready in a state of painful excitement. "I suffer from the least thing," he wrote, "*it is terrible.*" [20] He went on from one favorite part to another, insisting as he came to each that he had never surpassed this latest representation of it. Howe, an actor who was then appearing with him — as Horatio, for instance, to his Hamlet — writes that "he was evidently counting very much on the end, for he generally made a remark, 'Thank heaven, the last time but five, or four,' as the case might be." [21] Yet it was a wrench for him to give up Virginius, in Sheridan Knowles's play, and his thoughts went back to the first night, in 1820, "when Richard Jones came round from the front of the theatre, Covent Garden, into our dressing-room and, laying his hand on my shoulder, exclaimed, 'Well, my dear boy, you have done it now!' " [22] At last, after *King Lear* on February 3, we could feel that his "professional life" was over: "I have only to act one night more for my own benefit, in regard to which I am bound to no man; I have acquitted myself of my dues — I am free!" [23]

For his farewell, he chose Macbeth. It was of all his Shakespearian parts the one he had played most often.[24] It was associated with some of his greatest triumphs: with that night in 1836 when, to his astonishment, Covent Garden had received him with something like rapture after his bout with the detestable Bunn; or that more recent night, at the close of his second period of management, when at Drury Lane "the whole house" had risen with long-continued "shouting and waving of hats and handkerchiefs," changing at last "to a stamping of feet, which sounded like thunder." [25] Now, on February 26, 1851, Mrs. Warner, an able and experienced actress whom Macready respected, was to be his Lady Macbeth, and Samuel Phelps came from Sadler's Wells to do Macduff.[26]

In contemporary notices of the performance, much attention is given to the precautions which had been taken at the theatre to prevent overcrowding. Most of the seats — "not only the dress circle, but the upper circles and even the slips" — had been numbered, and were taken long in advance. The scramble for unreserved places is described in the *Theatrical Journal* of March 6:

> As early as 2 o'clock in the afternoon, the doors of the theatre were surrounded by vast numbers of persons eager to gain admittance to the pit and gallery — the boxes having all been engaged many days previous, and which could only be entered by tickets — hundreds of which were sold at the exorbitant sum of three pounds. At half-past 6 o'clock the multitude assembled could not be less than three thousand persons. . . . The neighbourhood presented a most animated appearance, for the windows of the houses were thronged by the fair sex, who appeared to take great interest in viewing the nobility's carriages as they arrived. Vinegar yard was quite blocked and the density of the throng may be most adequately expressed by an exclamation uttered by one of the street witnesses, that "Jenny Lind was nothing to it." That the persons who had taken places might reach their seats an artificial road was formed by a body of policemen.

Despite the presence of the police, however, "the light-fingered gentry" were busy in the crowd.[27] "It might have been supposed," adds the *Journal*, "that, with the dense and excited mass, not a word of *Macbeth* would have been heard"; on the contrary, "so well had the arrangements for public accommodation been made, and so great was the evident respect for Mr. Macready, that, to use a popular phrase, a pin might have been heard to drop during the whole performance."

Toole, the comedian, was one of those who stood for hours before the entrance of the theatre. On a visit to Macready, after the latter's retirement, he told him of this, and Macready, who was much pleased, said "he believed he had played 'Macbeth' on that last night as well as ever he had played it." [28] In his diary, he went further:

Acted Macbeth as I never, never before acted it; with a reality, a vigour, a truth, a dignity that I never before threw into my delineation. . . . I felt everything, everything I did, and of course the audience felt with me. I rose with the play, and the last scene was a real climax.

But though his earliest thought on this great day had been of the ending of his life as a player, "not one feeling of regret intermingled with the placid satisfaction accompanying my performance of every act, needfully preparative to the coming event, as I said to myself, 'I shall never have to do this again.' " [29]

There is much in the *Diaries* about Macbeth — ideas for single scenes or even phrases; chronicling of successes or failures. "The line 'fled to England?' I discovered capable of more prominent effect," he notes at one time; [30] and at another, "thought of an improvement in third act. Tenderness to Lady Macbeth." [31] The longest and most illuminating entry is one immediately following a performance at Plymouth in the spring of 1841:

I have improved Macbeth. The general tone of the character was lofty, manly, or indeed as it should be, heroic, that of one living to command. The whole view of the character was constantly in sight: the grief, the care, the doubt was not that of a weak person, but of a strong mind and of a strong man. The manner of executing the command to the witches, and the effect upon myself of their vanishing was justly hit off, I marked the cause. The energy was more slackened — the great secret. A novel effect I thought good, of restlessness and an uneasy effort to appear unembarrassed before Banquo, previous to the murder. The banquet was improved in its forced hilarity. . . .

Here "manly" is, I think, the key word; [32] nor have I found any evidence to show that Macready was influenced by the new heresy in character-interpretation which made Macbeth already evil, murderous in intent, at the beginning of the play.[33]

Of those who describe his Macbeth, Hazlitt (in 1820) and Hunt (in 1831) were familiar with the work of both Kemble and Kean. Lewes remembered Kean. Forster, an intimate friend of Macready's, was yet capable of detecting his faults, as were, indeed, Westland Marston and John Foster Kirk. Lady Pollack writes charmingly of Macready, whom she knew only at the close of his career, but is too impressionable to be quite convincing. No English actor, however, has had a more distinguished group of critics, and the measure of agreement among them is, when all is said, not unimpressive. Thus, Hazlitt found that "the *ideal* and preternatural" had evaded Macready. There was "not a weight of superstitious

terror loading the atmosphere and hanging over the stage."
He had in a word *"struck short* of the higher and imaginative
part of the character. . . . John Kemble was the best *Macbeth* (upon the whole) that we have seen." [34] Hunt missed
much the same things, finding Macready's performance wanting in "that grace and exaltation which is to the character
what the poetry is to the language." His passion lacked imagination. Before the murder, he "is (so to speak) *nothing* but
a misgiving anticipator of crime; and after it, nothing but
the misgiving or despairing perpetrator." [35] And Lewes might
be merely adding an illustration when, years later, he wrote
of the same Macbeth that "he stole into the sleeping-chamber
of Duncan like a man going to purloin a purse, not like a
warrior going to snatch a crown." [36] Even Forster admitted
(as we shall see) that in one scene "Mr. Macready fell flat"; [37]
and Kirk, unfamiliar with the heroic style (save as it survived
in Junius Brutus Booth), and so not missing it in Macready,
yet felt that "he lacked, above everything else, the tones that
should have appalled the ear and made the heart stand
still." [38]

He came on, in his first scene, a rugged, soldierly Macbeth,[39] who spoke first the spurious Davenant line,

> Command they make a halt upon the heath,

then, a little too casually perhaps,

> So foul and fair a day I have not seen.[40]

His impatience while Banquo questioned the Sisters was
palpable: rushing to the centre of the stage, he addressed
them himself "in a quick imperious tone." Their prophecies
seemed to "thrill through" him, "as he started away, and,

for a moment, 'stood rapt in the wonder of it.' " [41] Stood, as
Edward Fitzgerald remembered, with his mouth open:

Megreedy, with all his flat face, managed to look well as Virginius, didn't he? And, as I thought, well enough in Macbeth,
except where he *would* stand with his mouth open (after the
Witches had hailed him), till I longed to pitch something into
it out of the Pit, the dear old Pit.[42]

Other eyes saw admirable things only. Lady Pollock found
that the actor could, "without gesticulation or grimace," con-
vey Macbeth's amazement. "His wandering, unsettled tone
did more than all the efforts of those who played the witches
in showing the supernatural at work." He had "a singular
power of looking at nothing; and when he spoke 'into the
air,' we could almost see the hags pass away, and like a wreath
of vapour dissolve into the invisible element." [43] The soliloquy, later in the scene, was finely done. Westland Marston
speaks of "the air of brooding reverie" about it, "with a
strange sense conveyed in the fixed and fateful gaze of im-
pending evil." [44] John Coleman, the actor, writes to much
the same effect, adding that this Macbeth's "tell-tale face
revealed the working of his mind," and you realized that
"the horrid image" of which he spoke was actually "the gory
image" of Duncan murdered.

In the great scenes at the beginning of the second act,
Macready was very nearly at his best. Forster could praise
almost everything here: his dismissal of the ubiquitous Seyton
just before the Dagger Scene; his appearance, "as he stood
before speaking — like a man on the verge of fate"; his exit,
which was "ghastly and impalpable." Only in "the lines
immediately before the murder" was there a fault to find, in
the want of "sustained and unearthly grandeur." [45] Marston

was satisfied that the soliloquy was "a triumph of discrimination and emphasis": the transitions in it "could not have been more judiciously marked." If, as he felt, there was something wanting still, it was because "reasoning carried it over intuition; all had been too obviously reasoned out." [46] But this criticism Macready's art faced ever. As for the exit, so much disliked by Lewes, Marston in good Victorian style found a lesson in it:

The crouching form and stealthy, felon-like step of the self-abased murderer . . . made . . . a picture not to be forgotten. In contrast with the erect, martial figure that entered in the first act, this change was the moral of the play made visible.[47]

Too close to trickery was, however, Macready's habit of pausing in making this exit, so that for an instant his left leg alone remained in view of the audience.[48]

His return from the chamber of Duncan is described in *Tallis's Dramatic Magazine*: "He stood bending back in the attitude, and with the apparent suffering of a man who has been shot through the breast by an arrow — and this, with the two bloody daggers still grasped in his hands unconsciously, was a true and dreadful picture of remorse." [49] The subsequent dialogue with Lady Macbeth he carried on in a whisper, but one, it was often remarked, which was distinctly audible throughout the house,[50] and the scene ended with a climactic exit. Marston, indeed, thought this one of the actor's grandest moments: "I still vividly recall the terrible agony of his cry —

Wake Duncan with thy knocking; I would thou couldst!

as, with his face averted from his wife, and his arms outstretched, as it were, to the irrecoverable past, she dragged him from the stage." [51]

On the other hand, the poetry near the beginning of the
third act — where Banquo's approaching murder is hinted at
— Macready altogether sacrificed. Even Forster admits this.
The lines beginning,

> There's comfort yet! They are assailable,

were delivered (he says) "in an ordinary way, without any
absorbing sense of their beauty." [52] Leigh Hunt, quoting

> Light thickens, and the crow
> Makes wing to th' rooky wood,

tells us that Macready spoke the words "as merely intimating
a fact — a note of time — pointing with his hand as he did it,
and as he might have pointed to a clock"; and what follows
was "spoken with too much rapidity and indifference. . . .
Mr. Macready seems afraid of the poetry of some of his
greatest parts, as if it would hurt the effect of his naturalness
and his more familiar passages." It took an Edmund Kean
to give you "the grace and the nature too — the ideal with the
common." [53] Marston greatly admired Macready's playing of
the same scenes. But he speaks of "the furtive look" with
which Macbeth turned from his wife when she questioned
him about Banquo, and of "the sinister, ill-suppressed laugh,"
accompanying his answer [54] — details which imply, I am
afraid, a performance verging upon melodrama. It was Macready's idea, too, in the scene before, that Macbeth should
fondle Fleance, as he asks whether the child is accompanying
his father. [55]

His most individual touch — one that excited comment
when Macready first played the rôle, some thirty years before
— was introduced in the scene with the Ghost. Earlier Mac-
beths, like Kemble and Young, had defied the Ghost, dared,

or even bullied it. Not so, Macready. Overcome by terror, he retreated before it and at last, crying

> Hence, horrible shadow!
> Unreal mock'ry, hence!

sank into a chair and covered his face. Then after a moment he raised his eyes — and the ghost had disappeared:

> Why, so! Being gone,
> I am a man again.[56]

Manliness and energy distinguished Macready's fifth act, which rose, indeed, to a splendid climax in the combat with Macduff. A transition of the old Kean sort attracted attention early in the act:

> Hang those that talk of fear.
> How does your patient, doctor? [57]

the last words being violently contrasted, in their everyday colloquialism, with what went before. Neither Coleman nor Marston who describe this "point" liked it. Kirk, who appeared one night as the Physician to Macready's Macbeth — to get, as he says, "the actor's point of view" — pictures a style of playing still grandiose if no longer heroic:

Macbeth, at my entrance, left the attendants . . . and, striding across the stage with a step that seemed to shake the boards, stationed himself so near me that all the lines in his face appeared to be magnified, like those of a picture to the close gaze of a short-sighted man.

He made his demands "in tones that sounded like thunder"; then, receiving no satisfaction, "strode back to have his armor buckled on, turning, in the intervals of his stormy chidings, to direct some inquiry or splenetic remark to me, and at last rushing off to meet the approaching foe." [58]

On hearing "The Queen, my lord, is dead," Macready allowed his truncheon to slip from his grasp — an idea which may have been suggested by the dropping of Corporal Trim's hat in *Tristram Shandy*.[59] In this same scene, the episode of the Messenger was an awaited one. "We were struck, as of old," wrote a reviewer in the autumn of 1850, "by his terrific look and action, as he stands, half-drawing his sword, over the messenger who brings the hideous news that Birnam Wood *is* coming to Dunsinane." [60]

The fight was still ahead — a fight that in those days was looked forward to, eagerly, by audiences who enjoyed stage-combats, whether in Shakespeare or melodrama. With Macready it was *acted* too. Back in the eighteen-twenties the German Prince Pückler-Muskau had noticed that nothing about the combat was "hurried," yet this Macbeth had captured "all the fire, nay, all the horror of *the end*." [61] The transitions were strongly and clearly marked — in his face, especially — as he passed from an easy confidence through prostration of spirit to the final desperation with which he flung himself upon his enemy.[62]

Did he curse his Macduff, I wonder, on this last night of all, and did Macduff curse back? Phelps had come from Sadler's Wells to play the part, out of courtesy to Macready; and when Phelps was a young actor he had, as Macduff, heard himself damned, and had, quite surprisingly, replied in kind ("though a pious man, he allowed himself the indulgence of a few Cromwellian oaths"), and afterwards Macready had congratulated him on his performance — especially in the fight! [63]

A death-scene, almost like one of Kean's in its picturesque

detail, brought the performance to a close. Lewes, writing of it soon afterwards, speaks of a *"crescendo* of excitement." When, at last,

after an energetic fight — which showed that the actor's powers bore him gallantly up to the last — he fell pierced by Macduff's sword, this death, typical of the actor's death, this last look, this last act of the actor, struck every bosom with a sharp and sudden blow, loosening a tempest of tumultuous feeling such as made applause an ovation.[64]

A few days later same the inevitable "Banquet to Mr. Macready on his retirement from the Stage." Bulwer-Lytton's speech, as chairman, put the case for Macready strongly and well. Of one of his performances, the dramatist pointed out, "we don't so much say, 'How well this was spoken,' or 'How finely that was acted,' but we feel within ourselves how true was the personation as a whole." The "originality" which even Macready's detractors allowed him, included "depth of thought." He had attempted "to penetrate into the subtlest intentions of the poet"; was, indeed, "original because he never sought to be original, but to be truthful; because, in a word, he was as conscientious in his art as he is in his actions." [65]

It was as an interpreter of Shakespeare's heroes that Macready would have liked best to be regarded. Criticism in his time was concentrating upon a reverent analysis of the same great characters, and a performance of his own — say the final one of Iago — was, he believed, a commentary on the character such as other actors had not, could not have given.[66] He might even understand Hamlet better than the critics themselves.[67] Indeed, he sometimes talked of Shakespeare's personages as they did, as living beings, not mere characters in plays. Someone, in that earnest age, once referred in his presence to the deplorable selfishness of Bassanio in accepting Antonio's sacrifice. Macready defended him, and the other shifting his ground said:

"Well, Antonio was the better man, at any rate. He, as a friend, was admirable."

"I don't wish," replied Macready, "to detract in any way from his merits: it *was* very kind of him." [68]

He could not understand why there was laughter at this.

Many qualities in his acting point forward — the emphasis on conception of character, perhaps, most strikingly. Tragedy in his time yielded something of its former splendor to the homeliness of *Virginius*. One hears more about Macready's stage business, in Shakespeare, than about his delivery of the great speeches. The voice, once a superb instrument, lost a good deal of its music. Matthew Arnold, visiting the theatre in 1848, was repelled by "the self-consciousness of Fanny Kemble, the harshness of Macready." [69] There was complaint that he was neglecting Shakespeare's verse in concentrating upon its meaning. Kirk found that

the musical flow of the verse was almost utterly lost; the sense alone directed the elocution, leading sometimes to abrupt changes of intonation that had the effect . . . of a sudden change of key without modulation in a musical composition. On the other hand, no false note was ever struck, no shade of meaning was left undiscriminated, no measured or monotonous recitation ever wearied the ear.[70]

Fanny Kemble believed that it was Macready's "consciousness of his imperfect declamation of blank-verse that induced him to adopt what his admirers called the natural style of speaking it; which was simply chopping it up into prose." [71] But this was an extreme and no doubt a jaundiced view.

For four exciting seasons Macready was a producer as well as a star actor. As such, he achieved much — his restoration of Shakespeare's *King Lear* will be remembered gratefully as part of that achievement — and, once more, his work points forward, if only in the attention, unusual in that day, which he bestowed upon details. Thereafter, he devoted himself to his own characters. The pains he bestowed upon them seemed ludicrous to some of his contemporaries. Like any competent performer today, he insisted upon taking rehearsals seriously; wished to know the positions at any given moment of the other players on the stage; saw the advantages of wearing beforehand, long enough to become accustomed to it, the armor in which he must appear in a martial play like *Henry V*.[72] He was accused, by members of his profession, of being a "selfish" actor, one who thought only of what would enhance the importance of his own rôles.[73] At least, he sought with a dogged determination to act them well.

Irving as Shylock

ON October 20, 1905, Henry Irving, like David Garrick before him, was laid to rest in the Abbey. It was in keeping with what he had accomplished for himself and his calling. The knighthood Queen Victoria had conferred a few years earlier, adding to the formal "Rise, Sir Henry," her own words, "It gives me very great pleasure, sir," carried much the same meaning. He was one among the Great Victorians and, like Garrick once more, a national figure.

A few weeks after his death appeared a pathetic little volume of poetical tributes. The writers were without exception obscure men — provincial journalists, country clergymen, and the like. They praise Irving for the most part as a good and worthy man, one who had purified the stage, sowing "white lily-flowers where other pois'nous weeds," [1] one who would now, in a better world, be greeted by Tennyson as well as Shakespeare. A generation later, on the eve of the Second World War, came another commemorative volume, the splendid and desirable book, *We Saw Him Act*. This time, the writers, now a distinguished company, unite in praising Irving as an artist. For the demurrers and detractors, the Archers and Bernard Shaws, they express only contempt. It is as if, in their lifetime, there had been but one theatre, the Lyceum, and one supremely gifted actor, the man whose

memory they were honoring. The applause of other days
echoes anew. Surely, we must believe, it was deserved!

Yet no other player of comparable rank, not even Edmund
Kean, remained so long unrecognized; no other, when recognition came, was so widely or destructively criticized. Irving,
we are assured over and over again, could neither walk nor
talk. He was a painstaking and even inspired stage manager,
but quite incapable of tragic acting on any level of true
excellence. Some of those who remembered the old patent
theatre days simply could not understand the enthusiasm
of the inexperienced. Edward Fitzgerald, having looked in at
"the famous Lyceum Hamlet" early in the spring of 1879,
"soon had looked, and heard, enough."

It was incomparably the worst I had ever witnessed, from
Covent Garden down to a Country Barn. . . . When he got to
"Something too much of this," I called out from the Pit door
where I stood, "A good deal too much," and not long after returned to my solitary inn.[2]

By that time, however, Macready was a generation away;
and where, save in the provinces, and America, were there
any who respected the traditions for which he had stood?
Their doom already determined in Macready's own day, they
were discarded or forgotten. Phelps at Sadler's Wells had
carried them bravely forward. So, in a measure, had Charles
Kean. It was in the eighteen-sixties that actors of the old
school began to find themselves no longer wanted. In London, Shakespeare spelled ruin — save, momentarily, with the
foreigner Charles Fechter, who exulted in overthrowing tradition, which he called, not very happily, "that worm-eaten
and unwholesome prison, where dramatic art languishes in
fetters." [3]

Irving as a very young man was coached by a member of Phelps's company. During his long years of apprenticeship in the provinces, he had sometimes the good fortune to appear with traditional actors like Barry Sullivan and the young Edwin Booth. But he was scarcely qualified to go far in their ways, even if he had desired to follow them, which is more than doubtful. Rather, he learned from many sources, and applied his knowledge shrewdly, Fechter and melodrama teaching him the effectiveness of pure miming; [4] Charles Kean, a regard for historical accuracy. As a Shakespearian actor, he was very original, very "modern." Archer, indeed, exaggerated only legitimately when he asserted of English acting that "the objects and methods of Macready were very much the same as those of Betterton; the objects and methods of Sir Henry Irving, even when he deals with the same material, are utterly dissimilar." [5]

Those who held out for the older style of Shakespearian acting had only distant memories to cite, and standards which, in England at any rate, had long been unmet. Irving satisfied such influential conservatives as Clement Scott and William Winter. It was rather from the left, from men associated with the new movement in drama, that he continued to be assailed. With Garrick, as we have seen, began the preëminence of the actor in the English theatre. Lamb's paradoxical essay, "On the Tragedies of Shakspeare," is in the first instance a protest against the exaltation of the player at the expense of the poet. It was an actor's theatre still when, in the eighteen-seventies, Irving mounted a long-vacant throne. But, with the passing of time, another theatre, realistic in intent, very serious, very self-conscious, came into being — an author's theatre. Pinero, it was remarked, would already have arranged every detail of performance when one of his mature plays reached the actors, so that they had only to follow his instructions.[6] Shaw, in his sagacious little pamphlet *The Art of Rehearsal,* tells the dramatist how to get his own way with the players.

Now Irving gave nothing by Shaw, or Henry Arthur Jones, and such contemporary dramas as he did give (Tennyson's *Becket* is a dignified exception) were wanting in vitality. Shakespeare yielded him parts in which he could star [7] — though not enough of them — and he drew upon the store of elder tragedians and did *Richelieu* and *Louis XI.* No wonder there was grumbling! Jones, in his unfinished *Shadow of Henry Irving,* insists gloomily upon "the eternal distinction, an opposition sometimes amounting to a pull-devil-pull-baker rivalry between the Drama and the Theatre." He grants that "Irving's acting and management at the Lyceum remain the supreme achievement of the English Theatre in all its annals"; but "by very reason of his being such a great actor and with this incomparable position he was the greatest enemy of the English Drama." [8]

In the autumn of 1879, however, Ibsen and the new realism were still unknown to English playgoers, and they were full of enthusiasm for the Lyceum and its new manager. At the close of the season before, he had promised them a number of curious revivals and did, indeed, open with Macready's old war horse *The Iron Chest.* But soon after — as early as October 8 — he changed his plans and set to work on the first new Shakespearian play to be given at his own theatre, *The Merchant of Venice.*[9] On Saturday, November 1, a little over three weeks later, it was ready for performance, ran for two hundred and fifty nights, and remained thereafter in Irving's "working *répertoire.*" In all, he is said to have played Shylock over a thousand times.[10]

The preface to Irving's acting edition of *The Merchant of Venice* contains an admirably concise statement of his ideals as a producer:

I have endeavoured to avoid hampering the natural action of the piece with any unnecessary embellishment; but have tried not to omit any accessory which might heighten the effects. I have availed myself of every resource at my command to present the play in a manner acceptable to our audiences.

In the course of an interview some years later, when the actor was in America, he answered criticism that the play's success was chiefly owing to its *mise en scène* by pointing out how little time (twenty-three days!) he had had for its preparation. The elaborate mounting of plays at the Lyceum began, he said, with the productions of 1880–81.[11] Percy Fitzgerald explains that "the whole effect," which was of great beauty, "was produced by the painting, not by built-up structures"; there was "none of that overloading of illustration without *a propos*, which was such a serious blemish in later productions." He questions, it is true, whether there had not been some overemphasis on externals even in *The Merchant of Venice*. "At the same time, it must be said that this system of reviving the tone of the era seems quite *un*-Shakespearian. These revels and Venetian dances and gondolas, put in for 'local colour,' have little to do with high tragedy and dramatic interest." [12] But there were few playgoers, in 1879, who would have shared his doubts.

Irving's acting text seems, at first glance, badly mutilated. Not only are some entire episodes omitted — the discomfiture of the Prince of Arragon; Jessica's talk with Launcelot Gobbo, discreditable to Shylock; Portia's, with Lorenzo and Nerissa, just before she sets forth from Belmont; and, more

excusably, the scene in Belmont following her departure —
but others are cut so drastically as to seem no longer themselves. Thus the scene of Bassanio's choosing among the
caskets is reduced by more than a third, with over seventy
lines omitted — and Portia was Ellen Terry! It is all the more
striking that such mention of the text as occurs when Irving
first produced the play, and when, four seasons later, he
brought it to America, is usually complimentary. In particular, his "restoration" of the fifth act is frequently cited.[13]
Booth and a good many others had been accustomed to treat
the play as a sort of tragedy and lowered their curtain upon
the defeat of Shylock. Clement Scott noticed that on the first
night some of the spectators left at the close of the Trial
Scene. They were "ill-advised" to do so.[14] As the run proceeded, Irving, not without protest, dropped the fifth act altogether, and substituted an afterpiece by Wills.[15]

J. H. Barnes, "handsome Jack" Barnes, as he was called,
appeared as Bassanio in the production of 1879. In his autobiography, Barnes takes exception to the idea of Shylock as
a wronged man for whom we should feel only sympathy. He
had, he says, talked over the character with Irving in 1901,
and thought "he was almost disposed to agree with my view."
Could it be that the Shylock Irving "played and made so
famous" was not "absolutely the Shylock he would have
played if he had possessed a greater amount of physical
power?" During the early rehearsals, Barnes fancied that he
was aiming at this other, more truly Shakespearian character,
only to find it, at certain points, beyond his reach.[16] William
Winter quotes Irving as having said in his presence that
Shylock was "a bloody-minded monster — but you mustn't
play him so, if you wish to succeed; you must get some sympathy with him"; [17] and Robert Hichens, after a talk with

the great actor, was left with much the same impression, that Irving's treatment of the part had been conditioned by his desire to score heavily in it.[18] Both explanations — the shrewd surmise that audiences of his day would prefer a sympathetic Jew, and the realization that he himself could not, like Kean, bring them to their feet with outbursts of passion — are likely to have weighed with Irving. After all, he had the fortunes of the Lyceum to consider as well as his own prestige. And who could say with confidence that this carefully wrought interpretation of his was wide of the mark?

Those who wrote of that first Shylock of 1879 divide, with few exceptions, into three groups. Some — and they are the largest group — were enthusiastic about Irving's conception of the part; a few wholly disagreed with it; and still others maintained that the actor had presented not one Shylock but two, that the impersonation was inconsistent with itself. One Shylock, according to *The Times*, was "erect, composed, dignified," and "almost by his bearing compelling our sympathies where they are most keenly raised against him." The other was "a screaming incoherent old man, who seemed to have lost his wits together with his daughter and his ducats." *The Saturday Review* agreed that the scene in which the Jew bewails his losses was out of keeping with the rest. *Punch*, perhaps with greater subtlety, was satisfied that "Mr. IRVING's conception of the character, its truth to SHAKSPEARE, and to nature," lay in its very inconsistency.

If Mr. IRVING is firm one moment, tottering another, now hobbling, now striding: now bent and broken, anon upright and sturdy; if at one time he raves and scolds like a virago, and at another is calm, impassive, and unrelenting as destiny, — I say that this is SHAKSPEARE's own *Shylock*, a character all lights and shades.[19]

Yet Dutton Cook found the performance "altogether consistent and harmonious" — this Shylock, "old, haggard, halting, sordid, represents the dignity and intellect of the play"; [20] and another critic felt that the part, as Irving represented it, had taken on "a sad and romantic interest, an almost tragic elevation and grace." [21] Among the dissentors several have famous names. Ruskin, who had been quoted in *The Theatre* as having told Irving that his impersonation was "noble, tender, and true," protested that although admiring "Mr. Irving's own acting of Shylock . . . I entirely dissent (and indignantly as well as entirely) from his general reading and treatment of the play." [22] Henry James referred to the conception as "a sentimental one," then turned his attention to matters of technique. Irving as the Jew, he wrote comprehensively, was "neither excited nor exciting." [23] In later years, both Shaw and Henry Arthur Jones joined the attack. "He was simply not Shylock at all" (writes the former) and in the Trial Scene "positively acted Shakespeare off the stage." [24] And Jones calls the final exit,

undoubtedly a great piece of acting. It was, however, quite ex-Shakespearean, if not anti-Shakespearean. It illustrates a frequent habit and method of Irving — that of getting his greatest effects not in, and by, the text and obvious meaning of his author, but in his own extraneous bits of business.[25]

A densely crowded audience waited for their first sight of the new Shylock. They saw him enter with Bassanio, at the beginning of Scene 3, against "a view of the Palace of St. Mark, with a quay on which porters are landing bales of merchandise." [26] A man of between fifty and sixty, old but not decrepit, he was dressed in a sober brown robe, with an oriental, shawl-like girdle and a black cap across which ran a yellow line. In his hand, as was traditional, he carried a stick. The face was gaunt and wolfish, with a wisp of iron-grey beard.[27] Certainly, as even James admitted, he looked the part! [28]

In Boston, on an evening some years later, Irving talked about Shylock, and had much to say about this first, long scene.[29] He traced the Jew's changing moods. "He is, to begin with, quiet, dignified, diplomatic; then satirical; and next, somewhat light and airy in his manner, with a touch of hypocrisy in it." Although "his first word is more or less fawning," he presently,

breaks out into reproach and satire when he recalls the insults that have been heaped upon him. "Hath a dog money?" and so on; still he is diplomatic, for he wants to make reprisals upon Antonio: "Cursed be my tribe if I forgive him!" He is plausible, even jocular. He speaks of his bond of blood as a merry sport. Do you think if he were strident or spiteful in his manner here . . . they would consent to sign a bond having in it such fatal possibilities?

Clement Scott, who for all his limitations was a good critic of acting, calls attention to many details in Irving's perform-ance of the scene. "Scarcely a moment of the dialogue was unrelieved by some variety of intonation or facial expression," such as "the half-laughing sneer that a pound of man's flesh was not so profitable as that of mutton, or of goats," or "the recital with the fervour of interest of some old passage in the history of Jacob." [30] In the long aside beginning:

How like a fawning publican he looks!

the actor dwelt "with concentrated bitterness on the expres-sions of hatred to Antonio . . . and here, in the implacable determination of

'If I can catch him once upon the hip,
I will feed fat the ancient grudge I bear him,'

we have the prologue, as it were, to the intense revengefulness
of the last scene." [31] Irving himself raises the interesting question of when the idea of the bargain first occurs to Shylock —
of when, to speak more accurately, the coming of the hideous
thought should be indicated by the actor. He had chosen the
moment at which Antonio, turning upon the Jew, declares
"he is 'like to spit upon him again,' and invites him scorn-
fully to lend him the money, not as to his friend, but rather
to his enemy. . . . From that moment I imagine Shylock
resolving to propose his pound of flesh." [32] Putting on a show
of servility, he came close to his victim and touched him
lightly on the breast. Antonio recoiled in disgust and Shylock, sensitive to the rebuke, bowed low.[33] He could afford
to wait.

During the second act, Shylock has little to do. But just
at the end, Irving invented for him and invented brilliantly.
Jessica's elopement had been elaborately staged. The scene
showed the Jew's house, "with a bridge over the canal which
flows by it, and with a votive lamp to the Virgin on the wall.
There a barcarolle is sung by some Venetians on a gondola,
and a number of masqueraders rush merrily past." [34] As the
sound of their laughter and music died away, the curtain
descended. (Can it have been that at this point some of the
critics scurried for the lobbies? At any rate, what follows
passes unmentioned in a good many contemporary accounts
of the performance.) After a few moments, the curtain was
raised once more, showing the same scene, but now silent and
deserted. Shylock appeared, "lantern in hand, advancing,
bent in thought," and as he drew close to the house — still

unaware that it is now empty — the curtain fell.[35] In later performances, he sometimes knocked at the door.[36]

Edmund Kean had made Shylock's scene of mingled menace and lamentation, at the beginning of Act III, the climax of his performance. Irving could not. The expression of violent emotion in torrents of speech was denied him. On the first night, moreover, he was upset by a bad slip of memory on Tubal's part (*Punch* fancies what would have happened to the unfortunate actor had he been with Macready!). Irving had not yet learned how to make the most of his powers. He ranted "after a fashion and in a language wholly unintelligible." [37] Yet Sir Theodore Martin assures us that as a spectator he was able to forget "the cracked and screaming tones, and the occasional want of articulateness, in the powerful action, the visible intensity of the feeling, the thoroughness with which the ruling idea is worked out." [38] Scott too, though admitting there were faults, remained cordial.

The expression of incontinent rage and prostration of nervous energy, was occasionally not in tune. The great speech was started in too high a key, and, though it won the finest burst of applause of the whole evening, Mr. Irving was not at this moment seen at his best. . . the strain was very great and a little painful.

A moment later, however, came "the calm and almost inspired delivery of the pathetic words: 'No satisfaction, no revenge . . . no tears but of my shedding . . .' and, from that instant, all went well again." [39] In America, a few years later, Irving was thought to have reached a "summit and climax" in his speaking of the same words.[40] It is not, perhaps, without significance that in talking of the traditional playing of this scene he then dwelt upon the desirability of avoiding excess. Shylock would be unlikely to give his terrible resolve "a loud and noisy utterance." [41]

Irving's best scene was still to come — that of the trial. The setting was a splendidly painted hall adorned with portraits of Venetian worthies. It was "lined with mediaeval soldiery in their quaint costumes"; and spectators, including a little knot of eager Jews, watched the proceedings.[42] Shylock, entering slowly, remained "standing almost motionless, his hands hanging by his sides . . . his grey, worn face, lined and hollow, mostly averted from the speakers who move him not; except when a gleam of murderous hate, sudden and deadly . . . burns for a moment in the tired, melancholy eyes" — as he asked, for instance,

> Hates any man the thing he would not kill?

At the taunts of Gratiano, "and the amiable maundering of the Duke," a "slow, cold smile, just parting the lips . . . passes over the face, but does not touch the eyes or lift the brow." [43] The stillness, or even listlessness, of this Shylock is remarked on again and again. While he listened to "the Duke's speech in mitigation," we are told, somewhat inexactly, he had "the horrible stillness and fascination of the rattlesnake." [44]

It was noticed that Irving, unlike many earlier Shylocks, laid no emphasis upon the grim action of whetting the knife.[45] When Bassanio made his offer of twice the amount owed —

> For thy three thousand ducats here is six —

Shylock's refusal was accompanied by his tapping the bag of jingling coins three times with the point of his knife; and it was again with the knife's point that he later showed the young judge what was and what was not specified in the bond, leaning eagerly over the other's shoulder as he did so.[46]

With the deadly "A sentence! Come, prepare!" the scene leaps to climax — and the next moment, Shylock is defeated. In Irving's performance, he stood as if dazed, his utter collapse marked by the dropping of the scales and knife from his hands.[47] The "last effort to clutch the gold . . . his cunning, business-like, 'Give me my principal, and let me go!' " was "an admirable point." [48] Then came what was to be one of Irving's most famous moments — equalled, it may be, only by the frenzied action at the close of the Play Scene in *Hamlet*. It is well described by *The Spectator*:

> Shylock is Mr. Irving's finest performance, and his final exit is its best point. The quiet shrug, the glance of ineffable, unfathomable contempt at the exultant booby, Gratiano, who, having got hold of a good joke, worries it like a puppy with a bone, the expression of defeat in every limb and feature, the deep, gasping sigh, as he passes slowly out, and the crowd rush from the Court to hoot and howl at him outside, make up an effect which must be seen to be comprehended.

And still speaking of this exit, the writer adds that the impression it produced "upon the vast audience was most remarkable; the thrill that passed over the house was a sensation to have witnessed and shared." Is it any wonder if some preferred, as we have seen, not to stay on, after that, for Shakespeare and his fifth act?

In Shylock, Irving's mannerisms were found less conspicuous, less obstructive to a full success, than they were in most of his other rôles. After all, a certain strangeness of speech and gait may be granted the Jew, and even become him.

A great deal has been written about these mannerisms, and

116

they remain mysterious. The late Sophia Kirk, daughter of the John Foster Kirk who knew and wrote about Macready, once told me of going with her brother to see Irving for the first time. They had heard he had a wooden leg. But which leg? After comparing notes at the close of the performance, they were satisfied — *both were*! Yet Irving could upon occasion walk well, and gracefully, just as he was capable, at rehearsals, of pronouncing "God" otherwise than "Gud."

All sorts of explanations were offered. Were the mannerisms deliberately assumed, as some of Irving's admirers insisted to the last, or were they involuntary? And if involuntary, were they due to mere nervousness, as on such unfortunate first nights as that of *King Lear*? Ellen Terry suggested as a means of overcoming self-consciousness, that he avoid long waits at the side before his entrances, and in *The Merchant of Venice* he followed her advice successfully.[49]

Apologists for Irving, when not actually extolling his mannerisms,[50] made light of them. At first distracting, they might be readily forgotten as one became accustomed to them. (Booth once spoke of this.[51]) Such too was Irving's dignity, his absorption in his characters, his command of audiences, that ridicule of him found no expression in the theatre. "Never once at the Lyceum," writes Sir Max Beerbohm, "did I hear a titter. Irving's presence dominated even those who could not be enchanted by it." [52] It was possible, notwithstanding, to feel the enchantment and still deplore Irving's lapses of speech as a grave defect in his art. The Bostonian critic Henry Austin Clapp states the conservative position admirably. The mere "mannerisms," as they were called, Clapp takes as evidence that the actor had not mastered his craft; and the demand that they be lightly dismissed from consideration was much as if an acquaintance were to recommend for confidential clerk a young man who was a little weak on the score of honesty and accuracy, but, aside from these trifling mannerisms, had every desirable qualification. . . . If there were such a crime as lingua-matricide, Mr. Irving would have suffered its extreme penalty long ago; for night after night he has done foul murder upon his mother-tongue.[53]

The voice itself, he goes on to describe as possessing "very little resonance, and almost no richness of tone; it is high-pitched, and has a narrow range; he seems absolutely incapable of *sustained* power and variety in speech." There were others who agreed. Henry James found the voice "without charm . . . a thick unmodulated voice";[54] and Bernard Shaw described it, in comparison with Barry Sullivan's, as "a highly cultivated neigh."[55]

Thus it was that the grandeur of the Shakespearian music, which earlier actors would summon up, however mechanically, through their declamatory method, was flatly denied Irving. But had not much the same thing been true of Macready before him? How came it about, then, that Irving could so startle and offend — or startle and delight — as he did, for instance, on his first visit to America?[56] The explanation lies, I believe, as much in the sensational success of his methods as in their novelty. He was picturesque himself, and a master of pictorial effect. Clapp was inclined to say that Irving's face was "without exception the most fascinating" he had "seen upon the stage. Once beheld, it will not out of the memory."[57] His hands were beautiful and he used them with extraordinary skill.[58] Above all, he possessed in a degree only matched, perhaps, by Garrick among English actors, that quality of personal attraction which writers on the theatre despair to explain. You could not help watching

Irving while he was on the stage. You saw him after the fall of the curtain — it might be for years to come — as the Jew, or Hamlet, or the half-crazed burgomaster, Mathias, in *The Bells*. And what is more remarkable this might hold good even when the actor's view of a character was not your own.[59]

Alfred Darbyshire, the architect, has a tale to tell of Irving's obscure days as a minor actor at Manchester under Charles Calvert. Darbyshire "was watching a rehearsal at the Theatre Royal, when someone came up to Calvert and asked the question, 'Why on earth did you engage that raw fellow?' (pointing to Irving). Calvert replied by touching his forehead with his forefinger." [60] And Irving had brains. With little education, and no interests, seemingly, outside those of his profession, he thought, observed, and invented with a devotion to the theatre which was sometimes considered fantastic. No detail was beneath his notice. Robert Ganthony, a very minor actor who did Stephano in *The Merchant of Venice*, gives an anecdote by way of illustration.

If genius be the faculty of taking pains, Irving must be a genius, for if it were the last performance of a play, and he saw something that would improve it, he would adopt it. Months after we had been playing the "Merchant" he called me to him and said, "It would be better, Ganthony, if your spurs jingled a little more as you entered and crossed the stage." I accordingly had two metal discs put in each, the sound from which should have satisfied all the requirements of dramatic art.[61]

For Irving was a producer as well as an actor, and it is not always easy to distinguish one side of his achievement from the other. Is the homecoming of Shylock across that Venetian bridge to be regarded as a feat of stage-management or an unusually elaborate piece of original "business"? It scarcely matters, really, since as we have seen this *Merchant of Venice* kept Shylock ever to the fore. Yet if in some sense a production at the Lyceum was no more than a frame for Irving himself, it was a frame splendidly wrought and gilded — a work of art. And though his methods of presenting Shakespeare may seem to us who only read of these performances, cumbersome and even a little prosaic, they appeared quite otherwise to audiences of his own day. Thus Irving's Romeo, I read in an anonymous little book on the actor, published in 1883, could not altogether pass unchallenged, nor could his Benedick,

but for pure enjoyment of a play — or *going to the play* as we say — an evening spent in the society of those beautifully-dressed, admirably-graceful ladies and gentlemen, in that Lyceum-land where, as in the Isle of the Lotus-eaters, it is "always afternoon," is perfect. When we leave we have indeed "been to the play — not merely looked on at a performance, but *been* there — to the home of chivalry, romance, ease, and wealth, where nothing sordid can ever enter, though malice and all uncharitableness creep in to make it human.[62]

Edwin Booth as Iago

"WELL, old boy, we are at last in the great world, where I shall soon be known or lost in the fog. A few weeks will decide." Booth is writing from a Kensington hotel on August 25, 1880. Still in his forties and near the height of his powers as an artist, he might well have been more confident. Save to the few who still talked of Forrest, he was America's greatest actor. England, his father's country and Kean's, was still to be won.

He was already a little tired. "I can't get up an ounce of steam, try as I will," his letter continues.[1] Tragic misfortunes, of which the death of his beloved Mary Devlin and the mad crime of his brother, the assassin of Lincoln, were but the most terrible, had aged him; nor was their sum even now complete. A second wife, desperately ill — dying as it proved — and at times insane, had accompanied him to England.

With a hastily assembled English company, which left much to be desired, though among them was John Ryder, a stalwart of earlier days, Booth opened the new Princess's Theatre on November 6. As safest for his voice after a long rest, he chose *Hamlet*.[2] Years later, Booth admitted that he would have done better to open with *King Lear*.[3] Or there was *Richelieu*. He "could not act *Hamlet* the first night":[4] it was, he told his friend Winter, "the most inflexible performance that he ever gave." [5]

The critics showed little enthusiasm. Granting the actor intellect, they complained of his coldness and artificiality. His use of gesture was excessive.

He was apt to spoil the fine effect of certain passages by his adherence to the old trick of "taking the stage" at the end of speeches which are finished off with what the old school of acting considered "a point." [6]

The memory of Charles Mayne Young is invoked for purposes of a detailed comparison [7] — Young was a tragedian of the Kemble school. The American was even likened to Charles Kean! [8] That his declamation was admirable is generally allowed, though exception is taken to his accent: "The pronunciation of a word is one thing; the key in which it is spoken, another. The exquisite speech of English private life — there is never too much of that at the theatre. . . ." [9]

As Booth turned to other parts, in the weeks following, to Richelieu and Iago, to Bertuccio (in *The Fool's Revenge*) and Lear, the tone of the critics changes. Even at the outset, J. Palgrave Simpson had come forward in *The Theatre* to defend his art as "eminently natural." Sala in *The Illustrated London News* decided that this actor was "the finest Bertuccio and, next to Macready, the finest Lear and the finest Richelieu" he had seen. *The Athenaeum* declares that the later scenes of *King Lear* might

count among the most distinct triumphs of art the present generation has had the opportunity to contemplate. . . . No English-speaking actor since Macready has possessed a method so admirable as Mr. Booth.

Punch, indeed, remained obdurate. "In manner, Mr. Booth frequently reminds us of Mr. Phelps, only without the growl," is not intended as a tribute; and when the news came that Irving had engaged the American to appear with him at the Lyceum: "The prices are to be doubled; it strikes us they should be halved." [10]

Meanwhile, Booth himself had been making the best of what he admitted was a long "uphill drag." In part, he blames the "gush" of his own countrymen in London: "There's no restraining the eagle when he feels like screeching & he 'scroched' too much for me." [11] English actors were cordial. Old Ryder, who had played with Macready, came to him deeply moved after *Richelieu* to declare that he had upset his idol.[12] Then, early in the new year, Irving called, and Booth liked him — "a very pleasant fellow and kindly inclined." [13] Irving, he remembered, had once supported him at Manchester; and he had tried before leaving America to reach some arrangement with him in connection with the present visit. Negotiations had broken down, however, and Booth had pretty well decided that the Englishman had the "big head." [14] Now they talked over plans, and Irving suggested that they should appear together in *Othello*, at the Lyceum, alternating in the parts of Iago and the Moor.[15]

The advantage, as Booth saw it, was on his side, with Irving running all the risks. Irving would have the responsibility of producing the tragedy. He had not played Iago before. He must continue to perform his part in Tennyson's *Cup* on the nights, three a week, when *Othello* was not given. "He has done a friendly thing," Booth writes, "and I hope he will reap a good reward for it, here and in America, if he should ever go there." [16] At the earlier rehearsals Booth, quite characteristically, sent his dresser to represent him.[17] When he did go himself, Ellen Terry found him "very gentle and apathetic." [18] He was much interested, nevertheless, and upon his return to America described with a certain wonder what he had seen. Irving, he said, "as a stage-manager" was despotic.

He sits on the stage during rehearsals, watching every movement and listening to every word. If he sees anything to correct or alter, he rises and points out the fault, giving the proper form, when the scene is repeated. He commands all points, with an understanding that his will is absolute law . . . whether it concerns the entry of a mere messenger who bears a letter, or whether it is the reading of an important line by Miss Terry. From first to last he rules his stage with an iron will, but as an offset to this he displays a patience that is marvellous.[19]

The first performance, with Booth as Othello, Irving as Iago, was on Monday, May 2. Then, a week later, Irving was the Moor and Booth his ancient.[20] Ellen Terry played Desdemona; Terriss, Cassio; and Pinero, Roderigo.

One hears of the "tumultuous applause" bestowed upon the performers by a great audience; of the many artists and authors who were present; of the "Boothians," "Irvingites," and "Terryites." The popular parts of the theatre were "densely crowded." [21] G. R. Foss, the actor, tells of being at the pit door from one o'clock in the afternoon (pit seats were to be had for two shillings). "There were no queues in those days; it was a football scrum, all hard shoving and the devil take the hindmost. But it was well worth it." [22] Thinking over the play afterwards, a critic could take comfort in the thought

that our much abused and derided theatre has really produced something to which, without vanity, we may point as a proof that this nineteenth century of ours, despite the jibes of *Punch*, is not wholly unworthy to enjoy the heritage of Shakespeare;

and, albeit "with the utmost trepidation," he "would hazard the doubt whether, even in the happiest days of the poetic drama . . . this noble play can ever have been *as a whole* much more satisfactorily presented." [23] It may be added that Irving's Iago — an unconventional characterization abounding in brilliant detail — was very generally preferred to Booth's Othello.

Public interest showed no sign of waning with the exchange of rôles. Booth's Iago was warmly praised. *The Times* actually liked it better than Irving's — "less startling," indeed, "less spirited," but as a whole "more artistic." [24] Sir Theodore Martin finds this Venetian "much more likely than Mr. Irving's to impress those around him with the belief of his 'exceeding honesty.'" The evil in the character flashed out upon occasion "with tenfold force by contrast with the careless ease of his general bearing. Every word told without having undue stress laid upon it." The "soliloquies were those of a man really thinking aloud." [25]

Mowbray Morris, in an essay first published in *Macmillan's Magazine*, describes the two Iagos with at least an appearance of fairness to both:

The American Iago, clear, cool and precise, admirably thought out, never deviating a hair's-breadth from the preconceived plan, design and execution marching hand in hand with ordered step from the first scene to the last; a performance of marvellous balance and regularity, polished to the very finger-nail. The Englishman's startling, picturesque, irregular, brilliant sometimes, sometimes less brilliant than bizarre, but always fresh and suggestive, always bearing that peculiar stamp of personality which has so often saved the actor in his sorest straits.

It was marred, in the writer's opinion, by a single fault — and this fault, one so far from being regarded as such that it was often counted a virtue — "*a perpetual striving after something new.*" [26]

That there was development in Booth's conception of the rôle is asserted by a writer in whom I have great confidence, Henry Austin Clapp. Booth (he says) had fitted his performance "to his physical limitations," making Iago "a light, comfortable villain" and bringing out his human qualities. "Later he darkened the hues of his conception, and steadily increased its force . . . and profundity." Malice gave place to a satanic malevolence. There was now an "absolute self-consistency," an "unfailing relation of every point and particular . . . to the total scheme." [27]

Many, however, of the distinguishing traits of Booth's earlier Iago, as we know them from the detailed description by Lucia Calhoun in the sixties, lasted on unchanged. There was plausibility. This villain indulged in

no stage winks and grimaces. Save in his soliloquies he makes no confessions to himself. If Othello had suddenly turned upon him, at any moment in their interview, he would have seen only the grave, sympathetic, respectful, troubled face that was composed for him to see.[28]

So Dutton Cook, writing of Booth at the Princess's, could "remember no *Iago* at once so natural and plausible, so intellectual and so terrible"; [29] and Towse agrees that he was "entirely plausible. . . . His most pernicious lies to Othello — concerning Cassio's dream and the handkerchief, for instance — he administered in the most deceptive form, that of an involuntary confidence." [30]

Booth himself is quotable on this same matter of plausibility. In one of the memorable notes which he contributed to the Furness Variorum *Othello* in 1885, Iago is advised:

Do not smile, or sneer, or glower, — try to impress even *the audience* with your sincerity. 'Tis better, however, always to ignore the audience; if you can forget that you are a "shew" you will be natural. The more sincere your manner, the more devilish your deceit. I think the "light comedian" should play the villain's part, not the "heavy man"; I mean the Shakespearian villains. Iago should appear to be what all but the audience believe he is. Even when alone, there is little need to remove the mask entirely. Shakespeare spares you that trouble.[31]

Unpretentious as the words are, they are yet full of meaning. In another note, returning to the idea of Iago's seeming sincerity, he warns:

Don't *act* the villain, don't *look* it or *speak* it (by scowling and growling, I mean), but *think* it all the time. Be genial, sometimes jovial, always gentlemanly. Quick in motion as in thought; lithe and sinuous as a snake. A certain bluffness (which my temperament does not afford) should be added to preserve the military flavour of the character; in this particular I fail utterly, my Iago lacks the soldierly quality.[32]

"Versatility" was another characteristic of Booth's performance in the sixties. His Iago was an accomplished actor. To Othello, "the truthful, respectful adherent and friend"; to Desdemona, "the courteous servant"; to Cassio, "the open and generous fellow-soldier"; to Roderigo, "a dashing buck." To Emilia alone he remained "the inscrutable, black-browed schemer, whom she distrusts, but does not understand." [33] This swiftness of adaptation, this power of moulding himself to what others suppose him to be, distinguished the characterization at all times. The possibility that, except of course in the soliloquies, the part might be done throughout in a "bluff, vigorous, and off-hand manner" did, indeed, occur to

one English critic. But to have played it so would have been
to miss "the constantly-changing interest, grace, and vivacity
of Mr. Booth's performance." [34] It was exactly in bluffness,
moreover, that Booth (as we saw) found himself wanting.

When Iago dropped his mask there were "grave and even
terrible" moments.[35] Lucia Calhoun tells of one such, near
the close of the tragedy: "I bleed, sir, but-not-killed" became
as Booth spoke it "the mocking defiance of a devil, indeed."
In later years, the baleful and the fiendish in the character
were brought out increasingly. It "seemed to be enveloped
in an aura of evil"; [36] to pervade the tragedy "like an incarna-
tion of the Evil Principle." [37] Otis Skinner remembered it as
"radiant with devilish beauty"; [38] White, the Shakespearian
commentator, spoke of the hate burning in the eyes — the face
at times looked "snake-like." [39]

In the last act, especially, the diabolical was manifest. Cassio and Roderigo lie wounded; Iago stands over them. It is
night and the street is deserted. Suddenly, the villain stabs his
miserable dupe.

> *Rod.* O damn'd Iago! O inhuman dog!
> *Iago.* Kill men i' th' dark? Where be these bloody thieves?
> How silent is this town!

Here, according to Booth's invention, Iago would have killed
Cassio as well, and actually raised his hand to do so, only to
be stayed by the sight of Lodovico and Gratiano approaching.
"Ho! murder! murder!" he cries instantly; but the deed remains uncompleted.[40] Or again, near the close of the tragedy,
when Othello would know why "that demi-devil" had en-
snared him body and soul, and the Venetian only says:

> Demand me nothing. What you know, you know.
> From this time forth I never will speak word,

Booth's utterance was accompanied by a hideous grinding of his teeth, as if, indeed, torments could never make him speak.[41] He was then led away, to stand, waiting, till suddenly the Moor stabbed himself. At that, Iago started forward as if to gloat over the destruction of his enemy. William Winter wrote approvingly that the actor "made this prodigy of wickedness live in the actual form of nature, as it lives in Shakespeare's page." [42] There were those, however, to whom the device seemed strangely old-fashioned and melodramatic. Richard Dickins, in his scarce little book, *Forty Years of Shakespeare on the English Stage*, is of this opinion. Booth's performance at the Lyceum seemed to him

not in harmony with the rest of the picture, not in sympathy with the dominating mind. . . . I would illustrate this by saying that his Iago brought down the final curtain standing over Othello, pointing triumphantly at the dead body and gazing up at the gallery with a malignant smile of satisfied hate.[43]

Passages of quiet intensity, where Iago actually does or says little, Booth could also make memorable. Thus Irving was endlessly praised for the realistic byplay he introduced in the scene where Iago, watching the innocent familiarities of Cassio and Desdemona, comments viciously upon them. Irving ate grapes. "The action is easy and natural enough," Mowbray Morris writes,

yet how much less really natural to the character than Mr. Booth's still, respectful attitude, leaning against the sun-dial, alert to execute any command, seeming careless what goes on so long as he is ready when wanted, yet ever watching his prey with sly, sleepless, vigilance.[44]

Nor did his "silent hatred" of Emilia in Act IV, scene 2, escape remark.[45]

In the notes, already referred to, which Booth sent to Furness for the Variorum *Othello*, he repeatedly warns the performers against theatricality. "O, you are well tun'd now," says Iago, when the lovers are happy in being reunited,

> But I'll set down the pegs that make this music.

And the words "should be spoken with calm assurance; not too pointedly. He knows he will make the discord, — so does the audience." [46] Just before the Temptation Scene in the third act, Iago's "I like not that" is annotated: "Don't growl this, — let it barely be heard by the audience"; and as the attack is opened, Iago's disquieting "Indeed" is not to be made conspicuous: "Contract the brows, but do not frown, — rather look disappointed, and merely mutter in surprise, 'Indeed!' " A little later, the villain begins:

> Good name in man and woman, dear my lord,
> Is the immediate jewel of their souls. . .

and Booth writes: "Don't fire this directly at Othello, but trust to the 'whiff and wind' of it, for your effect on him, and on the audience too, although it may not gain applause from them as do the scowls and growls of the stage-villain." Still another caveat against overplaying appears in the note on Cassio's speech about his lost reputation: "In Cassio's speech . . . don't preach; be not violent; avoid rant; yet be impassioned, — feel thoroughly disgusted with yourself, and you'll be natural. Walk about, but don't stamp or 'saw the air.' "

The idea that an actor should feel the emotions he is expressing reappears in what is perhaps the finest, certainly the most idealistic, of all the notes. The Duke has attempted in vain to console Brabantio. Then they turn to state affairs.

Othello leaves Desdemona with Cassio, who regards her with tender, yet respectful admiration. Iago, at back, watches them curiously, but let him not be obtrusive; he must keep in the background and assume this expression, and feel the curiousness, even if only one person in the whole audience sees or understands it; the "censure," as Hamlet calls it, of that one is worth all the rest.

But did Booth, himself, "feel the curiousness"? Was he like Macready in experiencing the emotions of his characters? It is impossible to be sure. We hear of how greatly his performances varied. At times, we are told by one who observed him closely, "he was somewhere else, and his art moved in a mist." [47] Was it that at just such times emotion had completely failed him?

Finally, the sensitiveness of Booth's feeling for the play is repeatedly suggested by his annotations. Cassio greets Desdemona in courtly terms upon her safe arrival in Cyprus. Then he turns to Emilia:

> Welcome mistress. —
> Let it not gall your patience, good Iago,
> That I extend my manners. 'Tis my breeding
> That gives me this bold show of courtesy.

So saying, he kisses her — kisses her face, as Booth points out, "not, as is frequently done, her hand" — and "Iago winces slightly, for he 'suspects Cassio with his nightcap.'" When, again, they are talking of Desdemona just before the Drinking Scene — "What an eye she has! Methinks it sounds a parley to provocation" — "Iago watches Cassio intently." In each case, the rightness of the action called for is obvious. Such notes as these have almost the value of original stage-directions.

It was the soundness of the actor's conceptions, rather than their originality, which won praise. As Hamlet, he made clear where the Prince was merely feigning madness, where he was in reality perilously near to being deranged.[48] In Richard III, as in Iago, he restricted his confidences in the audience to the soliloquies and asides.[49] Reading of Booth, one is sometimes reminded of Phelps — though Booth himself did not at all like the comparison [50] — but more often of Betterton.

In range, to be sure, he was inferior to either. Though he liked to play Benedick, and especially Petruchio, he was not at his best in comedy. The humor which shines through his letters seems to have deserted him on the stage. Winter, thinking no doubt of his Hamlet, calls Booth a specialist "in passionate melancholy and poetical delirium." [51] Skinner finds it strange that "with such gentleness as his" he yet achieved his "greatest effects . . . in parts of sinister and diabolic character." [52] In England, nevertheless, he added to his reputation when he passed from the rôle of Iago to that of King Lear. And Lear, like Othello, lay a little beyond him physically — or so it was thought.

Of middle height, no more, he was slenderly built, free and graceful in movement. His face with its sculpturesque features and dark, flashing eyes, was like his body perfectly under control. So extraordinary were his eyes that children sometimes "kept the look of them as almost the sole recollection of plays in which they had seen him." Booth's Shylock had once been to Copeland "nothing but a pair of eyes, large, dark, awful, and bright — above all, bright, and seeming to give out light." [53] So, it will be recalled, Kean's eyes had haunted those who saw them.

In England, Booth's art was considered old-fashioned, and

there is no questioning his conservatism. Out of weariness and discouragement, he came to tolerate in his own productions such characteristic evils of the American starring system as carelessness in rehearsing and palpable inadequacy in the players who supported him. His Shakespearian texts were, it is true, freshly edited, but they were still cut and dismembered (in Booth's *Richard II* the waits between acts amounted to a full third of the evening) [54] and their prudishness was ridiculous. *The Athenaeum,* after admitting that "we have ourselves gone pretty far in Bowdlerizing our acted drama," finds that the Americans are

leagues ahead of us. . . . If such a word as "lechery" may not even be mentioned, if a phrase like "A halter pardon him! and hell gnaw his bones!" is too "shocking," and if "She repeals him for her body's lust" needs to be expressed by a euphemism, we care not how soon the attempt to play Shakespeare is abandoned.[55]

In a brief but memorable essay on Edmund Kean, Booth defends imitation. Why, he asks, is the word used "as a slur upon the actor alone?" He too, having his old masters, will show wisdom in being guided by them. "Tradition, if it be traced through pure channels, and to the fountain head, leads one as near to Nature as can be followed by her servant, Art." [56] And it was said of Booth with not too much exaggeration that "the tradition of his father and of Edmund Kean was his law." [57]

He was, of course, no mere copier of others. A letter of his to a subordinate actor, dated August 9, 1866, is interesting in this connection. Booth is explaining why he had made no effort to have the younger man retained at the Winter Garden.

I may as well be frank with you and state that my principle reason for remaining "neutral" was owing to a fatal habit which I saw growing upon you . . . an unfortunate custom (to which all young actors are prone) of imitation. It took me several years to rid myself of the fault; all my Father's mannerisms and imperfections I acquired by being so constantly with him — when they were pointed out to me I watched myself closely and rooted them out.[58]

When, years later, he was asked how his father's acting compared with his own, "he hesitated and then said: 'I think I must be somewhat quieter.' " [59]

Increasingly he had sought to avoid extravagance, fustian, theatricality, and it was exactly as he succeeded in avoiding them that his acting became natural. As Hamlet, in the scene with Rosencrantz and Guildenstern after the Mousetrap, he used at one time to fling the recorder into the flies — "though you can fret me, you cannot play upon me." [60] Even at the Princess's he had unwarrantably delayed Hamlet's first entrance so as to appear more conspicuously, and be applauded, only just before he is addressed.[61] Such claptrap devices he gave up one by one, achieving a style more truly dignified, and in a sense classical, as his art matured. A purer taste was finding expression within the tradition, founded by Kean, of dazzling brilliance and passionate intensity. Still another English reviewer came nearer, I believe, than the rest to accuracy of appreciation. In *Dramatic Notes* for 1880–1881, Booth's acting is distinguished from that of "the robust school represented in the past by Edwin Forrest, and at present by Mr. John McCullough."

His method, on the contrary, is almost coldly intellectual, and yet ornate and polished to an extreme degree. His elocution is impressive, and many words fall from his lips with an hitherto undiscovered beauty. But the scholarly studiousness which may be observed in his acting is not the limit of his resources, nor are the natural advantages of a handsome face, a sonorous voice, and a graceful form. Mr. Booth is an emotional and inspirational actor, and the very delicacy of his art leads him to curb and refine the expression of qualities, which are often simulated by mere boisterousness.

At one point, Booth clearly excelled his contemporaries. In England the speaking of verse had come to be regarded as a lost art; there was Ryder, to be sure, though Ryder was not among the great; there had been Phelps. But the unique beauty and expressiveness of Booth's reading were immediately recognized.[62] Nor was his "elocution" forced or mechanical. Rather, it sprang from a perception that in Shakespeare's verse sound and sense, the movement of the lines and their meaning, are inseparably related. To the service of the poet, he brought a fine intelligence and an ear attuned to the music of words. His enunciation was beautifully distinct. He used a "wise economy of emphasis." [63] "He says he has no ear for music," wrote Madame Modjeska, "but any mistake in blank verse jars upon him as a false note." [64] It was a fastidiousness becoming to one who took pride in preserving what was best in a splendid heritage.

Enter William Poel

TO see Edwin Booth was to see an actor of royal descent great in his own right. Yet at the Lyceum he seemed old-fashioned in comparison with Irving, and he had no successor worthy of the name. In Shakespeare's plays as the American and Barry Sullivan still gave them, it was the single tragic rôle that mattered. Honors might be divided in *Othello* and *Macbeth*; but who cared about the bloat Claudius when Booth was Hamlet, or about Richmond when Sullivan confronted him as Richard? Enough if the subordinate could spout a little, and fence, and that he never for one instant diverted attention from the star.

That Shakespeare was a master of dramatic construction, that a play of his might in performance be more than its chief scenes loosely strung together, had long been forgotten. Against the integrity of the text stood the prudishness which made a variety of strangely assorted words unspeakable on the stage and the delight of the eye in pompous recreations of "Shakespeare's Venice." Scholars who condescended to visit the theatre found comfort in the fact that adulteration was no longer permitted. Tate's *Lear* was a thing of the past. Even Cibber's *Richard III* was beginning to be replaced by attenuated versions of the original. At the Lyceum there was a sense of progress and well-being. Irving, whatever one thought of him as an actor, was giving Shakespeare's plays with a magic and a magnificence new to the English stage. To question the rightness of such productions as these, took courage.

Few could have foreseen in that same spring of 1881 when Booth and Irving met in splendid rivalry that an obscure performance by amateurs, a few weeks before, would be eagerly remembered by the future. This was, in truth, a very humble affair, a single matinée at St. George's Hall, where *Hamlet* in a queer antiquarian version had been presented without scenery. On February 12, the *Academy* remarked that "the issue of the cheap facsimiles of the Shakspere quartos by Mr. Griggs and Mr. Furnivall has already led to one unexpected good result . . . a member of the New Shakspere Society, Dr. W. Pole, and some amateur friends have resolved on giving, what Shakspere students and critics have long desired to see" — a representation of the First Quarto edition of *Hamlet*, "preserving its order of scenes, following its stage directions and omissions, and correcting only the manifest blunders of its text." A misstatement in this notice was swiftly corrected. Dr. Pole, F.R.S., "engineer, musician, and authority on whist," disclaimed any connection with the venture. It was his son, William Poel, to use his stage name, for the young man was an actor, who was responsible. Furnivall of the New Shakspere Society was likewise interested, since there were theories about this unorthodox Quarto which could be tested by seeing it played.

The *Academy* has another cordial notice on April 9. The performance is to be "next Saturday afternoon, April 16"; Elizabethan costumes are to be worn; instead of elaborate scenery there will only be "perhaps a little tapestry . . . This all sounds as if it were going to be distinctly interesting." A scholarly review followed on the twenty-third. Nothing, indeed, is said of the staging, but the First Quarto proved to be a complete and actable play,

and the performance itself was certainly up to the average of amateur performances of a high class. The only failure was the Ghost. The honours of the afternoon rested with Ophelia. . . . Hamlet was personated by Mr. W. Poel, who took on himself the burden of getting-up the play, training the minor actors, and superintending every detail. He looked the pale and thoughtful student to the life, and in some passages moved his audience to warm applause; but his voice and he were hardly up to the requirements of his part — who, indeed, is? — and his emphasis was sometimes faulty.

The programme carries on one side of its single leaf a facsimile title-page of the Quarto and on the other the names of the players.[1] There was some doubling of parts. Mr. R. Templeman's name stands against Barnardo, Lucianus, and the "other clowne," better known as Second Gravedigger. Mr. J. B. Partridge undertook both "Leartes" and "Gilderstone." A boy appeared as the Player Queen, but actresses as Gertrude and "Ofelia," and Miss Helen Maude (Maud Holt, who became Lady Tree) carried a lute instead of the customary flowers in the Mad Scene.[2]

Writing many years later, Poel claimed for the production that it was "the first revival of the draped stage . . . in this country or elsewhere." [3] There was no vestige of scenery, nor even locality boards; only a raised platform, on which for instance the dumb show was presented.[4] At intervals, the curtain descended for a few moments, but there was no intermission — another instance of daring — and the performance lasted only two hours.

The conservatives were up in arms at once. The *reductio ad absurdum*, an argument which was often to be used against Poel in the years to come, is attempted in *The Saturday Review*. Why not go further still and play the play by daylight or candlelight? Ophelia and Gertrude should be acted by boys. The costumes, to be consistent, ought certainly to have been modern, not Elizabethan: "Hamlet should have superintended the play in evening dress and killed Laertes in a fencing jacket." Furnivall in an address at the beginning had asked the audience's indulgence — and it was all too liberally bestowed.

The audience not only tolerated a version of *Hamlet* which botchers and pirates had done their best to reduce to a *caput mortuum*, but, with the exception of an occasional titter, they listened with a gravity of dubious merit while that degraded text was declaimed in a manner beneath criticism. Only once was there a general laugh.

Poel himself is allowed credit for having "perfectly solved the problem of giving a *Hamlet* without the Prince of Denmark"; the company as a whole displayed "the airy confidence of ineptitude." "It is high time," the writer concludes, "that people who set up an idol and dub it Shakspere should be made to understand that the antics they may be pleased to indulge in before it are not to be taken seriously." Another reviewer, Dutton Cook, is chiefly concerned with the perversities of the Quarto text, which "certain sages or wiseacres" have chosen to venerate. The production was "necessarily of a very incomplete kind," and "the attitude of the general audience was one of apathy tinctured by a disposition to deride." Some stir attended the appearance of Fortinbras, a character usually omitted from ordinary acting editions of the tragedy. But to many the performance was very wearisome and depressing; while a strong feeling prevailed that, upon the whole, the experiment was of an absurd and reprehensible sort, involving, as it did necessarily, some degradation of the poet in whose honour it purported to be undertaken.[5]

William Poel was born on July 22, 1852. When he was about twenty he saw his first play, *The Merchant of Venice*, with Ryder as Shylock. Afterwards, he read it and was struck by the difference between what he had just seen and what he read. He was dissatisfied with his work in a contractor's office and decided to adopt the stage as a career. Chiefly he wanted to study Shakespeare.[6] He had been an actor for about five years when his *Hamlet* was given at St. George's Hall.

In 1887 began his long association with the Shakespeare Reading Society, of which Irving was at one time president. Bernard Shaw affords us a glimpse of this group at a later time, "seated like Christy minstrels" on a platform. They gave, too, a regularly staged performance of *Macbeth*, when he was deeply interested in their Lady Macbeth, a very young and quite inexperienced Lillah McCarthy.[7] Meanwhile, Poel had produced *The Duchess of Malfi* for Grein's "Independent Theatre," on October 21, 1892, and *Measure for Measure* at the Royalty a year later. *The Duchess of Malfi* came almost as a relief after Grein's disturbing experiments with Ibsen. It was tactfully adapted for the Victorian stage, handsomely mounted in the prevailing mode, and in most respects wholly uncharacteristic of Poel.[8] With *Measure for Measure* he returned eagerly to his Elizabethan ways, and controversy began anew.

A small proscenium had been built, with a platform or gallery in the background. Changes of scene were marked by the drawing of transverse curtains. On the sides of the stage, and in the theatre's dismantled side-boxes, sat gentlemen in Elizabethan costume who, during the one ten-minute interval, regaled themselves with Elizabethan clay pipes.[9] Wonder was expressed, sarcastically of course, how that "most vital element of dramatic representation" in Shakespeare's time, boys in the women's parts, could have been forgotten. As it was, instead of good acting there was "an intelligent, but monotonous and lifeless, recitation of the parts." [10]

A subtle and dangerous enemy now appears in William Archer. As yet, it is true, he somewhat withholds his fire. Certain details in the staging were wrong: the curtain was much too far forward; the doors shown in De Witt's newly discovered drawing were wanting. Then there was the choice of the play. *Measure for Measure* has no directions calling for entrances "above," though such entrances were arbitrarily introduced in this production. "There is no other play of Shakespeare's in which so much of the dialogue is absolutely unspeakable before a modern audience." Hence large excisions were necessary. "Several of the performers simply improvised at will when their memory failed them." [11]

For a friendly account one turns to *The Academy*, which had once been kind to Poel's *Hamlet*:

While we are far from urging the abandonment at the ordinary theatre of so much that draws the general public to a Shaksperian play — the elaborate and beautiful scenery to which audiences have become accustomed — we must chronicle the fact that the extremely intelligent audiences gathered to see "Measure for Measure" scarcely seem to have missed the absence of scenery, so closely, with the prompt and rapid action now inculcated, has it been possible to follow the story of the play. If the dialogue sometimes seemed to be spoken too hurriedly, that was, probably, because the amateurs, with all their good intentions, had not learnt completely how to be both swift and intelligible. . . . They have presented the play with dignity, and enacted it with a quaint charm.[12]

That the performers sometimes spoke too rapidly even for this sympathetic reviewer is interesting. Poel had his own ideas about the reading of verse. Elizabethan actors had been praised, he shows, for the nimbleness of their speech, and a return to their method was imperative. The heavy stressing of a more recent time — Mrs. Siddons's "Give ME the daggers" — could scarcely have been used at the Globe. (Edwin Forrest took six full minutes to get through "To be, or not to be" — and was praised for his deliberation!) [13] Rather, all "redundancy of emphasis" is to be avoided, and "the audience should never be made to feel that the tones are unusual." [14] Yet Shakespeare, Poel believed, counted upon contrasts in the voices of his speakers, just as he was ever "conscious of the need for variety in sound and in time as means to sustain dramatic interest. In fact, the atmosphere, so to speak, of Elizabethan drama is created through the voice, that of modern drama through the sight." [15]

Many of Poel's arguments in advocating a return to the Elizabethan stage are almost commonplaces today. The bareness of that stage was a challenge to the imagination of dramatist and spectator alike. Nor is it readily conceivable that Shakespeare would enjoy having his poetical descriptions superseded by the obtrusive art of the scene-painter. In his theatre, a poet could use his gifts, could count, too, upon an audience undistracted by "outward decorations and subordinate details." [16] The same lack of scenery concentrated attention on the player, "with whose movement, boldly defined against a simple background, nothing interfered." His action,

142

"placed close before the eye, deprived of all perspective . . . acquired a special kind of realism" — that "of an actual event, at which the audience assisted." [17] Finally, the construction of Shakespeare's plays, freely flowing, unconfined by act-divisions, is incomprehensible without reference to the stage for which he wrote. Instead, therefore, of adapting him we should endeavor to bring "our own minds within reach of those influences from which the Elizabethan playgoer undoubtedly obtained the greatest enjoyment," honoring the poet by carrying out his intentions.[18]

So the Elizabethan Stage Society was established, including among its members Sidney Lee, Stopford Brooke, Israel Gollancz, Edmund Gosse, and Walter Crane. In June 1895 they did *Twelfth Night*, following this, in December, with *The Comedy of Errors* in Gray's Inn Hall where it had been presented three centuries before. Among the more exciting of the Society's later productions were: Marlowe's *Faustus*, given with a prologue by Swinburne on July 2, 1896 (*The Times* found the play "scarcely fitted for representation on the modern stage, where its free introduction of sacred characters jars a little upon one's sense of propriety"); *The Merchant of Venice*, with the Prince of Arragon episode retained and Shylock played as a comic character, late in 1898; *Richard II*, with Granville-Barker as the King, in November 1899; and *Everyman*, Poel's greatest triumph, in July 1901. Later still, in 1912, he produced a memorable *Troilus and Cressida* with Edith Evans as Cressida.

The work of the Society was brilliantly defended by Bernard Shaw. It was uncomfortable, of course, to have him as an ally. At one time, he was railing at the Elizabethan dramatists — the "blank-verse beast" Marlowe and the rest — at another, scolding Shakespeare himself and ridiculing those who revered him for the wrong things. Yet, not from principle but from actual observation, Shaw became convinced that it was thus, on the platform stage, that Shakespeare should be given. There the actor, placed as he was in the midst of his hearers, enjoyed an immense advantage; and the play, as it could never have been "as a picture framed by a proscenium," was brought home to the audience. "We are less conscious of the artificiality of the stage when a few well-understood conventions, adroitly handled, are substituted for attempts at an impossible scenic verisimilitude." [19] In the first scene of *The Tempest*, where a stage ship would, Shaw felt, be merely monstrous, we are willing to pretend that a gallery is one. Stimulated by Shakespeare's poetry, the imagination can accomplish wonders. And it is the more poetic of his plays — *A Midsummer Night's Dream* and *The Tempest*, rather than *Othello* — which do best without scenery.[20] "The only Shakespearian performances by which he had been really moved," Shaw once said, were "those of the Elizabethan Stage Society." [21]

William Archer was simply irritated. Once and once only, writing of their *Twelfth Night*, he attacks without caution. Restoration of the Elizabethan stage will be a most imperfect restoration without Elizabethan actors and, above all, an Elizabethan audience. Shakespeare will not be made to live for the modern playgoer "by a form of representation which appeals only to the dilettante and the enthusiast." This was not to defend contemporary practice. Shakespeare, Archer admitted, was "horribly maltreated on the modern commercial stage," to accommodate "the scene-painter and the machinist." But to argue from the abuse of a thing to its disuse is fallacious. "Because scenery is stupidly overdone . . . we are forcibly to put back the clock, and, instead of refining a living art, make hopeless efforts to revive a dead one!" There is no necessary reason why the text should be sacrificed in the modern theatre: "It is as easy to change a scene as to draw a 'traverse.'" And to the question, "Do appropriate scenery and costume help and stimulate the imagination of a theatrical audience?" he answers: "Emphatically, yes; and, on the other hand, glaring anachronism of costume, and the absence of any sort of pictorial background, tend to disconcert and hamper the imagination, and to distract attention from the matter of the play." [22]

After this, it is difficult to take seriously the professions of friendship toward the enterprise which Archer continually makes. His later criticism is, however, concerned increasingly with details of execution rather than with ideals. He discovers a streak of perversity (or is it merely a want of common sense?) in Poel's staging:

When one thinks of the toil that must be involved in organising and preparing these frequent performances — in negotiating with civic and legal magnates for the use of their Halls, in animating the ambition, soothing the vanities, reconciling the jealousies, overcoming the laziness of a large company of amateur and unpaid actors, in arranging for the dresses and the music, and, finally, in so rehearsing long plays that, despite the performers' inexperience, they go (as a rule) with perfect smoothness — when one thinks of all this, one feels it base ingratitude to say a word in disparagement of the results achieved. . . . There is not another man in London who could do what he does — and there is scarcely another man who, from the artistic point of view, could make such a hopeless mess of it. . . . He seems to study the Elizabethan stage in order to do precisely the reverse of what reasonable conjecture, if not actual stage-direction, assures us that the Elizabethans did.[23]

There were, too, the large deletions in some of Poel's acting texts — and "the Society's whole reason for existence vanishes when it begins to flourish the blue pencil." [24]

Although Archer points out a few mistakes in Tree's *Julius Caesar* of 1898 — a production as different from those of the Elizabethan Stage Society as could well be imagined — he is on the whole enthusiastic, finding the play "superbly staged." [25] Another writer, St. John Hankin, is not enthusiastic at all, and his criticism suggests that he knew and liked the work of Poel. At any rate, Tree in replying to Hankin alludes to "learned amateur societies who will present Shakespeare in such a way as to commend him to the few, while boring the many." Rather, it is "the business of the manager to present Shakespeare in such a way as to commend him to the many, even at the risk of agitating the few." [26]

In more formal pronouncements of a later time, Tree would have illusion the great end of theatrical art. "All that aids illusion is good, all that destroys illusion is bad." Shakespeare himself, he argues, was dissatisfied with the stage of his own day, and "not only foresaw, but desired, the system of production that is now most in the public favour." Did he not write the choruses in *Henry V*, the satirical play-scene at the end of *A Midsummer Night's Dream*? [27] For answer, if any answer is needed, there is a letter full of good sense which Shaw contributed to the scene-painter Joseph Harker's book, *Studio and Stage*, in 1924:

Every play should be performed as its author intended it to be performed. It is no reply to this that Shakespear would have written for scenery if he could. It might as well be said that he would have written for the cinema if he could. The fact remains that he did not, and that the stage for which he wrote his plays is the

146

only one to which they are adapted, and on which they make the effects he planned.[28]

As one thinks of Poel's work, still further names come to mind. There was Sir Max Beerbohm, who had no use for it. *Twelfth Night* by the E.S.S. in 1903 greatly depressed him: "You are allowed to shed a tear or two when you see the owls building their nests in some palace that was erst a setting of gaiety and pride and riches." When Shakespeare wrote, "the science of scenic production was in its infancy." An Elizabethan audience might accept defects and limitations which are impossible for us to tolerate. "We cannot forget what we have learned." [29] Poel, again, made his Chorus in *Samson Agonistes* come down through the audience to reach the stage. Familiar as such an entrance would be today, it was then strange, and to Beerbohm ridiculous. "Aesthetically, of course, there could be no reason for it, since it must obviously destroy all aesthetic illusion, and send us all into paroxysms of internal laughter." [30]

On the other hand, no critic has left a more sensitive appreciation of Poel's art than C. E. Montague.[31] To be at *Samson Agonistes* as Poel gave it was, he found, to be possessed of a new pleasure. "One seemed to be in at the birth of a thing that some day might be valued for ancientry." The groupings of the characters were a joy in themselves — it was as if Poel "had had every one of his groupings painted to a finish in his mind and then transferred it, touch by touch, to its place on the purple background, all under the strong influence of Italian mediaeval and Renaissance theories of pictorial design." In *Everyman*, "the acting had a maintained ecstasy of simple seriousness, every actor seemed to have the same grave, thrilled sense of the momentousness of what they

147

were all handling. . . . They spoke like people who felt they were bringing tremendous news." In *Faustus*, there was the same sincerity and a never-failing tact. "The least slip in judgment was sure to raise laughter, and nobody laughed."

Montague recognizes limitations as well. Poel could not rid himself of the proscenium arch. "What he gave us was not an Elizabethan stage as it was to Elizabethan playgoers, but a picture of an Elizabethan stage seen through the frame of a modern proscenium." Wanting was that "fusion or interpenetration of stage and auditorium" which was "the essence of the Elizabethan theatre." Yet a great deal was accomplished.

We saw better than ever the needlessness, as well as the destructiveness, of the quite modern method of taking Shakspere's shortest scenes. They are usually scurried through by actors who maintain a precarious footing on a strip of boarding between the footlights in front and a bellying sail painted with landscape, which swells out at them from behind.

On Poel's stage, one scene flowed into another "without the slightest jolt or scrappiness." The upper stage proved to be a fine asset. "As for scenery, one did not think about it, either in the way of missing it, or of being glad it was away. But if any people did imperatively need to be distracted from the play, they could look at the dresses, which were quaint and rich to admiration." [32]

"I started the Elizabethan Stage Society," Poel once said, "in order to go straight to the Shakespearean text." [33] The plays, in shockingly mangled versions, were being exploited as mere vehicles or shows. He demonstrated that under sympathetic direction they need be neither; that they are far more interesting — more actable, even — if their integrity is respected. He fought long against ignorance and prejudice. In a paper read in 1893, the year of his *Measure for Measure,* he could say without risk of contradiction that "the ordinary reader and the every-day critic" were quite without "historic knowledge of the Elizabethan Theatre; and however full the Elizabethan dramas may be of allusions to the contemporary Stage, the bias of modern dramatic students is so opposed to any belief in the superiority of past methods of acting Shakespeare over modern ones, as to effectively bar any serious inquiry." Few had so much as dipped into the subject of the interrelation of the drama and the stage. They "have read the plays," he continued bitterly, "they have heard something said about old tapestry, rushes, and boards, and they have at once become convinced how 'thoroughly handicapped' were our greatest dramatists by the methods of representation then in vogue." [34]

"Poel," writes Mr. Harcourt Williams, "never abandoned his original conception of Shakespeare as a consummate craftsman of the practical theatre." [35] We are no longer startled by the conception, but it was startling enough when Poel first defended it. Shakespeare in the study was almost everything else. On the stage, to be sure, he had lent dignity to the art of the great actors, but he was not to be trusted. It was Poel's revolutionary discovery that he could be trusted. As with the criticism of great plays, so with their representation, a sensitive regard for the author's intention is ever to be preferred to mere impressionism or virtuosity.[36]

Shakespearian Playgoing

I N America, the old way of producing Shakespeare was not given over abruptly. Change came, but not without opposition. Granville-Barker's *Midsummer Night's Dream* (in 1915) seemed to conservative critics like William Winter and the late Professor Odell something like sacrilege, and they wrote against it violently. Tradition lingered on in the performances of Robert B. Mantell. It was not my good fortune to see Mantell. I did, however, see Fritz Leiber; and Leiber, who had been a prominent member of Mantell's company, continued to give Shakespeare very much in the style of the elder tragedian. There were, for instance, the "strong curtains," inherited from melodrama. Shakespeare as often as not ends a scene quietly, well beyond its climax; but then, Shakespeare could always be cut, and always was. So Lear, in Leiber's version, rushed out into the storm crying "O fool, I shall go mad!" and down came the curtain, with what follows, as Cornwall and the daughters talk callously of the wildness of the night and order the doors to be shut, wholly omitted.[1] The Orchard Scene in *Julius Caesar* ended, similarly, with Portia in Brutus's arms —

O ye gods,
Render me worthy of this noble wife! [2]

150

Richard III formed part of Leiber's repertory in 1930, and on my way to see it I wondered whether I would hear Colley Cibber's famous claptrap,

Off with his head. — So much for Buckingham;

or even, perhaps, "Richard is himself again." Indeed, it might be my last chance to hear them. Both were spoken, sure enough, but that was only a beginning. I suppose a Cibber purist would not have been satisfied — Richard's dying speech was omitted, and the murder of Clarence, wanting in the Laureate's version, was rather clumsily restored — but it remained the Cibber text, practically in its entirety. Leiber even included the appalling scene in which Richard visits Lady Anne, now Queen, and tries to induce her to take her own life, and played it so well that not a soul laughed.[3]

Two later productions, both at certain points archaic, I remember with pleasure. The first was of *Hamlet*. Having read, early in May 1945, that the play was to be given in Bridgeport, Connecticut, with a young actor, Mr. Tom Rutherfurd, who had been well received in Canada, I determined to see it. The journey proved worth making, for not only was this new Hamlet interesting in his own right but, also, he introduced a good deal of business once associated with the rôle but long since laid aside. At one moment it was Kemble who came to mind, at another Garrick. In the scene with Polonius, he madly tore a leaf from the book he carried, crying, "Slanders, sir." [4] At sight of the apparition in Gertrude's closet he contrived to overturn the chair. And some at least of these revivals justified themselves instantly.[5]

Sir Godfrey Tearle's *Othello* at Stratford in 1949 was the second. This was in general a dignified adaptation of traditional methods, though the cutting of the text was ruthless.

As part of a repertory which included two plays put on by Mr. Michael Benthall and one by Mr. Tyrone Guthrie, it came as something of a relief. If we were not excited by brilliant invention we were at least never distracted. The chief characters held quiet possession of the centre of the stage. The Venetian Senators required no silencing as Othello began to address them. They stood rather stiffly in a formal semicircle and listened without fretting. We in the audience listened too.[6]

With the old-fashioned Shakespearian production against which Poel rebelled are associated three things chiefly: the excessive emphasis placed upon the star actor; the arbitrary cutting of the text; and the use of settings which localized, pictorially, the action of the play. On the other hand, those producers who have more or less consciously returned to the practices of the Elizabethan stage would have Shakespeare's own lines conjure up backgrounds. If scenery is introduced at all, it should suggest, not represent. They have sought speed, as well, with scenes no longer sharply defined but following one another in virtually unbroken sequences. And, finally, such producers have desired a closer proximity and intimacy between actors and audience than was permitted by yesterday's theatre and its picture-frame stage. Only at one point has this complex ideal been widely accepted. Continuity of performance is taken for granted when the plays are given today. We no longer waste a great part of the evening (in the productions of Sir Herbert Beerbohm Tree it might be as much as three-quarters of an hour)[7] gazing at an unresponsive curtain while the scenes are being shifted. Nor is it without interest that our present practically uninterrupted sequences were achieved well before the cinema had begun to influence the stage. Yet controversy still rages as to the desirability of doing without scenery. And though the low comedian now unashamedly addresses us, and the speakers of soliloquy are no longer concerned to murmur what is on their minds, as if they must remind us at all costs that they are supposed to be merely thinking aloud, they are still, in most productions, at too great a distance from their auditors to be on familiar terms with them. "In a 'picture-frame' theatre," Mr. Tyrone Guthrie writes, "it is impossible not to put a picture in the frame. The whole intention of the building's design is to isolate and emphasize a visual impression." [8]

My first experience of how satisfactorily Shakespeare could be done without scenery I owe to Sir Philip Ben Greet, who, in the course of several visits to Boston about twenty years ago, put on *Hamlet* (in the First Quarto version), *As You Like It*, and *The Comedy of Errors*, in each case before plain curtains. It is my impression that these productions owed something to Poel. The choice of the First Quarto *Hamlet*, as earlier of *Everyman*, in which the Ben Greet Company won a wide success, implies as much. They were unpretentious performances but not without freshness. It was curious, for instance, to find that the Dromios, now that they were dressed in Elizabethan clothes, had lost their classical remoteness and become Shakespearian clowns. Audrey, too, was a pretty, barefooted girl who scampered up and down the aisles in company with her Touchstone (Russell Thorndike was admirable in this rôle) and instead of a turnip, which she regularly consumed on the Victorian stage, munched apples.[9] The general method has proved its worth repeatedly. It admits of, without demanding the subtleties of modern lighting, but only as means to an end — the concentration of our attention on essentials, on the players and the play.

The Ben Greet Company usually gave Shakespeare out of

doors, and it is at least arguable that the pleasure discovered in open-air performances helped to overthrow the idea that there was but one way in which the plays should be given, the way of scenic magnificence. "This is the Forest of Arden" . . . the words became magical, once more, under the stars. Yet in such performances our sense of illusion may be succeeded by one of dissatisfaction. Thus, through most of *A Midsummer Night's Dream*, this bit of well-trodden lawn and irregular background of shadowy trees before us will have summoned up, better, it may be, than painted scenery could ever have done, the haunted wood of the play. And, at the end, we wish them gone!

> The iron tongue of midnight hath told twelve.
> Lovers, to bed.

We are indoors — or would be — in a great house, now quiet, to which Robin comes with his broom and the fairy train brings benediction. For a modern audience it is as hard to dissociate as to imagine.[10]

The best performance I have seen out-of-doors left, however, no regrets. This was of *The Tempest* at Regent's Park in the summer of 1949. The initial problem of the storm at sea was solved by means as ingenuous as they were appealing. A tiny rocking-horse ship was drawn on from the side, the sailors and noblemen walking quietly behind it, the waves mimed by dancers. The banquet became a table-cloth with attached dishes, first held out temptingly, then whisked away, by Prospero's spirits. Throughout, detail was simplified, subordinated. Such business as was introduced if not actually called for by the lines seemed their natural accompaniment. The setting itself was presently forgotten, becoming as negative as plain curtains might have been; or, rather, its beauty became a part of the beauty of the play and indistinguishable from it. The poet's words received their due. There was not, as I heard remarked afterwards, a bad voice in the cast.[11]

The most recent method of staging the plays is, curiously enough, the most austere. I refer, of course, to the "arena" or "theatre-in-the-round" productions, which at the moment are still something of a novelty. *Julius Caesar*, represented after this fashion in New York, two years ago, proved an exciting experience.[12] A small stage, bare except for the broken stump of a column and three or four low stone blocks, stood in the very midst of the audience. It was lighted, a little glaringly, from above, and four aisles, used by the players for their entrances and exits, converged upon it. In comparison, the Elizabethan stage, with its big apron, its "study" and gallery, its windows and traps and permanent doors, was almost luxuriously appointed. A new convention had, also, to be accepted, that of the actors' constantly shifting their positions in order to avoid having their backs turned on any of us for too long a time. But actors are always restless and one soon became accustomed to their roaming about. Certainly, their proximity led to a swifter response, a more immediate identification. In the scene of the orations, there was no visible mob, only a clamor of voices behind and above us, so that at times the little theatre seemed filled with sound, while we ourselves had become those to whom Brutus and Antony were speaking, almost beside us.[13]

The brave attempts that I have seen to give Shakespeare's plays on the stage for which they were designed have been incomplete for the most part but ever illuminating. I was fortunate during the Festival summer of 1951 to see *The Taming of the Shrew* and *Pericles* at the Maddermarket Theatre, Norwich, and *The Tempest* at the recently built

Mermaid Theatre in St. John's Wood. Exception might be taken to the Maddermarket stage on at least two counts: a gratuitous second curtain was sometimes drawn just behind the two Elizabethan pillars; and the platform did not reach out into the midst of the spectators. Yet so small was the theatre itself (seating only a little over two hundred persons) that a happy sense of intimacy existed from the beginning. To this was added, especially in *The Shrew*, an unencumbered speed. The play fairly danced along! Even with the epilogue from *The Taming of a Shrew* included, and with relatively inconspicuous cutting, it was over in less than two hours. All of Shakespeare's plays have been produced by Mr. Nugent Monck at the Maddermarket, and out of long experience he has gained an enviable sureness of touch. Everything about the production seemed natural. Sly, now dozing, now all attention, sat of course on the upper stage. He was even permitted to improvize a little: as, "I haven't a lot of room here," to his lady, just as the players were beginning. The table from which Katherine was not to eat was shown by drawing the inner-stage curtain, as was the banquet of the last scene, a fine sight; and the Pedant, as he should, peered out of a window, above one of the two permanent doors, while he talked with Vincentio below.[14]

The Mermaid, a semiprivate theatre even smaller than the Maddermarket, claimed little more for itself than to furnish "a stage on which Elizabethan actors would have felt at home." [15] It reproduced, nevertheless, the three essentials of Shakespeare's stage — its projecting platform, gallery, and "study" — and again employed, unnecessarily, a second curtain. The richly painted "tiring house," and the bright curtains with their tapestry figures, were very pleasant to the ʌve. The single false note was, I thought, a quite modern ballet in the interrupted masque. The upper stage once more proved its value. Mounted there, Prospero was no longer in the way, as he usually is, during the first meeting between Ferdinand and Miranda, or, later, when the banquet vanishes. It was good, too, to see the Trinculo, Mr. Toke Townley, an experienced low comedian, take advantage of the platform-stage to get on friendly terms with his audience. The most illuminating moments came, however, at the very beginning. I praised the treatment of the opening scene at Regent's Park. There, out-of-doors, a bold recourse was had to symbol — the miming of the waves, the tiny rocking-horse ship. But in Shakespeare's theatre, it now appeared, the illusion of reality might have been wellnigh complete. The scene began with a clap of thunder and howling wind. In each of the two windows a ship's lantern swung back and forth. Ropes and a rope ladder were lowered from somewhere above the gallery. A trapdoor opened and became a hatchway; the upper stage, the upper deck. Sailors, shouting orders, clung for support to the pillars, or swarmed up the tackling. It was as if the ship were there before our eyes! Yet, as crew and passengers departed and the ropes dropped out of sight through the trap, it was gone again, in an instant. The curtains to the inner-stage opened, and we were on Prospero's isle, with Miranda beginning:

> If by your art, my dearest father, you have
> Put the wild waters in this roar, allay them.

Illusion and beauty marked the Elizabethan production of another comedy which has often defied picture-frame staging, *A Midsummer Night's Dream*. As this was represented under the direction of Mr. Ronald Watkins at Harrow School, the transformation of the stage at the beginning of the con-

157

cluding scene was complete. The same rushes which had served so well in the woodland episodes still covered the platform. But candles in sconces were now fastened to the pillars, instead of green branches. "The study," newly discovered by drawing a curtain, seemed with its stately portraits an extension of the great chamber where Theseus and his guests, among them a quite exquisite boy-Helena, assembled to witness the "tedious brief scene," while the upper stage became a corridor along which they passed to bed upon the completion of the night's revels.[16]

Thus far, we have been concerned, really, with only two sorts of production: that which, following tradition, has asserted the priority of the actor; and that which, reverting to Elizabethan precedent, has sought to fulfill the intentions of the author in important matters of stage-craft. With the advocates of Elizabethan staging for Elizabethan plays I have strong sympathy. Granville-Barker in particular seems to me wholly convincing as, having ruled out mere antiquarianism and demanding neither boy-actresses nor daylight, he urges us to "follow the road which Shakespeare and his fellows went. When we come to the end, we may follow him beyond — if we can." [17] In many recent productions, however, it is not the actor who has come first, nor certainly the author and his play.

The dignity of the director as an independent artist has come to be recognized, in England and America, at any rate, only within the last two generations. The actor's theatre had no place for him. Exits and entrances, details of business and sometimes of reading, were governed by tradition, of which the prompter was the chief custodian. An increasing feeling of responsibility for the production as a whole can be traced, it is true, from Kemble and, especially, Macready, through

Phelps and Charles Kean, to Irving and Beerbohm Tree. But all these men were actors first of all, a fact which even Irving never for a moment forget. When, near the close of the last century, playwrights once more began to assert themselves, it was only to be expected that Shaw, as we have seen, should be hostile toward Irving, friendly toward Poel. For Poel was devoted to the interests of his author, and would rather restore than invent.[18] With too many later directors it has been quite otherwise.

A memorable instance of the making over of a Shakespearian play to suit a particular intention was the production of *Julius Caesar* at the Mercury Theatre, New York, late in 1937. In this, no scenery was used and the brick wall of the building remained clearly visible beyond the stage. Sometimes, the characters were isolated by intense, concentrated lighting. There was no intermission and the acting time was an hour and forty minutes. The modern costumes and, indeed, the make-up of the actor who represented Caesar, suggested that the play was one of immediately contemporary fascism and its opponents. It began with music, silenced by the Dictator, who emerged from darkness: "Bid every noise be still." Soliloquies, apparently regarded as an outmoded convention, were got rid of, that of Cassius, for example, at the end of the second scene, becoming a dialogue between himself and Casca. Through the scene of the orations, where Mr. Orson Welles as Brutus by refusing to declaim brought out the contrast between his appeal to the intellect and Antony's to the emotions, the drama moved swiftly and strongly. It reached its climax, however, in the episode of the poet Cinna which follows. Here the character, at first merely futile and rather ludicrous, became one for whom we feared. The evil ruffians whom he addressed, repeating pitifully, over and over, "I am Cinna the poet! Cinna the poet!" gradually closed in upon him. A claustrophobic terror was created. Then came a rush, an obliteration, and darkness once more. The last two acts were so garbled as to be practically meaningless, There was no Ghost, no Octavius, and it might almost be said no battle. Caesar had been assassinated, certainly, and afterwards a political reaction had set in. Beyond that, one was left groping. Even the Quarrel Scene fell flat.[19]

A more grandiose project of Mr. Welles's, under the title *Five Kings*, will be remembered by few playgoers today — by fewer still, I imagine, with any pleasure. In this, the attempt was made to combine as a single play passages from both parts of *Henry IV* and from *Henry V*, ending with the courtship of the French princess. In a forlorn endeavour to clarify the action, Robert Speaight read, copiously and often, from the chronicles. (Fortunately, we were allowed to hear him in some of the *Henry V* choruses, as well.) Mr. Welles himself, as Falstaff, significantly chose "Empty the jordan" for his entrance line and played the part, almost to the end, as low comedy.[20]

At least, in such productions, we are under no misapprehension. The director is not inviting us to see a play of Shakespeare's. Rather, he is exploring. What can be done, he seems to ask, in order to make a new play out of this antiquated material; a new scenario for these old characters, their lines not being actually rewritten but freely manipulated or left out? It is as if a problem were proposed, and we were to judge how well it had been solved. When, however, the play we are witnessing is presented as if it were Shakespeare's own, we may begin to stand on our rights. Then, surely, the less we are conscious of the director, the better. Yet his intrusions may not be prompted solely by egotism. He may lack faith in us, or in the skill of the playwright, or both. Or he would modernize and domesticate what has seemed to him remote and perhaps a little incomprehensible. Anyway, the dull old play needed livening up.

Some of Michael Benthall's productions may serve for illustration.[21] Externally, they are elaborately pictorial. At times, indeed, to one acquainted with theatrical history, they bring to mind productions of long ago, this *Midsummer Night's Dream* suggesting the descriptions of Charles Kean's, and this *As You Like It*, the aberrations of Augustin Daly. The cuts and, even more, the transpositions in *As You Like It* were a persistent annoyance. The songs in the play were shifted about and reassigned promiscuously, and the cuckoo and owl songs from *Love's Labour's Lost* were thrust in for good measure, just as they used to be on the Victorian stage. Pantomimic episodes — as of the exiled Duke and his followers launching arrows at an unseen and certainly unharmed stag — were also introduced, behind a gauze-cloth. Sensitiveness to the finer moments seemed wholly wanting. Rosalind's faintness at sight of the bloody napkin, and the sudden reality of "I would I were at home" became farcical. She swooned three several times, while Oliver and Celia were busy making love, and the scene ended with Oliver's carrying off Celia in his arms. Of a piece with this, or nearly so, was the treatment of Prospero's friend and "true preserver" the "good Gonzalo," in *The Tempest*. Apparently, Mr. Benthall shares the view of this character expressed by Antonio and Sebastian. At any rate, he was represented as an elderly ninny, a sort of doting Polonius; and when he rebukes the two villains, their comment,

> *Antonio.* What a blow was there given!
> *Sebastian.* An it had not fall'n flatlong (II, 180),

was illustrated, with really astonishing literalness, by Gonzalo himself falling down! It might be added that in order to obtain a visual climax, a hundred-and-twenty lighted candles, more or less, were displayed in the last scene of this play (a large cluster of them stuck in Prospero's hat); that a new character was invented for *Cymbeline*, an execrable dwarf, the illegitimate son, as it seemed, of the wicked Queen; and that not even the *aubade*, "Hark, hark! the lark," was allowed to be heard in peace, since business, characteristically, was introduced while it was being sung.

For an invigorating restatement of ideals, I turn to an essay by Noel Annan in *The Cambridge Journal*. As Shakespeare is commonly given today, he decides, the clear meaning of the lines is repeatedly sacrificed. "The only thing that is always forgotten is the play. The play is *not* the thing — but the ideas of the producer, such clever ideas, are everything." And after laying down "a series of priorities," with Shakespeare's poetry coming first, he pleads for "less egotism, more reverence; less by-play, more seriousness; less naturalism, more of the grand style"; at all times, sincerity: "and let the producer end the dichotomy between the verse and acting so that they fuse into one another." [22]

Mr. Annan says little or nothing about a return to the Elizabethan stage. Yet it is this return, this restoration of what once was, that is often spoken of as if it were an end in itself, rather than a means. Thus, the very bareness of the stage frees us imaginately. The words themselves create atmosphere where atmosphere is wanted. Such scenery as would represent what the poet describes is impertinent, rashly competitive, and ultimately destructive of illusion. But is this true of scenery which merely suggests? I think not. Certainly, there was little harm, for instance, in the delicately tinted screens, moved about by pages, which Donald Wolfit used as backgrounds for the forest scenes in *As You Like It*: in the bringing on of a dove-cote and a bit of wattle-fence when, in a Memorial Theatre *Henry IV, Part 2*, Falstaff was to be entertained by Justice Shallow; or in the single green screen which served quite adequately to suggest a garden and its trees in the production of *Richard II* at the Brattle Theatre, Cambridge.[23] These were settings pleasant to the eye, pleasant to remember, and never for an instant distracting.

It may be hoped that from a wider familiarity with the Elizabethan stage we shall learn much about Shakespeare's plays and how they can be represented to better advantage. Meanwhile, it is characteristic of the age that less attention is being paid to Shakespearian acting — as if, once the physical conditions of the playhouse were made right, this art, which in a measure they are bound to condition, would take care of itself. But will the players themselves be willing to wait?

The success of Irving, as Henry Arthur Jones noted, made Shakespeare safe for the non-Shakespearian actor.[24] And the non-Shakespearian actor, equipped as he was to do only one kind of play, not unnaturally sought in Shakespeare for the values to which he was accustomed. A playwright's theatre found itself dominated by the playwrights' exclusive concern for realism. Today, however, this theatre may already be passing, along with the simplicity of the naturalistic ideal which gave it dignity.

Two styles of acting were contrasted, during the summer of 1951, in two productions of the same play. At the Old Vic, Mr. Roger Livesey, as Chorus to *Henry V*, was affable and familiar after the manner of a Music Hall Chairman, and seemed deliberately to make homely what was majestic, and, to turn, so far as he might, the poetry into prose. At Stratford, on the other hand, Mr. Michael Redgrave, rushing upon the stage, spoke vehemently with sweeping gestures. We were to share a poet's vision, he insisted, to see with our own eyes "the stately tents of war." That he did not quite succeed is beside the point. It was the gallant attempt that mattered.[25] Or there was the difference, a very real difference, between Gielgud's Hamlet of 1936 and his Leontes of 1951. The Hamlet had been intellectual and passionate, precise and brilliant, and it is a stirring memory still. The one conspicuous fault was a tendency to break up the speeches, to sacrifice line to phrase. He paused, for instance, before "mirror" in "To hold, as 'twere, the mirror up to nature" — "as if," I remember an older actor grumbling, "there were any other word he could have used, except 'glass!' " [26] In Leontes, his style, though still refined, was freer and more expressive. At least once, in soliloquy, he boldly addressed the audience:

> There have been
> (Or I am much deceiv'd) cuckolds ere now;
> And many a man there is (even at this present,
> Now, while I speak this) holds his wife by th'arm
> That little thinks she has been sluic'd in's absence
> And his pond fish'd by his next neighbour — by
> Sir Smile, his neighbour (I, 2, 190),

and the lines, spoken thus, far down-stage, were more rather than less truly dramatic. Nor was there any shirking of vocal climax, as in the trumpet music of

> Why, then the world, and all that's in't is nothing;
> The covering sky is nothing; Bohemia's nothing;
> My wife is nothing; nor nothing have these nothings,
> If this be nothing (I, 2, 293).

164

Most daring of all was the action following the disclosure of the Oracle. He seemed at first stunned, then staggered across the stage (the boards sounded), then sank upon the throne and groaned once. Some great actor of another age, a Macready, say, or a Kean, might have been puzzled by Mr. Gielgud's Hamlet. He would, I am sure, have understood and admired his Leontes.[27]

It is unrewarding to speculate as to the future of an art. But if acting is really in process of change, that change is likely to be bound up with the development of the drama. So, at any rate, it has been repeatedly in other times, whether we think of Quin and neo-classical tragedy, or of Fechter and melodrama. And if plays in verse, plays once more by poets, should succeed in establishing themselves on our stage we might hope to find a rapidly increasing number of actors capable of recognizing Shakespeare's verse for what it is: an instrument splendidly designed to clarify and reinforce meaning; or, rather, itself a part of the meaning. No one would advocate a return to the snail-paced declamation of yesterday's veterans. The style, shall we say, of Edwin Forrest and his disciples admits of no revival. Yet to pretend for a moment that Shakespeare can be played adequately with the ever-changing, ever-significant movement of the verse unperceived or neglected is ludicrous.[28] Fortunately, there are at least a few actors today, like Gielgud and Alec Clunes and Maurice Evans, who have shown themselves sensitive to its subtleties and unafraid of committing themselves to its guidance.

Something was said at the beginning of the chapter about Fritz Leiber's company. On one of their visits to Boston, in March 1930, they were followed within a fortnight by the company from the Memorial Theatre, Stratford, at that time

under the direction of Mr. W. Bridges-Adams. The performances they gave shone the more brightly by comparison. Not
that I had found fault with Leiber himself. He was a good
actor, though I had seen better — Mr. Walter Hampden, for
instance — but Shakespeare's plays as he produced them never
seemed quite themselves. I went to them out of curiosity,
chiefly, with little expectation of sustained pleasure, with
no sense, certainly, of adventure. It was very different with
the performances I was now to see. Under Bridges-Adams,
who had at one time been assistant stage-manager to Poel,
the plays were acted swiftly, with something like Elizabethan
continuity, and they were acted with few cuts. It was not
by accident that this producer was nicknamed "Unabridges-
Adams!"

Richard II, with George Hayes as Richard and Wilfrid
Walter as Bolingbroke, was given a single time on March 31.
For nearly all of us in the audience — an audience which
filled even the boxes, and included "rows of standees" at
the back of the orchestra [29] — this was a first performance.
Gielgud had appeared as Richard at the Old Vic, earlier this
same season; but in America the play had long been absent
from the stage. Indeed, we had been brought up to think of
it as memorable for its poetry, but very undramatic. It was,
some of us had read, "poor" in "theatrical effect"; it lacked
"action," was "barren in striking situations." Above all, its
hero had not the right stuff in him. That other Richard,
Richard III, might be only crudely drawn, but he was "a
fit figure for a play." [30] George Pierce Baker had found
Richard II "weak, dilatory, and selfish," as beyond question
he is. "The actor's instinct tells him there is no good acting
part in the play." And Baker had quoted from the Deposition
Scene a passage which he described as "beautiful but exceed-

ingly self-conscious," Shakespeare having still to learn that a
single word, or gesture, would have been "far more prob-
able." [31] The lines were these:

> Now is this golden crown like a deep well
> That owes two buckets, filling one another,
> The emptier ever dancing in the air,
> The other down, unseen, and full of water.
> That bucket down and full of tears am I,
> Drinking my griefs whilst you mount up on high (IV, I, 184).

Richard's crying "no, no!" or merely standing there in mute
anguish would, I suppose, have satisfied probability — the
narrowly restricted probability of yesterday's realism. The
young Shakespeare had permitted his Richard to speak, as
Richard himself might have longed to speak, with a poet's
subtlety, a poet's distinction.

"Within recollection," H. T. Parker declared in *The
Transcript*, next day, "Shakespeare's verse has not been
spoken so variously and vividly upon a Boston stage." There
was, what is rare in the theatre, a sense of style. The garden-
ers, in the scene in which the Queen hears the "black tidings"
of Richard's downfall, were not mistaken for comic countrymen. (Under Margaret Webster's direction, a few years later,
the chief gardener came in humming the Gravedigger's song
from *Hamlet*.)[32] Capturing the mood of the whole passage,
the Stratford players gave it as something remote from ac-
tuality, something far-off and long ago, and it was deeply
affecting.

Yet there are, in the same play, moments of entire reality.
As, in the Deposition Scene, once more, Richard's "Mark,
silent king. . . ." A reader almost forgets Bolingbroke, who
says so little here, biding his own time. When, however, we

see him, this impassivity, this silence, must, we perceive, have become intolerable to Richard. Or, back in the second act, there is the poor, fluttery, well-meaning Duke of York, hearing one piece of bad news after another, and at last that his sister, the Duchess of Gloucester, is dead. He is with the young Queen:

> God for his mercy! what a tide of woes
> Comes rushing on this woful land at once!
> I know not what to do. I would to God
> (So my untruth had not provok'd him to it)
> The King had cut off my head with my brother's.
> What, are there no posts dispatch'd for Ireland?
> How shall we do for money for these wars?
> Come, sister — cousin I would say — pray pardon me (II, 2, 97).

He is almost a comic character; a pitiful one, by the same token, and very real. "Come, sister . . ." his mind turning back, even as he speaks, to the past; to that final piece of news, which as yet he has scarcely taken in.

Reality, then, at least by brilliant flashes; irony, as well. The third act, especially, is full of it; as when Richard's speech on the divine protection of kingship seems answered, in a bitter sense, by the tidings Salisbury brings immediately after. In the Bridges-Adams production, the flippant laughter of the King and his favorites as they approached John of Gaunt's sick room actually mingled with the close of the "England" speech.

I have lingered a little on this performance, partly out of the mere pleasure of recollection, partly because it so often illumined the play. But it was an event, too. Parker, our best critic, wrote of it that "within memory" Shakespeare had not had "such a gala evening in Boston." And some who were there told me they had never before enjoyed a Shakespearian performance so much.[33]

Among the plays given by the Stratford Company on their next visit was *Measure for Measure*.[34] Again, under Bridges-Adams, it was given with few cuts — even in the low comic scenes. Now Mrs. Overdone and her friends are not in the least edifying, and very harsh things have been said about them. Dowden explains that they are "less important individually than as representatives of the wide-spread social corruption and degradation which surround the chief characters." In Vienna, " 'corruption boils and bubbles.' " [35] And to Mr. Mark Van Doren, "the air of Vienna is poisoned. . . . The city stews in its vices; bawds and pimps swarm in the streets, the prisons are crowded with moral vermin." [36] When, accordingly, Pompey and the rest began to speak the lines set down for them — in Boston, twenty years ago — a certain uneasiness was perceptible in the theatre. And then, from the gallery, there came a resounding laugh — no snicker — a good, honest, masculine laugh! And, at once, the tension was released, the spell broken. For, on the stage, these characters had become richly amusing in their own right, and we proceeded to enjoy them unreservedly for the rest of the evening. "If," Sir Walter Raleigh asks, "the humorous scenes are needed only, as Professor Dowden says, 'to present without disguise or extenuation a world of moral licence and corruption,' why are they humorous?" And in a fine passage he goes on to consider these wretches as "live men, pleasant to Shakespeare." Their world "is not a black world; it is a weak world, full of little vanities and stupidities, regardful of custom, fond of pleasure, idle, and abundantly human. No one need go far to find it." [37]

I recall two further moments. The first was where the

disguised Duke tells Isabella, what is of course untrue, that her brother has been executed. More than one reader has found it hard to accept the contrivance at this point. In the theatre, the difficulty not only remained but became of greater consequence. There, the violence of Isabella's distress could not be ignored. And though she has few words to speak, there is only one way in which they can be spoken. However, another difficulty vanished. This was just at the end, where Claudio is restored to his sister. Dr. Johnson had found it "somewhat strange, that *Isabel* is not made to express either gratitude, wonder or joy at the sight of her brother"; [38] and in our own time this silence of hers has been taken as evidence of faulty revision.[39] But the young Isabella of this Stratford production, Hilda Coxhead, needed no words. Her love for Claudio, her joy in his safety, were expressed by means of action. So, at the end of the eighteenth century, a greater actress had expressed them. "Claudio *discovers himself,* — Isabella *runs and embraces him*" is the stage direction in John Kemble's edition of *Measure for Measure*; and Mrs. Siddons was the Isabella of his production.

Much of what we learn from seeing Shakespeare acted might have occurred to us, as readers, if only our imaginative powers were livelier. This was brought home to me when I first saw *King John* and, years later, *Troilus and Cressida*. A striking scene in the former is the one in which John allows Hubert to perceive that he wants young Prince Arthur put out of the way. No reader misses his purring repetition of the name Hubert here. But I, at least, had not realized before, that all the time they are talking of him the little boy is actually there, on the stage, watched over by Elinor. And his mere presence makes the murderous conference far more horrible.[40] *Troilus and Cressida*, well produced at the Brattle

Theatre, Cambridge, was full of surprises; that this most difficult of the plays should have *acted* at all — should have held as it did the rapt attention of an audience — being the greatest surprise of all.[41] The prophetical and commemorative passages, as that of the first meeting of Hector and Achilles, were all the more impressive for one's knowledge of the story. The plot involving Ajax proved easy to follow. In fact, there was no want of coherence in the play as a whole through the great scene of betrayal and disillusionment "before Calchas' tent." In this I was struck, as never in reading it, by the strangely musical employment of the voices: those of Diomed and Cressida, contrasted with those of Troilus, Ulysses, and Thersites. No scenes could be less alike than Act V, scene 2, of this play and Act V, scene 2, with its "Good shepherd, tell this youth what 'tis to love," of *As You Like It*. Yet, formally, they agree in the sense both give us of "pattern," of effects deliberately calculated for the ear.[42]

In *Troilus and Cressida* was an instance, too, of the effectiveness of Shakespeare's use of off-stage sounds — those significant clocks and cocks and trumpets and knockings and alarum-bells in the plays — an instance which, again, I had not previously noticed. For, just as the debate of the Trojan leaders is interrupted, by the entrance of Cassandra, so that of the Greeks, earlier, is abruptly broken off. A sudden trumpet sounds; and with it, and the words "From Troy," comes fresh momentum, an exciting change of speed.

In this matter of off-stage sounds, we should I think, be ready to accept innovation, so long as innovation is in keeping with the spirit, if not the letter, of Shakespeare's lines. Thus, Mr. John Burrell, the producer of the Old Vic's celebrated *Henry IV, Part 1*, of 1946, felt free, during Falstaff's soliloquy in the fourth act, to allow us to hear the march past of those scarecrow recruits whom even Sir John himself describes with something like shame. A mournful chanting it was! Once "Greensleeves," as I was told, it had gradually been worn down into a sort of rhythmical grumbling. And although there is nothing in the text to demand its inclusion, it justified itself in an instant.[43]

But to go back to our failure to imagine. There are things we learn from seeing the plays which could scarcely have occurred to us in the study. The perfect intelligibility of the intricate plot of *The Comedy of Errors*, when the play reaches the boards, is an example (that holds true even when the Dromios are actually indistinguishable).[44] Or there are subtleties of detail, such as the effect on a character of things said in his presence though not, perhaps, addressed to him. What his face would reveal, we may have thought of, vaguely, but the good actor will have anticipated us, even if we have. In the second act of *Othello*, Cassio in his cups becomes solemn, all at once.

> *Cassio.* Well, God's above all; and there be souls must be saved, and there be souls must not be saved.
> *Iago.* It's true, good Lieutenant.
> *Cassio.* For mine own part — no offence to the General, nor any man of quality — I hope to be saved.
> *Iago.* And so do I too, Lieutenant.
> *Cassio.* Ay, but, by your leave, not before me. The lieutenant is to be saved before the ancient (II, 3, 105).

His new rank is very dear to him, we discover: "The lieutenant . . . before the ancient." But it is less of Cassio that I am thinking, than of Iago, and Iago's face as he listens. The merest flicker of pain and hate will be enough. But a look

. . . and with that look (in the theatre) our minds leap back to the very beginnings of the tragedy and its almost forgotten initial motive.[45]

Other instances come to mind — as the look of bewilderment and consternation on Speed's face when Valentine protests that his banishment was for having killed a man [46] — but two instances, most vividly: in *Henry V* and *The First Part of Henry IV*. I was unfortunate, when the Old Vic Company gave *The First Part of Henry IV* in New York, to see it without Ralph Richardson. There were delightful performances, nevertheless, by Laurence Olivier (the Hotspur) and in many even of the very minor rôles; and the young actor, Frank Duncan, who played Vernon, made a point I had quite missed. Worcester carefully explains to Vernon, a little before the battle, that Hotspur must not be told of "the liberal and kind offer of the King"; and Vernon reluctantly consents to keep silent about it. But not only did his face reveal his shame, while Worcester was distorting the facts of the parley, but also, when at last he could speak out and described the gallant behaviour of the Prince, he took a manifest joy in telling this part of the story fairly.

> *Hotspur.*   Seem'd it in contempt?
> *Vernon.* No, by my soul. I never in my life
>   Did hear a challenge urg'd more modestly,
>   Unless a brother should a brother dare
>   To gentle exercise and proof of arms. . . .

So that Hotspur was provoked, naturally as it seemed, to irony:

> Cousin, I think thou art enamoured
> Upon his follies (V, 2, 51).

In *Henry V*, the King a little before Agincourt is hearing from Captain Fluellen about the fighting at the bridge, where the English, according to Fluellen, had lost

never a man but one that is like to be executed for robbing a church — one Bardolph, if your Majesty know the man. His face is all bubukles and whelks, and knobs, and flames o' fire, and his lips blows at his nose, and it is like a coal of fire, sometimes plue and sometimes red; but his nose is executed, and his fire's out (III, 6, 105).

Henry has broken with his former life and turned away his old comrades. But now, as he listens, recollections crowd upon him, of this same Bardolph, who "blush'd extempore," who had "fire and sword" on his side, as he ran away from Gadshill; of Bardolph, and Bardolph's master. So, at any rate, young Richard Burton made me feel when, as Henry, he stood musing while Fluellen talked; then, after a slight pause, but gravely and without hesitation, said quietly: "We would have all such offenders so cut off." [47]

When we see one of Shakespeare's plays for the first time it is likely that the mere physical action, the stage business, will at some point assume an unforeseen richness of meaning. Not but that we may carry away from the theatre to remember perhaps, long afterwards some single line, or phrase even, that on the actor's lips we had seemed to be hearing for the first time. Each of us has had that experience. So I recall Walter Hampden's "Alas, poor Ghost!" in the first act of *Hamlet*; and, in the Graveyard Scene, Gielgud's "Now get you to my lady's chamber, and tell her, let her paint an inch thick, to this favour she must come. *Make her laugh at that.*" There was the same actor's "O, she's warm!" in the last scene of *The Winter's Tale*; and Maurice Evans's

> Down, down I come, like glist'ring Phaeton,

in the Flint Castle Scene in *Richard II*; and Godfrey Tearle's

> Alarum'd by his sentinel, the wolf,
> Whose howl's his watch,

in *Macbeth*.[48] I recall, too, a line of Desdemona's, after Othello has mentioned the pain upon his forehead,

> I am very sorry that you are not well.

No words could be simpler than those, or nearer the pitch of prose without being prose. Yet they became as Gladys Cooper spoke them both pitiful and arresting. Finally, Cleopatra, at the close of the Arming Scene:

> He goes forth gallantly. That he and Caesar might
> Determine this great war in single fight!
> Then Antony — but now . . .

where, in the last two words, Katharine Cornell suggested all the weariness of the transition to reality.[49]

Yet it is where action is executed that we are likeliest to be startled: as the kneeling of Volumnia to Coriolanus in the climactic scene outside Rome; or Hubert's gathering in his arms the crushed body of the little Prince in *King John* —

> How easy dost thou take all England up! —

or, in *The Tempest*, Trinculo's creeping under Caliban's gabardine, so that Stephano is confronted by what he takes to be a four-legged monster with two voices, suffering from an ague. And just as in the matter of off-stage sounds, so in this of action, there is room for happy invention, provided always that such invention is readily conceivable in terms of the lines themselves and true to the spirit of the scene. In

Guthrie McClintic's production of *Antony and Cleopatra*, I
found my pleasure in one episode greatly heightened by a
piece of business introduced at the close. Antony and Octavius have met after a long period of estrangement. Lepidus
has been present, too. But the others, going out amicably
together, seemed to have forgotten him. Then, just as Antony
reached the door, he recollected: "Let us, Lepidus, not lack
your company"; and, with a glad cry, "Noble Antony, not
sickness should detain me," the poor nonentity toddled off
after them.[50] Or there was a moment of inspired commentary
in Donald Wolfit's production of *King Lear*.[51] Mr. Wolfit,
who invented the business, was Lear, and Geoffrey Wilkinson,
an old Stratford comedian whom I had seen in the part in
Bridges-Adams's time, was the Fool. They were alone together
near the end of Act I. Lear, about to set off on his journey,
carried a whip. The Fool in his jesting went too far:

> *Fool.* If thou wert my fool, nuncle, I'ld have thee beaten
>   for being old before thy time.
> *Lear.* How's that?
> *Fool.* Thou shouldst not have been old till thou hadst
>   been wise.

At this, Lear suddenly struck out, lashing him with the whip;
then, as the Fool cowered on the ground, spoke:

> O, let me not be mad, not mad, sweet heaven!
> Keep me in temper; I would not be mad! (I, 5, 44).

A Gentleman entered to say that the horses were ready. Lear
called to the Fool — "Come, boy" — and the Fool ran to him,
as a dog will come to you after being punished, and gave him
the whip he had dropped. Lear put his arm about him, and
they went out together.

BETTERTON

GARRICK AS LEAR

KEMBLE AS HAMLET

"A Bloody deed! almost as bad,
good Mother, as kill a King and
marry with his Brother."

MRS. SIDDONS
AS LADY MACBETH

THEATRE ROYAL, DRURY-LANE.

This present THURSDAY, February 20, 1817,

Their Majesties' Servants will perform SHAKESPEARE's Tragedy of

OTHELLO.

Duke of Venice, Mr. R. PHILLIPS,   Brabantio, Mr. POWELL,
Gratiano, Mr. CARR,   Lodovico, Mr. COOKE,   Montano, Mr. KENT,
Othello, Mr. KEAN,
Cassio, Mr. HOLLAND,   Roderigo, Mr. S. PENLEY,
Iago,   Mr.   B O O T H,
(His First Appearance at this Theatre.)
Antonio, Mr. Coveney,   Julio, Mr. Ebsworth,
Marco, Mr. Jamieson,   Paulo, Mr. Goodman,   Giovanni, Mr. Buxton,
Luca, Mr. G. Wells, Messenger, Mr. Minton, Leonardo, Mr. Evans.
Desdemona,   Mrs.   BARTLEY,
Emilia, Mrs. KNIGHT.

After which (for the 16th time) a new pastoral Ballet, composed by Mr. BYRNE, called

PATRICK's RETURN.

Principal Dancers.—Mr. OSCAR BYRNE,
Mr. MAY,   Mr. EBSWORTH,
Miss S M I T H,
Miss TREE,   Mrs. VEDY,   Miss HART,   Mrs. MAY,   Miss GLADHILL,
To which will be added (4th time at this Theatre) the comick Afterpiece of

The FOLLIES of a DAY.

Count Almaviva,   Mr.   R A E,
Page, Miss KELLY,
Figaro,   Mr.   H A R L E Y,
Antonio, Mr. MUNDEN,
Basil, Mr. FISHER,   Pedro, Mr. MINTON,
Countess, Mrs. ORGER,
Susan,   Mrs.   A L S O P,
Agnes, Miss Cooke.

Vivant Rex et Regina.—*No Money to be returned.*—LOWNDES, Printer, Marquis-Court, Drury-Lane.

The Publick are respectfully informed, that
Mr. BOOTH
is engaged at this Theatre, and will make his first Appearance
This Evening, in the Character of *Iago,* in the Tragedy of *Othello.*
Othello, Mr. KEAN.

*Due Notice will be given of the next Representation of the Comedy of the INCONSTANT,
which was performed on Saturday Evening with the highest Approbation.*

The NEW BALLET called PATRICK's RETURN,
*performed on Tuesday for the 9th time, was honoured with a most brilliant Reception;
it will be repeated this Evening, and every Evening till further Notice*

THE FOLLIES of A DAY,
performed last Night for the third time, was again received with most distinguished and universal
Applause,—it will therefore be repeated *this Evening.*

In Consequence of numerous Enquiries at the Box-Office for the next Representation of
TIMON OF ATHENS,
it will be performed on *Saturday next.*

SOUTHERN's Tragedy of OROONOKO,
(In which Mr. KEAN made his 9th Appearance in the Character of
Oroonoko,) was performed on Wednesday to a brilliant and overflowing
Audience, and honoured throughout with the most enthusiastick
Applause;—it will be repeated early in the next Week.

Mrs. ALSOP, (Daughter of the late Mrs. JORDAN,)
Will appear as SUSAN, in the FOLLIES of a DAY, this Evening.

Mr. KEAN
Will perform OTHELLO *this Evening* and TIMON on *Saturday.*

To-morrow, there will be no Performance at this Theatre
On *Saturday,* SHAKSPEARE's Tragedy of TIMON OF ATHENS. Timon Mr. KEAN.

A NEW TRAGEDY
is in Rehearsal, and will speedily be produced.

DRURY LANE PLAYBILL

MACREADY AS MACBETH
"If I stand here, I saw him!"

BOOTH AS IAGO

IRVING AS SHYLOCK

A SCENE FROM THE FIRST QUARTO *HAMLET* ON
POEL'S ELIZABETHAN STAGE

JOHN GIELGUD AS LEONTES

TROILUS AND CRESSIDA AT THE BRATTLE THEATRE,
CAMBRIDGE, MASSACHUSETTS

Jan Farrand as Cressida; Thayer David, Pandarus; Bryant Haliday, Troilus.

NOTES

NOTES TO INTRODUCTION

1. Thomas Gilliland, *The Dramatic Mirror*, II, 803 (see also *Oxberry's Dramatic Biography*, I, 116).

2. "On the Tragedies of Shakspeare" (1811) in Charles Lamb, *Dramatic Essays*, ed. Brander Matthews, New York [1891], p. 166.

3. A. G. K. L'Estrange, ed., *Life of Mary Russell Mitford*, New York, 1870, II, 336.

4. For the extremes to which such identification could be carried, see A. O. Kellogg, *The Hamlet of Edwin Booth: A Psychological Study*, New York, 1872.

5. Charles Townsend Copeland, *Edwin Booth*, Boston, 1901, pp. 72, 74.

6. *Ibid.*, 143. See also the Philadelphia *Press*, December 6, 1887, and *Ledger and Transcript*, February 19, 1889 (in the Harvard copy of Matthews and Hutton, *Actors and Actresses*, Vol. V, no. 4, pt. 2).

7. Herschel Baker, *John Philip Kemble*, Cambridge (Massachusetts), 1942, p. 83.

8. Davies wrote of Garrick's Lear after the actor's retirement from the stage, and it would have been absurd to exclude his testimony. I have sometimes wondered, however, whether at certain points he may not be recalling performances of a long time before, when he himself played Gloucester.

9. Mrs. Jameson, *Sketches of Art, Literature and Character* (1834), Boston and New York, 1866, pp. 468, 469.

10. Thomas Campbell, *Life of Mrs. Siddons*, London, 1834, I, 208 (cf. II, 140).

11. A. G. L'Estrange, *The Literary Life of the Rev. William Harness*, London, 1871, p. 61 (Harness had been "referring to the excellence of her intonation").

12. James Boaden notes a change in style, which he attributes to her interest in statuary as to theatrical conditions (*Memoirs of Mrs. Siddons*, Philadelphia, 1827, p. 334). See also Miss A. M. Cook, "Eighteenth-Century Acting Styles," *Phylon*, October 1944.

13. *The Torrington Diaries*, ed. C. Bruyn Andrews, London, 1938, IV, 18 (entry dated May 14, 1794).

14. Boaden, 267.

15. William Winter, *Shakespeare on the Stage*, New York, 1911, pp. 177–179; Richard Dickins, *Forty Years of Shakespeare on the*

English Stage [London,1907], p. 35. Irving's improvement in the scene with Tubal, which went so badly on the first night, is remarked as early as November 8, 1879, in *The Saturday Review*.

16. Winter, 180.

17. *Personal Reminiscences of Henry Irving*, New York and London, 1906, II, 9; Ellen Terry, *The Story of My Life*, London, 1908, p. 187.

18. Charles Durang, "History of the Philadelphia Stage" (collected articles from the Philadelphia *Sunday Dispatch*), ser. I, chap. LXXII.

19. Quite recently, attention has been called to Poel's work by a commemorative performance at The Old Vic, and a full-length biography by Mr. Robert Speaight is in preparation.

NOTES TO CHAPTER ONE

Thomas Betterton (1635–1710)

Betterton, who had been for a time a bookseller's apprentice, began acting immediately after the reopening of the theatres at the Restoration. From 1661 till 1682, he played leading rôles with the Duke's Company, and by the latter date had securely established himself as the foremost actor in England. In 1695 he rebelled against the Drury Lane patentees and, with Mrs. Barry and Mrs. Bracegirdle, headed a new company at Lincoln's Inn Fields, opening with Congreve's *Love for Love*. He remained on the stage until a fortnight before his death, appearing for the last time, as Melantius in *The Maid's Tragedy*, on April 13, 1710.

1. *The Tatler* (in Alexander Chalmers, ed., *British Essayists*), No. 71. Cf. Hazelton Spencer: "Here we have a striking endorsement of the historical critics' view of Hamlet as the beau idéal of active young-manhood" (*Shakespeare Improved*, Cambridge [Massachusetts], 1927, p. 9).

2. *Roscius Anglicanus*(1708), ed. Montague Summers, p. 21.

3. *Diary*, August 31, 1668.

4. *Apology*, ed. R. W. Lowe, London, 1889, I, 117; see also, e.g., *A Comparison between the Two Stages* (1702), ed. S. B. Wells, Princeton, 1942, pp. 105, 106.

5. *The Poetical Works of Alexander Pope*, ed. Joseph Warton, London, 1797, VII, 113 note. The performance probably began at six.

6. *Hamlet*, I, 4, 11; III, 3, 73; IV, 5, 124 (my Shakespearian references are to G. L. Kittredge's edition).

7. I, 2, 77; V, 2, 65. For a full account of the Restoration version — first printed in 1676, and probably the work of Sir William Davenant — see Spencer, *Shakespeare Improved*, pp. 174 ff.

8. *Apology*, I, 101. The ranting actor was Robert Wilks (cf. *The Laureat: or, The Right Side of Colley Cibber, Esq.*, London, 1740, p. 30).

9. Thomas Davies, *Dramatic Miscellanies*, London, 1784, III, 31, 32.

10. Pages 31, 32. The posture which Betterton assumed on the Ghost's entrance may well have been that described in Gildon's *Betterton* (see Sprague, *Shakespeare and the Actors*, p. 164).

11. *A Brief Supplement to Colley Cibber, Esq; his Lives*, in Cibber's *Apology*, ed. Lowe, II, 300, 301.

12. Letter of Villiers Bathurst, quoted in G. Thorn-Drury, *More Seventeenth Century Allusions to Shakespeare*, London, 1924, p. 48.

13. *Brief Supplement*, II, 301.

14. *Tatler*, No. 167 (May 4, 1710).

15. *Apology*, I, 103, 104. "Not," Cibber adds, but that "in some part of this Scene" Betterton did not display "that Warmth which becomes a Man of Virtue."

16. Aston, *Brief Supplement*, II, 299–301. Alfred Harbage has called attention to what Aston says of Betterton's arms ("Elizabethan Acting," *PMLA*, LIV [1939]).

17. *Dramatic Miscellanies*, III, 271, 272.

18. [Charles Gildon,] *The Life of Mr. Thomas Betterton, The Late Eminent Tragedian*, London, 1710, p. 16. And, as Betterton took the advice of authors, so they took his (cf. Dryden's introductions to *Troilus and Cressida* and *Don Sebastian*).

19. Shakespeare's *Works*, ed. Rowe, I, xxxiii, xxxiv; cf. his epilogue spoken at Betterton's benefit, April 7, 1709 (quoted in Gildon's *Betterton*, p. xiv).

20. Cibber, *Apology*, I, 109.

21. *Tatler*, No. 1.

22. *Brief Supplement*, II, 299, 300. For Betterton's voice and appearance, see also Cibber's *Apology*, I, 116, 117; and cf. the obscene "Satyr on the Players," in Downes's *Roscius Anglicanus*, ed. Summers, p. 55.

23. *Apology*, I, 109, 110.

24. Gildon's *Betterton*, p. 6; cf. James Wright, *Historia Histrionica* (1699), in Cibber's *Apology*, I, xxiv.

25. See Montague Summers, *Restoration Theatre*, London, 1934, pp. 97, 270, 271; and Allardyce Nicoll, *Restoration Drama*, Cambridge, 1928, pp. 32, 51.

26. *Spectator*, No. 42. For the tragedian's equipment, see Summers, *Restoration Theatre*, pp. 264 ff.

27. For truncheons, see also *Shakespeare and the Actors*, pp. 87, 88.

28. Benjamin Victor, *The History of the Theatres of London and Dublin*, London, 1761, II, 164.

29. Davies, *Dramatic Miscellanies*, I, 40, 41. Mrs. Pritchard, he adds, refused to follow Cibber's advice and *"tone* her words." Richard Cumberland recalls as a schoolboy seeing Mrs. Cibber (wife of the graceless Theophilus), who "in a key, high-pitched but sweet withal, sung or rather recitatived Rowe's harmonious strain" (*Memoirs*, London, 1807, I, 80); but Davies praises her speaking (I, 38).

30. Davies, *Dramatic Miscellanies*, III, 464, 466, 467.

31. *History of the Theatres*, II, 57, 58.

32. *Apology*, I, 101–103; II, 241, 242.

33. *Life of Betterton*, p. 105.

34. *The Fatal Vision*, sig. Aᵛᵒ. His sole exception is, curiously enough, Barton Booth!

35. *Brief Supplement*, II, 302, 303. On this matter of "cadenced speech," cf. Montague Summers, *The Playhouse of Pepys*, London, 1935, pp. 45 ff., and Alan Downer, "Nature to Advantage Dressed," *PMLA*, December 1943.

NOTES TO CHAPTER TWO

David Garrick (1717–1779)

Garrick, the son of a captain in the army, and the grandson of a Huguenot refugee, attended Dr. Johnson's school at Lichfield and later set up as a wine merchant in London. He acted, under the name of Lyddal, at Ipswich in the summer of 1741; then, with his Richard III at Goodman's Fields on October 19, fairly took London by storm. In 1747, he became manager (with Lacy) of the Drury Lane Theatre, which now entered upon a long period of prosperity. In 1763, he left England and travelled on the Continent, to triumph anew upon his return, two years later; and in 1769 he got up the Shakespeare Jubilee at Stratford. He gave his last performance on the stage, as Don Felix in *The Wonder*, on June 10, 1776.

1. *Early Diary*, ed. Annie Raine Ellis, London, 1907, II, 31.

2. Witness the demonstration in the House of Commons when Garrick came as a visitor in 1777 (Mrs. Clement Parsons, *Garrick and his Circle*, London [1906], pp. 363, 364).

3. Pages 18 ff. above.

4. I refer to tragedy. In comedy Quin could be varied and impressive. Elizabeth Montague, praising his Jaques in 1740, wrote that she had "never heard anything spoke with such command of voice and action as the 'seven stages [*sic*] of man'" and "he spoke the slippered pantaloon just like my Uncle Clark" (*Correspondence from 1720 to 1761*, ed. Emily Climenson, London, 1906, I, 47, 48).

5. Pages 200, 201. In a later passage, he accuses Garrick of pausing often "in the middle of a line where the sense is continued" (pp. 309, 310). For these pauses, see below, pages 25 ff.

6. Joseph Cradock, *Literary and Miscellaneous Memoirs*, 4 vols., London, 1826–1828, IV, 97, 98.

7. No. 34 (September 19, 1754), in Chalmers, ed., *British Essayists*.

8. This was John Campbell, the second duke, born 1678. Walpole's letter is dated May 26, 1742 (*Letters*, ed. Mrs. Paget Toynbee, Oxford, 1913–1915, I, 228, 229).

9. Charles Dibdin, *A Complete History of the Stage*, 5 vols., London [1800], IV, 232 note (quoting Steed, the Covent Garden prompter); Percival Stockdale, *Memoirs*, 2 vols., London, 1809, II, 168 (a "good old man" with whom he became acquainted in the playhouse).

10. Page 12 above.

11. *Lichtenberg's Visits to England*, tr. Mare and Quarrell, Oxford, 1938, pp. 9, 10.

12. For further details, see *Shakespeare and the Actors*, 138 ff.

13. *Lichtenberg's Visits to England*, 11.

14. Miss Margaret Barton makes the interesting suggestion that Garrick "owed much of his power of expressing thought by gesture and byplay" to the pantomime as perfected by Rich (*Garrick*, London [1948], pp. 125, 126); and a scurrilous writer in *The Monitor* accuses Garrick of having "introduced stage tricks and gestures, as *scientific*; which were originally the motions of mountebanks merry-andrews, and harlequins at Bartholomew-fair, to make the people laugh" (No. II [October 24, 1767]).

15. *Two Dissertations on the Theatres,* London [1756], part 1, pp. 69, 70.

16. F. G. Waldron, ed., *The Literary Museum,* London, 1792, appendix to *Roscius Anglicanus,* 22–24. See also *The Present State of the Stage in Great-Britain and Ireland,* London, 1753, p. 20.

17. [Thomas Longueville,] *Pryings among Private Papers,* New York and Bombay, 1905, p. 95. Dr. George M. Kahrl tells me that Garrick is more likely to be addressing Sir Francis Delaval than his brother, Sir John (the letter is dated "March 26 [1767]").

18. Gilbert Austin, *Chironomia; Or, A Treatise on Rhetorical Delivery,* London, 1806, p. 53.

19. Garrick, *Private Correspondence,* ed. Boaden, 2 vols., London, 1831–1832, I, 136 (letter dated January 24, 1762).

20. Davies, *Dramatic Miscellanies,* 3 vols., London, 1783, II, 157; and, for the wig, *The Connoisseur,* No. XXXIV (September 19, 1754); cf. "Sir" John Hill, *The Actor,* London, 1750, p. 226.

21. Letter dated "Rome April 11th 1764" in *Posthumous Letters from Various Celebrated Men, Addressed to Francis Colman, and George Colman, the Elder,* London, 1820, p. 255.

22. *Literary and Miscellaneous Memoirs,* IV, 247.

23. William Shirley in *The Herald* (quoted in *The Literary Magazine,* III [1758], 20).

24. Henry Crabb Robinson, *Diary, Reminiscences, and Correspondence,* ed. Thomas Sadleir, New York, 1877, I, 215 (June 16, 1811).

25. Francis Gentleman, *The Dramatic Censor,* London, 1770, I, 56.

26. As, for instance, the American refugee, Samuel Curwen, who wrote in his diary, November 29, 1775, that he had seen Garrick as Hamlet: "in my eye more perfect in the expression of his face than in the accent and pronunciation of his voice, which, however, was much beyond the standard of his fellow actors" (*Journal and Letters,* third edition, New York and London, 1845, pp. 39, 40).

27. Ed. R. W. Lowe, London, 1891, p. 52.

28. William Whitehead, *Poems,* York, 1788, III, 64, 65.

29. *A Letter to David Garrick, Esq.,* 31.

30. Arthur Murphy, *The Life of David Garrick,* London, 1801, II, 178.

31. Second edition, London, 1779, p. 47.

32. There are several versions: the one quoted is from *The Monitor,* No. II (October 24, 1767).

33. David Mason Little, ed., *Pineapples of Finest Flavour,* Cambridge (Massachusetts), 1930, p. 78; Cradock, *Memoirs,* IV, 243; Mrs. Parsons, *Garrick and his Circle,* 346.

34. *Letters*, ed. R. Brimley Johnson, New York, 1926, p. 51.

35. *Journal and Letters*, 55 (Curwen failed, later to see Garrick as Richard — "house filled"). Sir William Pepys speaks of "the state of suffocation" which had to be endured by those who saw Garrick on his final appearances (A. C. C. Gaussen, *A Later Pepys*, London and New York, 1904, I, 204).

36. *Letters*, 48, 49. John Taylor could remember that at Garrick's Lear "white handkerchiefs were seen among the ladies in every box" (*Records of My Life*, New York, 1833, p. 186).

37. *Letters*, ed. Mrs. Paget Toynbee, IX, 420 (October 8, 1776).

38. *The Public Advertiser*, June 10, 1776.

39. See especially, "Garrick's Long Lost Alteration of *Hamlet*," *PMLA*, September 1934; "Garrick's Production of *King Lear*," *Studies in Philology*, January 1948; and "David Garrick's Significance in the History of Shakespearean Criticism," *PMLA*, March 1950; cf. A. H. Scouten, "Shakespeare's Plays in the Theatrical Repertory when Garrick Came to London," *Studies in English* (University of Texas), 1944.

40. *Roscius Anglicanus*, p. 43 note (in *The Literary Museum*, ed. Waldron).

41. Davies, *Dramatic Miscellanies*, II, 263.

42. *Ibid.*, 267.

43. *Memoirs*, IV, 250.

44. Hill, *The Actor*, London, 1755, p. 151 (cf. 1750 ed., p. 69).

45. Waldron, ed., *Roscius Anglicanus*, p. 68 note.

46. *London Chronicle*, May 21–23, 1776 (cf. Cradock, *Memoirs*, IV, 249, 250). For Garrick's interest in historical costuming, see Stone, "Garrick's Handling of *Macbeth*," *Studies in Philology*, October 1941, p. 624, and R. G. Noyes, *Ben Jonson on the English Stage 1660–1776*, Cambridge (Massachusetts), 1935, p. 254 and note (cf. D. T. Mackintosh, "New Dress'd in the Habits of the Times," *T.L.S.*, August 25, 1927).

47. Samuel Foote, *A Treatise on the Passions*, London [1747], p. 22.

48. Letter from T. Newton, April 19 [?1742], in *Private Correspondence*, I, 7.

49. Gentleman, *The Dramatic Censor*, I, 370. According to William Cooke's *Memoirs of Charles Macklin* (second edition, London, 1806, pp. 104 ff.), when Garrick first essayed the part "he did not sufficiently enter into the infirmities of a 'man fourscore and upwards,' " and this was called to his attention by Macklin and another friend. I am distrustful, however, of the whole passage.

50. "Garrick's Production of *King Lear*," *Studies in Philology*, XLV, 102 (Foote had much the same idea, *Treatise on the Passions*, 22, 23).

51. Thomas Wilkes, *A General View of the Stage*, London, 1759, pp. 232, 241. See also Dr. Fordyce's letter, May 13, 1763, in Garrick's *Private Correspondence*, ed. Boaden, I, 158, and cf. Davies, *Dramatic Miscellanies*, II, 328.

52. Joseph Pittard, *Observations on Mr. Garrick's Acting; In a Letter to the Right Hon. the Earl of Chesterfield*, London, 1758, p. 8.

53. *Ibid.*, 11 (the lines are quoted as he gives them).

54. *General View of the Stage*, 233, 234.

55. Aaron Hill, *The Prompter*, No. 95 (October 7, 1735). For what follows, see also *Shakespeare and the Actors*, 286 and notes.

56. R.B., in *St. James's Chronicle*, September 26, 1769, who seems somewhat indebted to the author of *An Examen of the New Comedy, Call'd the Suspicious Husband* (1747).

57. Gentleman, *The Dramatic Censor*, I, 370. It was a picture, according to Davies, "worthy the pencil of a Raphael" (*Dramatic Miscellanies*, II, 280).

58. Colman, ed., *Posthumous Letters*, pp. 241, 242 (R. B. Peake, in his *Memoirs of the Colman Family*, I, 83, dates the letter "Paris, Oct. 8, 1763").

59. *The Adventurer*, No. 113 (December 4, 1753) in Chalmers, ed., *British Essayists*. The line, Dr. Stone notes, was one of Garrick's Shakespearian restorations ("Garrick's Production of *King Lear*").

60. *Dramatic Miscellanies*, II, 293. In *An Examen of the Suspicious Husband* (p. 37), Garrick had been accused of "really imploring *Regan*" here — of missing, that is, the irony (cf. the Philadelphia *Mirror of Taste and Dramatic Censor*, IV [1811], 123, 124).

61. Gentleman, *Dramatic Censor*, I, 370.

62. John O'Keefe, *Recollections*, Philadelphia, 1827, I, 42; Rogers, *Table-Talk*, ed. Dyce, New Southgate, 1887, p. 8 (quoting Jack Bannister).

63. Gentleman, *The Dramatic Censor*, I, 370.

64. *General View of the Stage*, 234.

65. Pittard, *Observations on Mr. Garrick's Acting*, 17. The line, one of Tate's, later removed by Garrick, comes soon after Edgar's entrance as Mad Tom.

66. Hill, in the *London Daily Advertiser*, quoted in C. H. Gray, *Theatrical Criticism in London to 1795*, New York, 1931, p. 113.

67. *Life of Garrick*, I, 27, 28.

68. Ed. 1776, p. 133.

69. George Horne, Bishop of Norwich, *Essays and Thoughts* (in *Works*, ed. William Jones, London, 1818, I, 279, 280).

70. *Dramatic Miscellanies*, II, 319, 320. Even Foote, who had criticized Garrick's Mad Scenes for their want of kingliness, admitted that his playing here would have done honor to "the Pencil of a *Rubens, or an Angelo*" (*Treatise on the Passions*, 23).

71. C. R. Leslie, *Autobiographical Recollections*, ed. Tom Taylor, Boston, 1860, p. 98.

72. O'Keefe, *Recollections*, I, 42 (also Davies, *Dramatic Miscellanies*, II, 318).

73. Bell's *Shakespeare* (1774), II, 76. Garrick's acting is graphically described by Tate Wilkinson in *The Monthly Mirror*, XIII (1802), 123, 124.

74. *Westminster Magazine*, January 1783.

75. "Rather than not play," Foote once said of him, "he would act in a tavern kitchen for a sop in the pan" (Davies, *Life of Garrick*, London, 1781, II, 272).

76. See, e.g., Laetitia-Matilda Hawkins, *Memoirs, Anecdotes, Facts, and Opinions*, London, 1824, I, 135, and *The Monthly Mirror*, N.S., I, 53 (January 1807).

77. *Reasons why David Garrick, Esq; Should Not Appear on the Stage*, London, 1759, p. 25.

78. Shirley in *The Herald* (quoted in *The Literary Magazine*, III [1758], 20).

79. Williams, *Letter to David Garrick*, 30.

80. F. A. Hedgcock, *David Garrick and his French Friends*, London [c. 1912], p. 267.

81. Gentleman, *The Dramatic Censor*, I, 58.

NOTES TO CHAPTER THREE

John Philip Kemble (1757–1823)

In 1771, Kemble was sent by his father, a Roman Catholic, to study for the priesthood at Douay. Four years later, however, he returned to England and became a strolling actor. In 1778, he joined Tate Wilkinson's company at York, played next in Dublin, and after the success of his sister, Mrs. Siddons, came to Drury Lane in 1783. He became manager of that theatre under Sheridan, in 1788, and later was manager of Covent Garden. In 1809, he held out courageously against the O.P.

("old prices") rioters but was forced at last to give in to their demands. His farewell appearance was as Coriolanus, in 1817. He lived subsequently on the Continent.

1. See especially a letter from Dublin in *The Gentleman's Magazine*, April 1783.

2. *British Magazine and Review*, September 1783.

3. *St. James's Chronicle*, September 30–October 2, 1783. Accounts of Kemble's reception vary greatly.

4. *European Magazine* for November 1783.

5. *London Magazine* for November 1783.

6. Richard Twining, letter dated October 4, 1783, in *Selections from Papers of the Twining Family*, London, 1887, p. 110. *The Morning Chronicle* finds Kemble's "action and deportment . . . gracefull, easy, and full of dignity," but he "*acts* the part in general too much, and appears to have studied stage-effect rather too elaborately."

7. *St. James's Chronicle*, as above.

8. *The Public Advertiser*, October 1, 2, 3, 1783. It is pointed out that the correspondent was not a regular writer for the paper, like "CLIO, THE ROSCIAD, and THE TRUNK MAKER."

9. October 1, 1783; see also *The London Chronicle*, October 2, and *The British Magazine and Review* for September.

10. *Dramatic Miscellanies*, III, 148, 149.

11. *European Magazine*, November 1783.

12. The old actress, Mrs. Crawford, quoted in Frederick Reynolds, *Life and Times*, London, 1827, I, 151.

13. Charles Dibdin, *Complete History of the Stage*, London [1800], V, 329.

14. James Boaden, *Memoirs of the Life of John Kemble*, 2 vols., London, 1825, I, 221.

15. They are minutely set down in a long letter, signed "*The* ROSCIAD," in *The Public Advertiser* of October 7. This letter, which Boaden seems to have known, is, I should say, the best contemporary account of the performance.

16. "Mr. Kemble," *The Port Folio*, XLI (1823²). The writer distinguishes this Hamlet of the actor's vigorous days from that of his old age. The pervading melancholy of the characterization impressed later critics, like Tieck (Theodore Martin, "An Eye-Witness of John Kemble," *The Nineteenth Century*, February 1880) and the very hostile John Galt (*Lives of the Players*, Boston, 1831, II, 256 ff.). See also *The Literary Gazette*, March 1, 1817.

17. Boaden, *Kemble*, I, 104.

18. *Public Advertiser*, October 7, 1783. "Beteem" is of course the accepted reading today.

19. [H. Martin,] *Remarks on Mr. John Kemble's Performance of Hamlet and Richard The Third*, London, 1802, p. 4.

20. Boaden, I, 97. For a defence of the reading, see *A Short Criticism on the Performance of Hamlet by Mr Kemble*, London, 1789, pp. 8 ff.; and for a satirical description of the actor's behavior at this moment, see [J. H. Leigh,] *The New Rosciad*, London, 1785, p. 13.

21. *Public Advertiser*, October 7, 1783.

22. *Universal Magazine*, October 1783.

23. *European Magazine*, November 1783; cf. *Remarks on Mr. John Kemble's Performance*, pp. 4, 5, and Boaden, I, 97, 98.

24. *Public Advertiser*, October 7, 1783.

25. *A Short Criticism*, 13, 14. This elaboration may have come only with later performances.

26. *Public Advertiser*, October 7, 1783.

27. *Ibid.*

28. I am again trusting *A Short Criticism* (p. 15), though this came out several years after the performance under consideration.

29. The Hamlet was Mr. Tom Rutherfurd, in Bridgeport, Connecticut, May 20, 1945.

30. "Artificial Comedy of the Last Century," in *Dramatic Essays*, ed. Brander Matthews, p. 161. Cf. also, Leslie, *Autobiographical Recollections*, ed. Tom Taylor, Boston, 1860, p. 21, and Thomas Gilliland, *A Dramatic Synopsis*, London, 1804, p. 123.

31. "An Eye-Witness of John Kemble," *Nineteenth Century*, February 1880.

32. By the way, he spoke "The *mobled* Queen — not in Doubt, as with Garrick — but in Sympathy" (*Public Advertiser*, October 7, 1783).

33. As "tricks" are further cited "many of his crossings, and breaks, and hesitations in the colloquy." See also, for this scene, *Shakespeare and the Actors*, 154, 155.

34. John Finlay, *Miscellanies*, Dublin, 1835, p. 226. "A.B." in *The Morning Chronicle*, October 2, 1783, took exception to "the circumstance of Hamlet's lolling, . . . resting not only his arm, but in great measure his person on Ophelia's lap," but this indelicacy was presently removed (*ibid.*, October 6).

35. *Public Advertiser*, October 7, 1783. Boaden recalls as "too formal . . . the stately *march* from Guildenstern to Rosencrantz" (*Kemble*, I, 102).

36. *Selections from Papers of the Twining Family*, 110.

37. *The Wandering Patentee*, York, 1795, II, 6. A little later in the scene (at lines 170–172), Gertrude was sternly rebuked (*ibid.*, and cf. *The New Monthly Magazine*, May 1, 1814).

38. *A Short Criticism*, 16, 17; *Public Advertiser*, October 7, 1783. *The London Magazine*, however, accuses Kemble of falling into "the most ridiculous grimaces" as he turned to the second picture (November 1783).

39. *Edinburgh Dramatic Review*, March 22, 1825, and the Kemble editions. A nicety of the actor's, remarked by Gilliland (*Dramatic Synopsis*, 122, 123), was his wearing a long cloak in this scene; for Hamlet's presence passes unnoticed until he makes it known.

40. *Universal Magazine*, October 1783; *Morning Chronicle*, October 1, 1783.

41. *A Short Criticism*, 20, 21. For Kemble's grace in this scene, as an enthusiast described it in 1802, see *Remarks on Mr. John Kemble's Performance*, 7, 8.

42. *St. James's Chronicle*, September 30 — October 2, 1783, and *European Magazine* for November.

43. *Universal Magazine*, October 1783.

44. *Quarterly Review*, XXXIV (1826).

45. *Records of My Life*, New York, 1833, p. 270.

46. *The Shakespearian Productions of John Philip Kemble*, Shakespeare Association, London, 1935.

47. *Miscellanies*, 244, 252, 253.

48. Cf. Leigh Hunt, *Dramatic Essays*, ed. Archer and Lowe, 8. Hunt rarely has a good word for Kemble, his prejudice extending even to the actor's "old black-letter books which no man of taste would read" (*The Examiner*, September 24, 1809, quoted in Leigh Hunt's *Dramatic Criticism 1808–1831*, ed. L. H. and C. W. Houtchens, New York, 1949, p. 29).

49. "Playhouse Memoranda," *Works*, ed. William MacDonald, London and New York, 1903, III, 43.

50. See *Shakespeare and the Actors*, 149.

51. Page 279. On Kemble's attitudes, see also C. A. G. Goede, *A Foreigner's Opinion of England*, tr. Horne, Boston, 1822, p. 438.

52. London, 1947, pp. 67, 68.

53. *Reminiscences*, I, 150. See, also, Thomas Holcroft, *Theatrical Recorder*, I (1805), 274: Kemble's "inspired moments . . . give, perhaps, the greater delight by bursting upon the audience when they are least expected."

54. Boaden, *Kemble*, I, 177.

55. *Reminiscences*, I, 148.

56. *Actors and Editors: A Poem*, p. lx. Mary Mitford, indeed, writes that Kean at the beginning was liked and praised by many "because he is not Kemble, whom I dislike as much as they do" (L'Estrange, ed., *Life of Mary Russell Mitford*, I, 223 [letter dated July 5. 1814]).

NOTES TO CHAPTER FOUR

Mrs. Siddons (1755–1831)

Sarah Kemble was the daughter of respectable provincial players and began acting while she was still a small child. At eighteen, she married William Siddons, a member of her father's company. She played at Drury Lane in 1775–76, Garrick's last season, but met with little success and was not reëngaged. Appearing, however, at York, Bath, and elsewhere, she made steady progress in her art and when at last, in 1782, she returned to Drury Lane it was to achieve an immediate and overwhelming success. In later years, she acted frequently with her brother, John Philip Kemble. Her retirement from the stage in 1812 was not final.

1. *Dramatic Miscellanies*, III, 250.

2. *Letters*, ed. Mrs. Paget Toynbee, XII, 386. The time was to come when Mrs. Siddons would be looking anxiously for new parts. In an unpublished letter in the Harvard Theatre Collection she writes, November 24, 1795: "I am now acting in a Grand *Pantomime* calld Alexander the Great in which I have a very bad part and a very fine Dress it is an odious thing b[ut my] brother plays very finely in it, and the show of fighting Ladies dancing Horses Elephants Drums Trumpets &c will *go it* several nights I suppose: well, any thing is better, than saying Isabella &c over and over again till one is so tird — How I do wish that somebody woud write two or three good Tragedies some wet afternoon!"

Isabella is, of course, Southerne's pathetic heroine, not Shakespeare's austere one.

3. Thomas Campbell, *Life of Mrs. Siddons*, London, 1834, II, 36–37. Abigail Adams, after seeing her as Lady Macbeth in 1786, felt that she was "too great to be put in so detestable a character" (*Letters*, Boston, 1840, p. 323). Cf. also Genest, VIII, 419, for her declining to play Shakespeare's Cleopatra.

4. *Kemble*, I, 243.

5. *The Gazetteer and New Daily Advertiser*, February 3, 5, 1785.

6. *London Magazine* for February 1785.

7. Campbell had seen this essay "some nineteen years" before he printed it in his *Life of Mrs. Siddons* (1834) — see II, 44.

8. *The Morning Post*, February 3, 1785.

9. *The Farington Diary*, ed. James Greig, London, 1922–1928, VIII, 107.

10. *Lectures on Dramatic Literature: Macbeth*, London, 1875, p. 20. The *Macbeth* lecture seems to have been given while Mrs. Siddons was still alive. See also James Boaden, *Memoirs of Mrs. Siddons*, Philadelphia, 1827, p. 256, and John Galt, *Lives of the Players*, Boston, 1831, II, 303.

11. Boaden, *Mrs. Siddons*, 256. The important annotations made by Professor Bell during a much later performance refer to her "exalted prophetic tone" here (H. C. Fleeming Jenkin, *Mrs. Siddons as Lady Macbeth and as Queen Katharine*, ed. Brander Matthews, New York, 1915, p. 39).

12. *Ibid.*, 40.

13. *Ibid.*, 41, and Boaden, 257.

14. *Mrs. Siddons*, 258.

15. Fleeming Jenkin, *Mrs. Siddons as Lady Macbeth*, 42.

16. *Ibid.* Planché, who inspires confidence by saying he could recall only two of her effects, remembers this one (*Recollections and Reflections*, London, 1872, I, 23).

17. Fleeming Jenkin, *Mrs. Siddons as Lady Macbeth*, 44, 45. Bell describes also an impressive moment of hers at line 61; but I suspect that this owed something to an innovation of Kemble's when he came to play Macbeth (see Boaden, *Mrs. Siddons*, 269). Smith had the part in 1785.

18. Fleeming Jenkin, *Mrs. Siddons as Lady Macbeth*, 45, 48–49.

19. *Mrs. Siddons*, 259. See also Fleeming Jenkin, 47; and *The Farington Diary*, I, 148, where on May 5, 1796, the tenderness of the beginning of the speech is discussed.

20. *Oxberry's Dramatic Biography*, I (1825), 138. Mrs. Jameson, *Characteristics of Women* (1832), Boston and New York, 1887, p. 448 note, asserts that the actress "adopted successively three different intonations" in speaking the words: first, one of "contemptuous interrogation"; later, one of "indignant astonishment," and emphasizing "we"; finally, the "low, resolute tone" of simple acceptance. But if she experimented thus, it seems strange that the fact passed unnoticed when, for instance, her

fatalistic reading was challenged and defended through several numbers of *The Monthly Mirror* in 1808 (N. S., IV, 189, 302; V, 42, 293). Boaden, too, would have been sure to talk garrulously about the different readings?

21. Fleeming Jenkin, *Mrs. Siddons as Lady Macbeth*, 48, 49.

22. William Robson, *The Old Play-Goer*, London, 1846, p. 21.

23. *Memoirs of a Journalist*, Bombay and London, 1873, p. 17. Cf. Bell's note: "Breathes with difficulty, hearkens towards the door. Whisper horrible" (Fleeming Jenkin, 51).

24. Lord Harcourt's letter, "on her first appearance," in *Correspondence of Horace Walpole and William Mason*, ed. J. Mitford, London, 1851, II, 404. See also *The Gazetteer*, February 3, 1785, for the impression produced by this "horrid expression."

25. Fleeming Jenkin, 53–55.

26. *Mrs. Siddons*, 259.

27. Knowles, *Lecture on Macbeth*, 21. Cf. Mrs. Siddons's essay: "and calmly and steadily returns to her accomplice" (Campbell, II, 21).

28. Fleeming Jenkin, 57.

29. Campbell, II, 22.

30. Fleeming Jenkin, 59.

31. See also *The Morning Post*, February 3, 1785, and *The London Magazine* for February 1785. Next autumn, attention was called to "the dress worn by Mrs. Siddons as Queen" as further evidence of the same liberality. "The petticoat was a gold tabby, trimmed with sables, and the robe a sattin of the most beautiful purple, lined with ermine" (*Gazetteer*, October 4).

32. *Piozziana*, London, 1833, p. 85.

33. *Recollections of the Mess-Table and the Stage*, London, 1855, p. 77. See also Genest, *Some Account of the English Stage*, VIII, 306.

34. *Bell's Weekly Messenger*, July 5, 1812.

35. *Morning Post*, February 3, 1785. The writer (perhaps John Taylor) found much of the scene played in too familiar a style. In 1816, Hazlitt wrote that her dismissing of the guests now lacked the "sustained and graceful spirit of conciliation" toward them, it had once had (*Dramatic Essays*, ed. Archer and Lowe, 106).

36. Boaden, *Mrs. Siddons*, 261.

37. Fleeming Jenkin, 65.

38. Campbell, II, 37–39.

39. *The European Magazine*, March 1785. For further references, see *Shakespeare and the Actors*, 270, and notes.

40. *Morning Post*, February 3, 1785 (see also February 7); cf. Yvonne Ffrench, *Mrs. Siddons: Tragic Actress*, London [1936], p. 138.

41. Boaden, *Mrs. Siddons*, 262.

42. *The Examiner*, July 5, 1812 (quoted in Leigh Hunt's *Dramatic Criticism*, ed. Houtchens, p. 72). Hunt yet praises "The deathlike stare of her countenance, while the body was in motion . . . and the anxious whispering with which she made her exit, as if beckoning her husband to bed."

43. Leigh Hunt's *London Journal*, I (1834), 118.

44. Fleeming Jenkin, 66 ff. At her exit, she "used, as it were, to *feel* for the light . . . while stalking backwards, and keeping her eyes glaring on the house" (Mangin, *Piozziana*, 127).

45. Pages 21, 22.

46. W. R. Alger, *Life of Edwin Forrest*, Philadelphia, 1877, II, 545.

47. How else could she have been called "a pantomime actress," and one excelling in passionate outbursts, "sudden exclamations," and "inarticulate sounds"? (Hazlitt's *Dramatic Essays*, ed. Archer and Lowe, 19, from *The Champion*, October 16, 1814).

48. *Memoir of Charles Mayne Young*, London and New York, 1871, p. 56. Cf. Macready, *Reminiscences*, I, 60, and Hazlitt, *Dramatic Essays*, 39, 164.

49. Hazlitt, 105; Hunt, *Dramatic Essays*, 153. Both were writing of performances near the close of her career.

50. Yvonne Ffrench, *Mrs. Siddons*, 164, 165.

51. *Dramatic Miscellanies*, III, 249.

52. Cf. Boaden, *Mrs. Siddons*, 138.

53. Holcroft, in *The English Review* (1783), quoted in Agate, *English Dramatic Critics*, 70.

54. *A Foreigner's Opinion of England*, tr. Thomas Horne, Boston, 1822, p. 430.

55. *The Monthly Mirror*, XVII (1804), 318 note.

56. Tom Taylor, ed., *Autobiographical Recollections of Charles Robert Leslie*, Boston, 1860, p. 21.

57. Cf. *Shakespeare and the Actors*, 82.

58. See a letter of hers in *The Athenaeum*, April 13, 1872, H. C. Robinson, *Diary*, II, 179, and Frank Archer, *An Actor's Notebooks*, London [c. 1911], p. 302. The disgruntled author of a scurrilous little book, *The Wonderful Secrets of Stage Trick* (1793) tells quite a different story.

59. *Memoirs*, ed. Lord John Russell, Boston, 1853–1856, V, 297.

60. Campbell, I, 215.

61. *Ibid.*, II, 35, 36.

NOTES TO CHAPTER FIVE

Edmund Kean (1789?–1833)

Kean's parentage and the date of his birth have not yet been established beyond doubt. His mother was pretty certainly a disreputable minor actress named Ann Carey. He acted and recited while still a child; played small parts at the Haymarket in 1806; then endured years of hardship as a struggling performer in the provinces. His chance came at last when he appeared as Shylock at Drury Lane, January 26, 1814, one of the great nights in the history of the English stage. He continued to act, insofar as dissipation and attendant illness permitted, until the end of his life. He visited America in 1820–21 and again in 1825–26.

1. According to *Oxberry's Dramatic Biography*, I (1825), 8, Kean's height was five feet, four inches.
2. *Letters of Edward Fitzgerald to Fanny Kemble*, ed. William Aldis Wright, New York and London, 1895, p. 50.
3. *On Actors and the Art of Acting*, New York, 1878, pp. 15, 16. See also Hunt, *Dramatic Essays*, 225.
4. *Literary Gazette*, February 22, 1817; Robert Walsh, *Didactics*, Philadelphia, 1836, I, 152, 157; Young, *Charles Mayne Young*, 55; James Henry Hackett, *Notes, Criticisms, and Correspondence upon Shakespeare's Plays and Actors*, New York, 1863, p. 127.
5. *Miscellanies*, Dublin, 1835, p. 215. The voice he thought "stronger than Kemble's," and bad rather than weak (p. 210). For an opposite opinion, see *Blackwood's*, for April 1818, and Anne Plumptre, *Narrative of a Residence in Ireland*, London, 1817, p. 61.
6. William Gardiner, *The Music of Nature*, London, 1832, pp. 48, 49.
7. Richard H. Dana, *The Idle Man*, No. 1, New York, 1821, p. 35.
8. Hazlitt repeatedly speaks of this. See also, John Ambrose Williams, *Memoirs of John Philip Kemble, Esq.*, London, 1817, p. 76; Leslie, *Autobiographical Recollections*, 198; Hunt, *Dramatic Essays*, 228. That Kean's subtleties were defeated by the immensity of the new theatre is noted by P. G. P. in *The Examiner*, May 15, 1814 (quoted in Agate, *These Were Actors*, 35) and by *The New Monthly Magazine*, March 1, 1814.
9. "Whether Actors Ought to Sit in the Boxes," *Table-Talk* (1822), in *Works*, ed. Waller and Glover, VI, 277; cf. *Dramatic Essays*, 91, 92.

10. Hackett, *Notes, Criticisms, and Correspondence,* 126.

11. *Miscellanies,* 208, 209.

12. *The Idle Man,* 46.

13. *The Champion,* December 21, 1817 (*Works,* ed. H. Buxton Forman, III, 4). Lewes, too, grants Kean a "musical ear and musical voice," which saved him from that "unpardonable defect, the dissociation of rhythm from meaning" (*On Actors,* 28).

14. *Miscellanies,* 210. See also *Blackwood's* for March 1818, for his colloquialism.

15. *Leaves from an Actor's Note-Book,* London, 1860, p. 23.

16. *Dame Madge Kendal, by Herself,* London [1933], p. 7.

17. For these badly neglected Brighton performances, see Mary Theresa Odell, *Mr. Trotter of Worthing and the Brighton Theatre,* Worthing, 1944, pp. 55 ff. The fact that Kean and Booth had already crossed swords before their encounter at Drury Lane stirs the imagination.

18. Asia Booth Clarke, *The Elder and the Younger Booth,* Boston, 1882, p. 18 (for the call and the carriage, see also *Literary Gazette,* February 22, 1817). Mrs. Clarke would have us believe it was not until after his performance at Drury Lane that Booth discovered he was to play none of Kean's parts, but only, say, Richmond to his Richard.

19. *Literary Gazette,* February 22, 1817.

20. For the audience, see Macready, *Reminiscences,* I, 139, 140; *The Morning Post,* quoted in Asia Booth Clarke, 20–22; Charles and Mary Cowden Clarke, *Recollections of Writers,* London, 1878, p. 15; *Literary Gazette,* February 22, 1817; Hazlitt, *Dramatic Essays,* 131; *Theatrical Inquisitor,* for February 1817.

21. *Notes, Criticisms, and Correspondence,* 307.

22. So William Godwin had exclaimed, rapturously, as he left the theatre (Charles and Mary Cowden Clarke, *Recollections of Writers,* 15). See also his letter to Booth in Asia Booth Clarke, *The Elder and the Younger Booth,* 44.

23. *On Actors and the Art of Acting,* 18.

24. *Leaves from an Actor's Note-Book,* 21 (cf. Walsh, *Didactics,* I, 154).

25. Thomas Moore, *Memoirs, Journal and Correspondence,* ed. Lord John Russell, Boston, 1853–1856, VI, 70 (Murray was Moore's informant).

26. James E. Murdoch, *The Stage,* Philadelphia, 1880, pp. 143, 144.

27. *Dramatic Essays,* 77. Kean's Othello "appeared more like a Mahratta chief than a native of Africa" (Finlay, *Miscellanies,* 244).

28. Lord Granville Leveson Gower, *Private Correspondence 1781 to 1821*, ed. Castalia Countess Granville, London, 1916, I, 457. The letter, which seems to have escaped the vigilance of Kean's biographers, is dated "May 6, 1804" (*sc.* 1814). Byron, going with Hobhouse and Tom Moore to see Kean as Othello, found that he "threw a sort of Levant fury of expression into his actions and face" (Lord Broughton, *Recollections of a Long Life*, London, 1909–1911, I, 125).

29. *Works*, ed. Buxton Forman, III, 4 (from *The Champion*, December 21, 1817). For Kean's power of transporting a sympathetic spectator beyond the present, see also Mrs. Trench, *Remains*, London, 1862, p. 283.

30. *Miscellanies*, 242, 243.

31. Vandenhoff, *Leaves from an Actor's Note-Book*, 22.

32. *On Actors*, 16, 17. Isaac Harby found Kean's reading of the speech "sketchy, hurried and ineffective" (*Miscellaneous Works*, Charleston, 1829, p. 274). On the other hand, Frances Williams Wynn was struck by "the burst of tenderness" in "And I *loved* her that she did pity them" (*Diaries of a Lady of Quality*, ed. Abraham Hayward, London, 1864, p. 112).

33. *Theatrical Inquisitor*, May 1814.

34. *New Monthly Magazine*, February 1, 1816 (see also Harby, *Miscellaneous Works*, 274; and Forster, in *Dramatic Essays by John Forster and George Henry Lewes*, ed. Archer and Lowe, p. 14).

That Kean was not deficient in dignity is maintained by a writer in *Blackwood's*, for March and April 1818, who cites as an instance the dismissal of Cassio, later in this act (see also the quotation from Fitzgerald, page 71 above).

35. *Dramatic Essays*, 17.

36. *On Actors*, 17.

37. *Miscellanies*, 239, 240. He insists that Kean expressed jealousy when Desdemona first pleaded for Cassio, that is, before Othello was left alone with Iago!

38. Fanny Kemble, in her unexpected tribute to Kean, speaks of "the unutterable tenderness of his reply to Desdemona's entreaties for Cassio" (*Journal*, Philadelphia, 1835, I, 147 note).

39. "Reminiscences of Edmund Kean," *Theatrical Journal*, February 19, 1868; see also Durang, "The Philadelphia Stage," from *The Sunday Dispatch* (1855), chap. lxx. In *The New Monthly Magazine*, February 1, 1816, attention is called to "the simple exclamation, 'And so she did.'" As this "bursts from him, . . . the tumult of thoughts that has been passing across his mind during the long pause that preceded it is manifest."

40. *Theatrical Inquisitor*, February 1817; *New Monthly Magazine*, July 1, 1816.
41. Mary Cowden-Clarke, *My Long Life*, New York, 1896, p. 82; *New Monthly Magazine*, July 1, 1816.
42. *Dramatic Essays*, 78.
43. *The Idle Man*, 45, 46.
44. *On Actors*, 133.
45. *The Times*, May 14, 1814.
46. *The Times*, February 21, 1817; *New Monthly Magazine*, July 1, 1816.
47. *Diary, Reminiscences, and Correspondence*, ed. Thomas Sadler, New York, 1877, I, 276 (May 19, 1814).
48. *Dramatic Essays*, 78 (cf. 17, 37).
49. *Dramatic Essays*, 207, 208. "His voice," Leigh Hunt wrote, "occasionally uttered little tones of endearment, his head shook, and his visage quivered" (*The Examiner*, October 4, 1818, quoted in Leigh Hunt's *Dramatic Criticism*, ed. Houtchens, 201). Kean's face, as he spoke the lines, and his "clasped hands" are mentioned by Isaac Harby as contributing to the effect, which was "irresistible" (*Miscellaneous Works*, 275).
50. *Actors and Actresses of Great Britain and the United States*, ed. Matthews and Hutton, III, 7. For Kean's "ll" and "rr," see also Thomas R. Gould, *The Tragedian*, New York, 1868, p. 28.
51. *Times*, February 21, 1817; *Theatrical Inquisitor*, X (1817), 141.
52. This I take to have been his reading. It is that of the Kemble and Oxberry editions.
53. *Works*, ed. Buxton Forman, III, 4.
54. *Dramatic Essays*, 207 (cf. *The Examiner*, October 4, 1818, quoted in Leigh Hunt's *Dramatic Criticism*, ed. Houtchens, 201, 202); see also *Diaries of a Lady of Quality*, 113. W. G. in *The Literary Gazette*, March 1, 1817, took exception to the "*sarcastic* tone of lightness" which Kean gave to the word "married" in the same scene:
> "I took you for that cunning whore of Venice
> That married with Othello."
55. *New Monthly Magazine*, February 1, 1816.
56. *Blackwood's* March 1818 (of the performance with Booth).
57. "His stabbing himself was a masterpiece" (Lord Broughton, *Recollections*, I, 125).
58. "An Actor," in *The Tatler*, September 23, 1831 (Hunt, *Dramatic Essays*, 229).
59. On Garrick and Kean, see *The Farington Diary*, ed. James Greig, VII, 237, 238, 241; VIII, 69, 74; also, Thomas Dibdin, *Reminiscences*,

London, 1827, II, 31, 32; Leslie, *Autobiographical Reminiscences*, 98 (cf. Adolphus, *Bannister*, II, 230, 231); Sheridan Knowles, *Lectures on Oratory*, London, 1873, p. 134 b.; Martin, "An Eye-Witness of John Kemble," *The Nineteenth Century*, February, 1880.

60. *Works*, ed. Buxton Forman, III, 5 (cf. George Darley, in C. C. Abbott, *Life and Letters of George Darley*, London, 1928, p. 22). Kean himself once remarked that "he always felt his part when acting with a pretty woman, and then only" (Lord Broughton, *Recollections*, I, 173). For Kean and the Romantic Writers, see D. J. Rulfs in *Modern Language Quarterly*, December 1950.

61. *On Actors*, 13.

NOTES TO CHAPTER SIX

William Charles Macready (1793–1873)

Macready for a time attended Rugby but left to assist his father, a provincial manager, and reluctantly became an actor in 1810. He came to Covent Garden in 1816 and made a considerable success as Richard III, three years later. It was not, however, until after the death of Kean that he began to win the recognition he deserved. In 1836 he left Drury Lane, after a pugilistic encounter with Alfred Bunn, the manager, and came to Covent Garden. He was manager of Covent Garden, 1837–1839, and of Drury Lane, 1841–1843. When he was playing in New York in 1849, his quarrel with Edwin Forrest led to the very serious Astor Place Riot. He did not reappear after taking leave of the stage as Macbeth in 1851.

1. *Lippincott's Magazine*, May and June 1884.

2. John Kemble, hearing his brother Charles talk enthusiastically of young Macready's promise, "took a pinch of snuff, and with a significant smile rejoined, 'Oh Charles! con quel viso!'" (Macready, *Reminiscences*, I, 129). To Lady Pollock, when she first saw him "in his middle age," his appearance was striking: "his jaw was square, there was a singular intensity in his eyes, he looked like a passionate thinking man" (*Macready as I Knew Him*, London, 1884, p. 5).

3. *Memories of Fifty Years*, New York, 1889, p. 132.

4. For an excellent account of Macready's development, see Alan Downer, "The Making of a Great Actor," *Theatre Annual*, 1948–1949.

5. See, e.g., *Edinburgh Dramatic Review*, April 24, 1824; F. C. Tomlins, *A Brief View of the English Drama*, London, 1840, p. 80; *Illustrated London News*, October 13, 1849.

6. *Diaries*, ed. William Toynbee, 2 vols., New York, 1912, I, 212.

7. *Ibid.*, I, 258 (October 21, 1835). See also, Macready's *Reminiscences*, I, 94, 95.

8. Both editions, that of Sir Frederick Pollock (1875) as well as William Toynbee's (1912), must be consulted. Toynbee's, though far more nearly complete, lacks important entries given by Pollock.

9. *Diaries*, ed. Toynbee, II, 355.

10. *Diaries*, ed. Pollock, I, 342. "If I am to excel," he wrote, October 13, 1934, "it must be by consistent labour" (ed. Joynbee, I, 188).

11. *Ibid.*, I, 13, 38 (February 21, May 28, 1833).

12. *Diaries*, ed. Pollock, I, 432.

13. *Diaries*, ed. Toynbee, II, 231 (October 30, 1843).

14. For a sane and convincing treatment of the problem involved, see William Archer, *Masks or Faces? A Study in the Psychology of Acting*, London and New York, 1888.

15. *Diaries*, ed. Toynbee, II, 272 (May 30, 1844).

16. *Ibid.*, I, 282 (March 1, 1836).

17. *Records of Later Life*, New York, 1882, pp. 635, 642.

18. *Diaries*, ed. Toynbee, I, 114. As Hotspur, the December before, he had noted "the *vast benefit* derived from keeping vehemence and effort out of passion. It is everything for nature" (*Ibid.* 85).

19. *Ibid.*, 23 (April 3, 1833). For a stout defence of "Macready pauses," see Wallack, *Memories of Fifty Years*, 125, 126.

20. *Diaries*, ed. Toynbee, II, 474 (November 13, 1850); cf. II, 476, 479.

21. Henry H. Howe, "An Actor's Note-Book," *The Green Room*, ed. Clement Scott, London [1881], p. 45.

22. *Diaries*, ed. Toynbee, II, 487 (January 16, 1851).

23. *Ibid.*, 492.

24. William Archer, *William Charles Macready*, London, 1890, p. 203, note.

25. *Diaries*, ed. Toynbee, II, 213 (June 14, 1843).

26. There was "a universal call for Phelps" at the end of the fourth act — which he very properly ignored (Clement Scott, *The Drama of Yesterday and To-day*, London, 1899, II, 38, quoting Godfrey Turner).

27. *John Bull*, March 1, 1851 (calling attention to the police reports). For the scene outside the playhouse, see also Lewes, *On Actors and the*

Art of Acting, 44 ff., and George J. Dawson, *Recollections of the Stage and Platform* [Guildford], 1913, pp. 34, 35.

28. J. L. Toole, *Reminiscences*, ed. Joseph Hatton, London, 1889, p. 332.

29. *Diaries*, ed. Toynbee, I, 495, 496 (February 26, 1851).

30. *Ibid.*, 39 (May 31, 1833).

31. *Diaries*, ed. Pollock, I, 339 (April 12, 1832). Finlay had missed just this quality when he saw Macready in the part earlier (*Miscellanies*, 281).

32. *Diaries*, ed. Pollock, II, 178 (April 26, 1841). "Manly" is a word often used of Macbeth by the actor (see *Diaries*, ed. Toynbee, I, 4, 8, 34).

33. Cf. George Fletcher, *Studies of Shakespeare*, London, 1847, pp. 109 ff. Fletcher had urged this view of the character in 1844, a good many years before the earliest exponent of it known to Professor Dover Wilson (see his recent edition of *Macbeth*, pp. xxxiv ff.).

34. *The Examiner*, June 25, 1820 (quoted in *Works*, ed. Waller and Glover, XI, 315, 316).

35. *Dramatic Essays*, ed. Archer and Lowe, 209, 210 (from *The Tatler*, March 15, 1831).

36. *On Actors and the Art of Acting*, 41. James Agate makes much of the last three descriptions in his introduction to *These Were Actors*, London [1943], pp. 14 ff.

37. Forster and Lewes, *Dramatic Essays*, ed. Archer and Lowe, 4 (from *The Examiner*, October 4, 1835).

38. "Shakespeare's Tragedies on the Stage," *Lippincott's Magazine*, June 1884.

39. Lady Pollock, *Macready as I Knew Him*, 116; John Coleman, "Facts and Fancies about Macbeth," *Gentleman's Magazine*, March 1889. The familiar picture of Macready at the moment of his entrance was, Coleman says, "revoltingly faithful" (Tallis the publisher had "ordered his artists not to idealise the tragedian").

40. Hunt dwells with disrelish on Macready's treatment of the words as a "mere commonplace" (*Dramatic Essays*, 210; see also an anonymous letter to *The Tatler*, *ibid.*, 234).

41. Coleman, in *Gentleman's Magazine*, March 1889.

42. *Letters to Fanny Kemble*, New York and London, 1895, p. 55.

43. *Macready as I Knew Him*, 117, 118. One is reminded of what Mrs. Siddons accomplished with the words "made themselves — air" (pages 59, 60 above).

44. *Our Recent Actors*, Boston, 1888, I, 75. The Macready-Davenport "1851" promptbook at Princeton shows how carefully Macbeth was kept isolated during the speaking of this soliloquy. Excellent use of this book has been made by Professor Downer in his article, "Macready's Production of Macbeth," *Quarterly Journal of Speech*, April 1947.

45. *Dramatic Essays*, 4. As a young actor Macready had "very properly" drawn a dagger here, not as was usual at the time a sword (Genest, *Some Account of the English Stage*, IX, 223).

Another innovation was commented upon when (again in 1823) he visited Exeter. This was his avoidance of a *start* upon sight of the phantom dagger, which now seemed "to rise gradually in his imagination" (William Cotton, *The Story of the Drama in Exeter*, London, 1887, p. 60). Durang is cited by Mr. Downer to much the same effect. I no longer take seriously *John Bull*, May 26, 1839 ("suddenly raising his head, he sees the dagger — and starts according to prescribed rule").

46. *Our Recent Actors*, I, 76.

47. *Ibid.*, 76, 77.

48. For references to this artifice, which is glanced at by Dickens in *Edwin Drood*, see *Shakespeare and the Actors*, p. 409, note 58.

49. November 1850, p. 18. For another description, see *Theatrical Journal*, August 8, 1840.

50. *New England Galaxy*, November 3, 1826; Pückler-Muskau, *Tour in England, Ireland, and France*, Philadelphia, 1833, p. 218; Forster, *Dramatic Essays*, 4.

51. *Our Recent Actors*, I, 78. Of Macready's Macbeth at Covent Garden, November 25, 1836, Charles Rice reports: "Perhaps the finest acting in the whole scene was in his delivery of the words —

'To know my deed — 'Twere best not know myself.

Wake Duncan with thy knocking! Oh, would thou could'st' —

which was followed by three distinct rounds of applause" (*The London Theatres in the Eighteen-Thirties*, ed. A. C. Sprague and Bertram Shuttleworth, London, 1950, p. 74).

52. *Dramatic Essays*, 5. The performance, as Macready himself recognized, was not a good one; but Forster had noted the same failure before.

53. *Dramatic Essays*, 210, 211.

54. *Our Recent Actors*, I, 78, 79.

55. *John Bull*, May 26, 1839.

56. See especially, *The Theatrical Observer*, April 8, 1823, and *New England Galaxy*, November 3, 1826.

57. This is Oxberry's reading and that of the other contemporary acting editions I have consulted. They agree in deferring the entrance of the Physician until just before he is addressed.

58. "Shakespeare's Tragedies on the Stage," *Lippincott's Magazine*, May 1884.

59. This moment was remembered by Fitzgerald, with more accuracy than reverence (*Letters to Fanny Kemble*, 65). Forrest was using Macready's business in 1837 (*The London Theatres in the Eighteen-Thirties*, 27).

60. *Tallis's Dramatic Magazine*, p. 18.

61. *Tour in England*, 219.

62. For this scene, see especially Forster, *Dramatic Essays*, 6, 7; *Theatrical Journal*, August 8, 1840 (cf. *John Bull*, May 26, 1839).

63. John Hollingshead, *My Lifetime*, 2 vols., London, 1895, II, 77, 78. Phelps was fond of telling the story (see Toole, *Reminiscences*, 207; Coleman, *Memoirs of Samuel Phelps*, London, 1886, p. 165; and cf. Macready, *Diaries*, ed. Toynbee, I, 349, 423).

64. *On Actors*, 45, 46.

65. *Diaries*, ed. Pollock, II, 376, 377. W. J. Fox, in a thoughtful essay on Macready in *The People's Journal*, December 5 and 12, 1846, had praised him in much the same terms.

66. *Diaries*, ed. Toynbee, I, 149, II, 488. "Yours," a critic once told him, "is the only intelligible Hamlet I ever saw"; Macready treasured the remark (*ibid.*, II, 490; *Diaries*, ed. Pollock, II, 453).

67. *Diaries*, ed. Toynbee, II, 273. Lewes made light of his contributions of this sort (*Dramatic Essays*, 131).

68. Lady Pollock, *Macready as I Knew him*, 35 ff.

69. *Letters to Arthur Hugh Clough*, ed. H. F. Lowry, New York and London, 1932, p. 72.

70. "Shakespeare's Tragedies on the Stage," June 1884.

71. *Records of Later Life*, 636; see also, R. H. Horne, *A New Spirit of the Age*, New York, 1844, p. 256. Archer should be read for the defence (*Macready*, 197, 198).

72. *Diaries*, ed. Toynbee, II, 6, 8, 9.

73. See especially, Vandenhoff, *Leaves from an Actor's Note-book*, 206 ff.

NOTES TO CHAPTER SEVEN

Sir Henry Irving (1838–1905)

Henry Irving (John Henry Brodribb) came from the west of England to London, where he became a City clerk. In 1856 he began his long apprenticeship as a provincial actor, in Edinburgh, Manchester, and elsewhere. Returning to London, he distinguished himself in character parts like Digby Grant in *The Two Roses* and, in 1871, leaped to fame as Mathias in *The Bells* at the Lyceum Theatre. There he continued to perform, notably as Hamlet in 1874, and took over the management in 1878, when he was joined by Ellen Terry. With her he made a series of very profitable American tours, beginning in 1883. He was knighted in 1895, but his later years were clouded with misfortune. He remained on the stage up to the day of his death.

1. *Tributes to the Memory of the Late Sir Henry Irving*, ed. Chas. F. Forshaw, London, 1905, p. 117.

2. *Letters to Fanny Kemble*, 138.

3. Fechter's acting edition of *Othello*, quoted in Henry Ottley, *Fechter's Version of Othello*, London, 1861, p. 9.

4. Macready, as we have seen, and other traditionalists, had not been above introducing pantomimic action of the kind associated with melodrama in their representations of Shakespeare's plays. For Fechter and Irving, see E. B. Watson, *Sheridan to Robertson*, Cambridge (Massachusetts), 1926, p. 378.

5. *The Theatrical World of 1897*, pp. 174, 175.

6. See, e.g., Hamilton Fyfe, *Sir Arthur Pinero's Plays and Players*, London, 1930, pp. 259 ff. For the plight of the playwright in a theatre dominated by actors, see William Archer, *About the Theatre*, London, 1886, pp. 52 ff.

7. As Shaw pointed out in 1894: "More people go to the Lyceum Theatre to see Mr Irving and Miss Ellen Terry than to see Shakespeare's plays; at all events, it is certain that if Mr Irving were to present himself in as mutilated a condition as he presented *King Lear*, a shriek of horror would go up from all London" (Introduction to William Archer, *The Theatrical World of 1894*, pp. xvi, xvii).

8. New York [1931], pp. 13, 15, 110.

9. *Hamlet*, produced by Irving the season before, had been given earlier at the Lyceum under the Bateman management. Percy Fitzgerald speaks of November 1, 1879, as "the first *regular*, official Lyceum *première*." "All," he notes, "was anticipation and eager interest. . . . The house was most brilliant" (*Sir Henry Irving*, Philadelphia [1906], p. 102).

10. Bram Stoker, *Personal Reminiscences of Henry Irving*, New York and London, 1906, I, 86.

11. Joseph Hatton, *Henry Irving's Impressions of America*, Boston, 1884, pp. 70, 71.

12. *Sir Henry Irving*, 103, 104.

13. See, e.g., *Illustrated London News*, November 8, 1879; Joseph Knight, *Theatrical Notes*, London, 1893, p. 303; and, for the comments of actors, Robert Ganthony, *Random Recollections*, London [*c.* 1899], p. 65, and Hatton, *Irving's Impressions of America*, 227.

14. *From "The Bells" to "King Arthur*," London, 1897, p. 169.

15. Austin Brereton, *Life of Henry Irving*, London, 1908, I, 309; Ellen Terry, *The Story of My Life*, London, 1908, p. 188.

16. *Forty Years on the Stage*, New York, 1915, pp. 104 ff. (also, Barnes's "'Irving Days' at the Lyceum," *The Nineteenth Century*, January 1923).

17. *Shakespeare on the Stage*, First Series, p. 175 (see also page 5 above). A note of Ellen Terry's to the same effect is quoted in Laurence Irving's new biography, *Henry Irving: The Actor and His World*, London [1951], p. 500.

18. *We Saw Him Act*, ed. H. A. Saintsbury and Cecil Palmer, London, 1939, p. 167. "You'll never do what you want," Irving once told Frank Benson, "the public will not let you. They would not let me, they will not allow you" (Benson, *I Want to Go on the Stage*, London [1931], p. 68).

19. November 15, 1879. J. Ranken Towse, writing in *The Century*, March 1884, of Irving's first representation of the part in New York, recurs to the idea of inconsistency. This time, however, it was the shift from Shylock's "grosser attributes" to pathos and dignity in "the last half of the trial scene," which is found objectionable (see also the same writer's *Sixty Years of the Theater*, New York and London, 1916, p. 244).

20. *Nights at the Play*, II, 225.

21. *The Theatre*, December 1, 1879.

22. N.S., I (1880), 63, 169. For Ruskin's protest, see also Laurence Irving, *Henry Irving: The Actor and his World*, 345–349. An anonymous reviewer in Labouchere's *Truth*, November 6, 1879, finds plenty

of evidence against the theory, which "Mr. Irving has to a certain extent adopted," that Shylock was a "martyr to popular prejudice."

23. *Scribner's Monthly*, January 1881 (quoted in *The Scenic Art*, ed. Allan Wade, New Brunswick, 1948, pp. 140, 141).

24. *Dramatic Opinions and Essays*, New York, 1910, II, 55, 56.

25. *The Shadow of Henry Irving*, 52, 53.

26. *The Theatre*, December 1, 1879. The porters are typical of Irving's improvements upon the ideas of Charles Kean (cf. J. W. Cole, *Life and Theatrical Times of Charles Kean*, London, 1859, II, 264).

27. For these details, see *The Spectator*, November 8, 1879, *The Theatre*, December 1, 1879, and Scott, *From "The Bells" to "King Arthur,"* 165.

28. *The Scenic Art*, 140.

29. This conversation, set down by Hatton, took place in December 1883, after Irving's first performance of *The Merchant* at the old Boston Theatre — still for some of us a memory of high, curving galleries! (*Irving's Impressions of America*, 227 ff.)

30. *From "The Bells" to "King Arthur,"* 166.

31. *The Saturday Review*, November 8, 1879. For the emphasis placed by Irving upon "Shylock's personal loathing of Antonio," see W. T. Arnold in *The Manchester Guardian*, November 22, 1881, (quoted in *The Manchester Stage 1880–1890*, Westminster [1900], pp. 90 ff.).

32. Hatton, *Irving's Impressions of America*, 229.

33. See, especially, *The Spectator*, November 8, 1879; Theodore Martin, "Theatrical Reform: The 'Merchant of Venice' at the Lyceum," *Blackwood's*, December 1879.

34. *The Theatre*, December 1, 1879.

35. *Saturday Review*, November 8, 1879.

36. It was left for Irving's successors to elaborate sensationally upon his idea. See *Shakespeare and the Actors*, 22, 23, and W. Bridges-Adams, "Shakespearian Tradition in the Theatre," *Quarterly Journal of Speech*, XVI (1930). I have suggested a possible origin in Verdi's opera *Rigoletto*.

37. *The Times*, November 3, 1879.

38. *Blackwood's*, December 1879 (it was Ellen Terry as Portia whom the writer was attacking in this finical essay).

39. *From "The Bells" to "King Arthur,"* 166, 167.

40. Winter, in *The New York Tribune* (quoted in *Mr. Henry Irving and Miss Ellen Terry in America: Opinions of the Press*, Chicago, 1884, p. 3).

41. Hatton, *Irving's Impressions of America*, 231, 232.

42. Scott, *From "The Bells" to "King Arthur,"* 167, *The Theatre*, December 1, 1879; for the Jews, Knight, *Theatrical Notes*, 303, Frederic Daly [L. F. Austin], *Henry Irving in England and America*, London, 1884, pp. 194, 195, and see Ganthony, *Random Recollections*, 83.

43. *The Spectator*, November 8, 1879.

44. *The Saturday Review*, November 8, 1879. Portia, too, would have liked to be very quiet in this scene, but had to give up the idea (Ellen Terry, *Story of My Life*, 163).

45. Martin, in *Blackwood's* December 1879.

46. *Punch*, November 15, 1879; *Saturday Review*, November 8, 1879; Fitzgerald, *Sir Henry Irving*, 105, 106.

47. Scott, *From "The Bells" to "King Arthur,"* 168. He goes on to say that Shylock's acceptance of Christianity was rendered conceivable "by the lost air of dreaminess that makes the lips answer while the mind is astray."

48. *The Spectator*, November 8, 1879.

49. Ellen Terry, *The Story of My Life*, 97, 98, 155. She would have us believe that he overcame his defects at last; and it seems clear, despite Percy Fitzgerald's opinion to the contrary, that time did bring improvement (cf. his *Sir Henry Irving*, 303). For a summary of many other explanations of Irving's "physical and vocal eccentricities," see Professor E. J. West's admirable study, "Henry Irving, 1870–1890," in *Studies in Honor of Alexander M. Drummond*, Ithaca, 1944.

50. Cf. Gordon Craig, *Henry Irving*, New York and Toronto, 1930, pp. 60 ff.

51. Daly, *Henry Irving*, 282.

52. *The Saturday Review*, October 21, 1905.

53. "Henry Irving," *The Atlantic Monthly*, March 1884 (reprinted in Clapp's *Reminiscences of a Dramatic Critic*, Boston and New York, 1902).

54. *The Scenic Art*, 36, 37.

55. *Ellen Terry and Bernard Shaw: A Correspondence*, ed. Christopher St. John, New York and London, 1931, p. xxvi.

56. The feeling that Irving's success threatened to overthrow the whole system of acting to which American audiences were accustomed is clearly present in some of the reviews quoted in *Mr. Henry Irving and Miss Ellen Terry in America: Opinions of the Press* (see, especially, those from the *Chicago Tribune*). Irving himself was talking a good deal, at this time, about the worthlessness of tradition (Hatton, *Irving's Impressions of America*, 74, 232).

57. "Henry Irving," *Atlantic Monthly*, March 1884. For his eyes, see Louis Calvert, *Problems of the Actor*, Boston, 1918, pp. 81, 82.

58. See, e.g., Stoker, *Personal Reminiscences of Henry Irving*, II, 63, 64; [H. A. Saintsbury], *Letters of an Unsuccessful Actor*, Boston [1923], p. 328; Seymour Hicks, in *We Saw Him Act*, 115; George Sampson, *Seven Essays*, Cambridge, 1947, p. 161.

59. Cf. W. Graham Robertson, *Life Was Worth Living*, New York and London [1931], pp. 55, 166. Robertson felt that Irving was "wrong about Shylock. His dignified, heroic, intensely aristocratic Martyr was magnificent and unforgettable, but it upset the balance of the play and it ruined Portia's Trial Scene."

60. *The Art of the Victorian Stage*, London and Manchester, 1907, pp. 82, 83.

61. *Random Recollections*, 90.

62. *Henry Irving: A Short Account of His Public Life*, New York, 1883, p. 138.

NOTES TO CHAPTER EIGHT

Edwin Booth (1833–1893)

Edwin Booth, born in Belair, Maryland, was the son of Kean's sometime rival, Junius Brutus Booth. He began to act early. After his father's death, he played for a time in Australia and California. In 1857 his Sir Giles Overreach was acclaimed in Boston, and in 1860 he more than held his own in competition with Edwin Forrest in New York. In 1861 he acted in England. After retiring from the stage upon the assassination of Lincoln by his younger brother, John Wilkes Booth, he was persuaded to return, and in 1869 opened a theatre of his own, in New York, which failed, however, in 1873. His second English visit of 1880–1881, was followed by one to Germany, two years later. He made his last appearance in 1891.

1. William Bispham, "Memories and Letters of Edwin Booth," *The Century*, November 1893. Booth had acted in London in 1861 without attracting much attention.

2. Jefferson Winter, "As I Remember," *Saturday Evening Post*, October 30, 1920 (cf. William Winter, *Life and Art of Edwin Booth*, New York and London, 1893, p. 107).

3. Edwin Milton Royle, *Edwin Booth as I Knew Him*, New York, 1933, p. 33.

4. Edwina Booth Grossmann, *Edwin Booth*, New York, 1894, p. 214.

5. Winter, *Life and Art of Edwin Booth*, 108.

6. *Saturday Review*, November 13, 1880. Booth's fondness for "taking the stage" in *Hamlet* is noted by the late Professor Copeland, *Edwin Booth*, Boston, 1901, p. 74.

7. *Illustrated London News*, November 13, 1880.

8. Dutton Cook, *Nights at the Play*, London, 1883, II, 274.

9. Frederick Wedmore, in *The Academy*, November 13, 1880.

10. *Illustrated London News*, May 7, 1881; *Athenaeum*, February 19, 1881; *Punch*, December 4, 1880, April 2, 1881. For praise of Booth's Lear, see also *The Saturday Review*, February 19, 1881.

11. Letter to Barrett, dated January 20, 1881, in Harvard Theatre Collection (cf. Otis Skinner, *The Last Tragedian*, New York, 1939, p. 195).

12. Copeland, *Edwin Booth*, 118; Skinner, *The Last Tragedian*, 48. Yet there were intrigues at the Princess's — see E. H. House, "Edwin Booth in London," *The Century*, December 1897.

13. Skinner, *The Last Tragedian*, 194.

14. *Ibid.*, 31.

15. House, "Edwin Booth in London." *Venice Preserved* and *Julius Caesar* were also mentioned.

16. Bispham, "Memories and Letters of Edwin Booth," *The Century*, December 1893.

17. Bram Stoker, *Personal Reminiscences of Henry Irving*, New York and London, 1906, I, 2; cf. I, 89.

18. *The Story of My Life*, London, 1908, p. 204. "I have never," she wrote, "in any face, in any country, seen such wonderful eyes." For the rehearsals, see also Brander Matthews, *Principles of Playmaking*, New York, 1925, p. 291.

19. Newspaper interview quoted in appendix to Frederic Daly, *Henry Irving in England and America*, London, 1884, p. 282.

20. Special matinées were added later in the engagement, which continued until the middle of June.

21. See, especially, *The Illustrated London News*, May 7, 1881.

22. *What the Author Meant*, London, 1932, p. 79. For the crowding "pittites," see also Sir John Martin-Harvey, *Autobiography*, London [1933], p. 42.

23. Mowbray Morris, *Essays in Theatrical Criticism*, London, 1882, pp. 94, 95.

24. Review by Mowbray Morris, May 11, 1881. Many writers, of course, gave the advantage to Irving.

25. "Then Meiningen Company and the London Stage," *Blackwood's*, August 1881.

26. *Essays in Theatrical Criticism*, 98.

27. "Edwin Booth," in McKay and Wingate, *Famous American Actors of Today*, New York and Boston [1896], pp. 36, 37; cf. his *Reminiscences of a Dramatic Critic*, Boston and New York, 1902, pp. 135, 136.

28. "Edwin Booth," *The Galaxy*, January 1869. Winter speaks approvingly, however, of "the subtle use of gesture and facial play" by means of which Booth made Iago's duplicity evident to the spectators (*Shakespeare on the Stage*, 271), and there were suggestions of the villain in his dress (*The Athenaeum*, January 22, 1881).

29. *Nights at the Play*, II, 303.

30. *Sixty Years of the Theater*, New York and London, 1916, pp. 190, 191.

31. Page 146. Mr. Lockridge has made good use of these notes (*Darling of Misfortune*, New York and London [1932], pp. 341 ff.).

32. Furness Variorum *Othello*, p. 214. "Lithe" is a term frequently applied to Booth's Iago, and for "sinuosity" cf. R. G. White, *Studies in Shakespeare*, Boston and New York, 1885, p. 265.

33. Lucia Calhoun, "Edwin Booth."

34. *Saturday Review*, January 29, 1881.

35. *Ibid.* When Iago was alone he seemed "more than a demi-devil" (May 14, 1881).

36. Towse, *Sixty Years of the Theater*, 190.

37. Cook, *Nights at the Play*, II, 303.

38. *Footlights and Spotlights*, New York [1924], p. 93.

39. *Studies in Shakespeare*, 265.

40. Winter, *Life and Art of Edwin Booth*, 113, 247.

41. See especially Katherine Goodale, *Behind the Scenes with Edwin Booth*, Boston and New York [1931], p. 110; Booth in Furness Variorum *Othello*, p. 324; Skinner, *Footlights and Spotlights*, 94.

42. *Life and Art of Edwin Booth*, 197; *The Shakespearean Plays of Edwin Booth*, ed. Winter, II, 111.

43. Page 40 (privately printed, presumably in London, *c.* 1907); see also Percy Fitzgerald, *Henry Irving: A Record of Twenty Years at the Lyceum*, London, 1893, p. 170.

44. *Essays in Theatrical Criticism*, p. 102.

45. *The Saturday Review*, January 29, 1881. The half-menacing words he addresses to her were spoken "almost as an aside" (*The*

Athenaeum, January 22, 1881; cf. Furness Variorum *Othello*, pp. 267, 268).

46. Page 114. I have known Iago to get a laugh here — to the actor's shame.

47. Royle, *Edwin Booth as I Knew Him*, 35. Winter and Copeland agree on the extreme inequality of Booth's acting.

48. W. T. Arnold in *The Manchester Guardian*, November 22, 1882 (quoted in *The Manchester Stage*, Westminster [1900], p. 40).

49. Copeland, *Edwin Booth*, 30.

50. Skinner, *The Last Tragedian*, 195.

51. *Life and Art of Edwin Booth*, 260.

52. *Footlights and Spotlights*, 172; cf. Towse, *Sixty Years of the Theater*, 190.

53. *Edwin Booth*, 13.

54. Typewritten promptbook at "The Players" (fifty-eight minutes out of a total of two hours and fifty-seven minutes).

55. January 22, 1881. William Winter was Booth's editor.

56. Matthews and Hutton, *Actors and Actresses*, III, 10, 11.

57. Winter, *Life and Art of Edwin Booth*, 96.

58. Manuscript letter in the Harvard Theatre Collection. In another hand, the actor addressed is identified as Charles Barron.

59. Skinner, *Footlights and Spotlights*, 93.

60. Winter, *Shadows of the Stage*, First Series, 77. For Booth's approaches toward naturalism, see especially Lockridge, *Darling of Misfortune*, 336 ff.

61. For this belated entrance, see *Shakespeare and the Actors*, 133, 134.

62. See, e.g., *The Times, Illustrated London News*, and *Athenaeum* on his Hamlet.

63. Copeland, *Edwin Booth*, 69, 70. See also Clapp, in McKay and Wingate, *Famous American Actors of Today*, 29–31. Sadly worn as they are, the two gramophone recordings made by Booth near the close of his life are still impressive.

64. *Memories and Impressions*, New York, 1910, p. 500.

NOTES TO CHAPTER NINE

1. A copy is in the Gabrielle Enthoven Collection.

2. See William Poel, *Monthly Letters*, London, 1929, p. 83, and *Shakespeare in the Theatre*, London and Toronto, 1913, pp. 171, 172; and cf. Granville-Barker, *Prefaces to Shakespeare*, Third Series, London, 1937, p. 137.

3. *Monthly Letters*, 82. Poel overlooks or disregards Webster's quasi-Elizabethan production of *The Taming of the Shrew* at the Haymarket in 1844.

4. Joseph Knight in *The Theatre*, May 1881.

5. *Nights at the Play*, London, 1883, II, 314–316.

6. Interview in *The Observer*, October 20, 1929. One of his earliest engagements was as "utility man" in a Dublin theatre. He mentions, also, touring with Osmond Tearle's company. In 1883–1884 he was stage manager with the Benson company.

7. Shaw, *Our Theatres in the Nineties*, New York, 1931, I, 136, 137; see also Lillah McCarthy, *Myself and My Friends*, New York, 1933, pp. 28 ff. The performance was in May 1895. For other plays read or acted by the Society under Poel's direction, see an anonymous pamphlet, *William Poel and His Stage Productions 1880–1932* (n.d.). Irving's connection is noted by Laurence Irving, *Henry Irving: The Actor and His World*, London [1951], p. 608.

8. This has not always been recognized; but see, e.g., Wedmore in the *Academy*, Clement Scott in the *Illustrated London News*; *The Athenaeum* (October 29, 1892), and *The Theatre* (November 1).

9. For Poel's stage, see especially *The Times*, November 11, 1893, and William Archer, *The Theatrical World for 1893*, pp. 266 ff.

10. *The Saturday Review*, November 18, 1893.

11. *The Theatrical World for 1893*, pp. 266 ff. Whether performances of *Measure for Measure* should be sanctioned is questioned in perfect seriousness by William Winter, *The Wallet of Time*, New York, 1913, I, 389.

12. November 18, 1893. For a somewhat different, and depressing account of the audience on the first night (November 9), see *The Theatre*, January 1, 1894.

13. Alfred Ayres, *Acting and Actors, Elocution and Elocutionists*, New York, 1894, p. 101. No other actor Ayres had heard took more than four minutes, and some less than three.

14. *Shakespeare in the Theatre*, 57, 58.

15. *Monthly Letters*, 95. For Poel's "interpretation of character in terms of vocal music," cf. interviews with Robert Speaight in *The Stage*, March 14, 1946, and Sir Lewis Casson in *The Shakespeare Pictorial Occasional Papers*, November–December 1945. How Poel taught his actors the tunes of their speeches was admirably demonstrated by Casson in the course of a commemorative performance at the Old Vic, July 11, 1952.

16. *Shakespeare in the Theatre*, 8.

17. "Some Notes on Shakespeare's Stage and Plays," *Bulletin of the John Rylands Library*, April–September 1916.

18. "Shakespeare on the Stage in the Elizabethan Manner," *The Times*, June 2, 1905.

19. *Our Theatres in the Nineties*, II, 194, Cf. I, 198–200. "Poel," writes Mr. Robert Speaight, "hammered home the dogma that convention is a necessity for art" (*Acting: Its Idea and Tradition*, London, etc. [1939], p. 91).

20. See especially his review of Poel's *Tempest* (*Our Theatres in the Nineties*, III, 253 ff.).

21. "Shakespeare on the Modern Stage," *The Times*, October 25, 1905 (account of a public discussion at the Guildhall School of Music: Shaw, Poel, Bourchier, Furnivall, and Grein were among those who spoke).

22. *The Theatrical World of 1895*, pp. 221 ff.

23. *Study and Stage*, London, 1899, pp. 231, 232.

24. *The Theatrical World of 1895*, 224.

25. *Study and Stage*, 77.

26. *The Academy*, February 5 and 26, 1898.

27. *Thoughts and After-Thoughts*, New York and London, 1913, pp. 57 ff. Oscar Wilde had written to much the same effect in his essay, "Shakespeare on Scenery," *The Dramatic Review*, March 14, 1885; cf. Brereton, *Life of Henry Irving*, I, 354, and Arthur Bourchier, *Some Reflections on the Drama — and Shakespeare*, Oxford, 1911, pp. 40, 41. It should be added that when Poel's disciple Sir Philip Ben Greet gave "Elizabethan" productions in America he met with much the same hostility as had been shown his master. See, e.g., *The New York Sun*, March 24, 1907.

28. Page 188. "The principle," as Shaw goes on to explain, "must be applied with constant regard to common sense and knowledge of essential points."

29. *Around Theatres*, London, 1924, I, 452 ff. (cf. I, 112).

30. *Ibid.*, II, 407. The performance was in December 1908. Poel had used such entrances earlier (cf. *Athenaeum*, December 14, 1895, November 18, 1899), when exigencies of space necessitated them.

31. "The Art of Mr. Poel" (*c.* 1908), in *Dramatic Values,* New York, 1925, pp. 222–243.

32. Shaw calls attention to Poel's achievements in costuming, and he repeatedly praises his use of Elizabethan music (see, especially, *Our Theatres in the Nineties*, III, 381).

33. Interview in *The Observer*, October 20, 1929.

34. " 'The Elizabethan Stage' (Part of a paper read before the Elizabethan Society, November 1, 1893)" in *The Theatre*, November 1893.

35. Harold Downs, ed., *Theatre and Stage*, London, 1934, pp. 541, 542.

36. Miss Muriel St. Clare Byrne has noticed the concentration upon a "somewhat romantic interpretation of character" as distinctive alike of acting and criticism in the nineteenth century ("Fifty Years of Shakespearian Production: 1898–1948," *The Shakespeare Survey*, II, 19). By the same token, Poel's emphasis upon his author's intention was that of many critics during his own later years, and a similar parallelism may be found between some of the productions discussed in the next chapter and the aberrations of the New Impressionism.

NOTES TO CHAPTER TEN

1. The performance I saw was at the Wilbur Theatre, Boston, March 11, 1930. The version used was in all essentials that of Edwin Booth, with the blinding of Gloucester omitted.

2. Arlington Theatre, Boston, November 4, 1927. In another old-fashioned production — by Henry Jewett at the Repertory Theatre, October 10, 1929 — it was curious to hear Caesar's Ghost pay final tribute to Brutus:

"This was the noblest Roman of them all."

What the source of this extraordinary idea was, I am at a loss to say.

3. Wilbur Theatre, Boston, March 18, 1930. Cibber, by the way, was nowhere mentioned in the programme. As for

"Off with his head. — So much for Buckingham!"

Mr. Walter Hampden could not resist including it in his production of 1934, yielding, he told me, only after rehearsals had begun.

4. See page 48, above.

5. Klein Memorial, Bridgeport, May 20, 1945.

6. August 17, 1949. Among the episodes omitted were Othello's swoon and the overhearing scene which follows. Bianca's part was reduced almost to nothing.

7. Gordon Crosse, *Fifty Years of Shakespearean Playgoing*, London, 1941, p. 44.

8. "Shakespearean Production," *The Year's Work in the Theatre 1949–1950*.

9. *Hamlet* was at Jordan Hall, December 9, 1929; *As You Like It*, at Sanders Theatre, Cambridge, January 13, 1931; *The Comedy of Errors*, at Jordan Hall, January 19, 1932.

10. The more formal the setting, the more readily it can be shaped anew by the imagination. Thus in the production of *The Two Gentlemen of Verona* by the Bristol Old Vic Company, as it was brought to London, June 30, 1952, a little balcony at one side of the stage and slender golden pillars served equally well for the scenes in Verona and Milan. It was only when in the same setting Valentine spoke of
"This shadowy desert, unfrequented woods,"
that difficulty began, almost at the end of the play.

11. July 22, September 5, 1949. Robert Atkins was the producer.

12. Arena Theatre, July 1, 1950.

13. In a letter addressed to the *New York Times*, July 30, 1950, it was curious to find the same arguments used against this production as had been used so often against Poel's productions in the eighteen-nineties. The writer, Mr. William T. Fowler, concludes: "One might, by extension, just as plausibly argue for a return to the Elizabethan practice of having the female roles played by boys and of having the actors garbed without regard for historical accuracy."

14. June 29, 1951. *Pericles*, the next day, was full of happy inventions, such as the repetition of the "sweet music," associated with the courtship of Thaisa, during the later scenes of recognition and reunion. For a brief, but excellent account of the Maddermarket, see Norman Marshall, *The Other Theatre*, London, 1947, pp. 92–97.

15. Programme note. The performance I attended was on September 22.

16. Possibly, the simulation of a log fire above a trap in the center of the platform was not altogether legitimate. The production, which is fully described in Mr. Watkins's delightful book *Moonlight at the Globe*, London [1946], was repeated on June 7, 1952, when I saw it.

17. *Associating with Shakespeare*, London, 1932, p. 27. See also two English books of 1950, C. B. Purdom, *Producing Shakespeare*, and

Ronald Watkins, *On Producing Shakespeare*. These are reviewed with considerable truculence by Hugh Hunt, in the autumn issue of *Drama*, 1951. He would have us believe that "Globe Shakespeare," like "Lyceum Shakespeare," is now "as dead as mutton." See also Margaret Webster in *The Shakespeare Quarterly*, January 1952.

18. Augustin Daly may be mentioned as another early director; but Daly gave no more heed to Shakespeare's intention than does the "creative" director of the present time.

19. November 27, 1937.

20. Chestnut Street Opera House, Philadelphia, March 25, 1939. Beside this *Five Kings* I should put as perhaps my *worst* Shakespearian memories: *Antony and Cleopatra* (with Tallulah Bankhead) at the Mansfield Theatre, New York, November 13, 1937; *As You Like It* (with Helen Craig) at the same playhouse, October 24, 1941; and the Theatre Guild's *Merry Wives of Windsor*, at the Locust Street Theatre, Philadelphia, March 23, 1946.

21. I refer to *A Midsummer Night's Dream* (August 13, 1949), *Cymbeline* (August 16, 1949) and *The Tempest* (August 7, 1951), at Stratford; and to *As You Like It*, at the Cort Theatre, New York, January 28, 1950. Mr. Benthall's production of *Antony and Cleopatra*, at the St. James's Theatre, London, June 19, 1951, was on the whole much more true to the play.

22. "The Marlowe Society Tradition," *Cambridge Journal*, July 1950. See also a letter by Guy Boas in *The Times*, September 11, 1952.

23. *As You Like It*, at the Century Theatre, New York, February 20, 1947; *2 Henry IV*, August 6, 1951; *Richard II*, July 23, 1948.

24. *The Shadow of Henry Irving*, New York [1931], pp. 109, 110.

25. Old Vic, June 23; Stratford, July 31, 1951.

26. Empire Theatre, New York, October 17, November 14, 1936. Irving paused before "nature" (Ellen Terry, *The Story of My Life*, 128, 129).

27. Phoenix Theatre, London, July 14, 24, September 8, 1951. *The Winter's Tale* is, to be sure, a very different play from *Hamlet*, and one more obviously calling for "the grand style."

28. See a really appalling statement by the Director of the State Theatre of Virginia, Mr. Robert Porterfield, in *Theatre Arts*, April 1951. "Our formula for producing Shakespeare," he writes, "is to have the script typed out as prose instead of poetry [*sic*]. This tends to kill the instinct for cadence and make the meaning more coherent to the actors and thus to the audience."

29. *Boston Evening Traveller* (Press Cuttings Book in the Shakespeare Memorial Library at Stratford, where I have also consulted Bridges-Adams's promptbook). The Theatre was the Hollis Street, of so many happy memories.

30. Brander Matthews, *Shakspere as a Playwright*, New York, 1913, p. 92.

31. *The Development of Shakspeare as a Dramatist*, New York and London (1907), 1916, pp. 152 ff.

32. St. James Theatre, New York, February 13, 1937. In Miss Webster's latest production of the play (at the City Center, New York, January 27, 1951), the Gardener's first order to his man evoked from the latter a completely modern "uh" — and, of course, the audience laughed.

33. Philip Hale, who as a critic of plays was no match for "H.T.P.," remained unconverted. He was troubled, in particular, by his inability to sympathize with either Henry or Richard. The audience, he admits, was "warmly applausive" (*Boston Herald,* in Press Cuttings Book).

34. Tremont Theatre, October 8, 1931.

35. *Shakspere*, New York, 1878, pp. 126, 127.

36. *Shakespeare*, New York [1939], p. 217.

37. *Shakespeare*, London, 1907 (1926), pp. 166, 167.

38. Edition of Shakespeare, 1765, I, 380.

39. J. Dover Wilson in New Cambridge Edition of *Measure for Measure*, 155, 156.

40. "Thursday Night Club" of the Church of the Transfiguration, New York, March 4, 1938 (James Bell played John).

41. December 10, 11, 1948. The director was Peter Temple.

42. See a brilliant essay by Geoffrey Tillotson, "Elizabethan Decoration," *Times Literary Supplement*, July 3, 1937.

43. Century Theatre, New York, May 11, 1946. Or there was the passing bell for Falstaff in the fine production of *Henry V* by Mr. Glen Byam Shaw, at the Old Vic, June 23, 1951.

44. As they certainly were in a production at Jolson's Theatre, New York, December 30, 1932.

45. Mr. José Ferrer caught the expression at the Colonial Theatre, Boston, September 20, 1943, but later the whole episode was over-played.

46. *Two Gentlemen of Verona*, IV, 1, 27, as produced by the Bristol Old Vic Company (Newton Blick as Speed) at the Old Vic, London, June 30, 1952.

47. Stratford, July 31, 1951.

48. Stratford, August 12, 1949.

49. I saw Gladys Cooper as Desdemona at the Plymouth Theatre, Boston, September 21, 1934, Katharine Cornell as Cleopatra at the Martin Beck, New York, November 29, and December 20, 1947.

50. See note 49. The Antony was Sir Godfrey Tearle.

51. Century Theatre, New York, February 21, 1947.

INDEX OF SHAKESPEARIAN PLAYS

INDEX OF PLAYERS AND PRODUCERS